Acclaim for *Immigrant, Inc.*

"This book, filled with stirring stories testifying to the ongoing power of the American Dream as a magnet, challenges us all to build an inclusive culture of welcome, access, opportunity, and empowerment. In so doing, we will renew and transform our society."

—Leonard M. Calabrese, President,
Catholic Community Connection

"*Immigrant, Inc.* is a much-needed book on the positive economic contributions of immigrants to the U.S. economy. All-too-often immigration naysayers focus on the alleged costs of immigration without any acknowledgement of the substantial economic contributions of immigrant entrepreneurs. Richard Herman skillfully balances the cost-benefit analysis with this timely inquiry."

—Kevin R. Johnson, Author, Dean, and Professor of
Chicana/o Studies, University of California at Davis, School of Law

"When Greater Cleveland reclaims its former status as an American mecca for those from around the globe seeking a better life and new opportunities, Richard Herman will deserve much of the credit. He has connected the dots for local public policy makers and thought leaders, convincing us that immigrant attraction is a critical, indispensable driver of urban revitalization."

—Peter Lawson Jones, Cuyahoga County Commissioner,
Cleveland, Ohio

"The United States is a nation of immigrants and yet it has not often understood the role immigrants have played in nation building. *Immigrant, Inc.* provides an important testimonial that uncovers the drive, the dreams, and the relentless nature of immigrants in America. Immigrants strive for the *American Dream*, even though they must tread a risky path that requires hard work, sacrifice, and frugality. High-skill immigration has today become a controversial issue. Yet, our admiration for immigrant-founded companies like Intel, Google, eBay, Yahoo, and Sun that have revolutionized technology, created employment for thousands, and contribute significantly to the US economy remains steadfast. In this book, the authors effectively break the disconnect between the creator and his creation and implore policymakers to protect the liberal and creative spirit of America."

—Suren G. Dutia, Chief Executive Officer, TIE Global
(The Indus Entrepreneur Association)

"Immigrant entrepreneurship is a competitive advantage for America. Policymakers and all of us who want our nation to prosper should read Richard Herman's powerful stories about immigrants revitalizing our economy."

—Rob Paral, Fellow, Institute for Latino Studies,
University of Notre Dame

"Herman and Smith's book is a must read for anyone who is concerned about the future of the United States and about the continuing nature of its global leadership. The book is an enthusiastic and convincing argument that the future of our great country is to go back to our unique roots — indeed it is a call for our renewal as, in President Kennedy's words, A Nation of Immigrants."

—Raj Aggarwal, Sullivan Professor of International Business and Finance,
College of Business Administration,
The University of Akron

"[Immigrant, Inc.] is an important and valuable contribution to the immigration debate, which is notoriously short on facts and long on rhetoric. The book offers compelling and deeply personal evidence of the many blessings bestowed on America by those who hunger to make a better life for themselves and their adopted homeland. Herman and Smith force us to rethink the stereotypes and misconceptions that dominate our approach to immigration, and to think critically about the need for an immigration policy built for the 21st century and beyond."

—Benjamin Johnson, Executive Director,
American Immigration Council

"Having worked with Richard Herman for years on issues of immigration, entrepreneurship, and opportunity, I know his passion and expertise very well. His vision and essential message are masterfully delivered in *Immigrant, Inc.*"

—Dick Russ, Managing Editor, WKYC-TV, Cleveland, Ohio

"We've all heard of the entrepreneurial power of modern-day immigrants to America. But this book goes further. It shows how newcomers to our shores, setting up their own firms, excelling in cutting-edge technologies, employing and working with native Americans, are essential to the United States' economic well-being, indeed its very future in a fiercely competitive 21st century world."

—Neal Peirce, Chairman of the Citistates Group and Syndicated Columnist, Washington Post Writers Group

"Richard Herman makes a passionate, persuasive case for immigration as a crucial investment in our country's future. This book is a timely call for clear thinking and positive action on an issue that goes back to the founding of the American Republic."

—Charles Michener, Author, former Senior Editor at The New Yorker and Newsweek

"The U.S. is at a critical juncture and faces global competition like it has never seen before. To stay ahead, it needs to focus on its core strengths which include innovation, entrepreneurship, and immigration. As Herman and Smith show, these are linked. Unfortunately, with the economic downturn, xenophobia is building and political clouds of nativism are swirling in Washington, DC. This book couldn't have come at a more timely moment. I hope that all policymakers read this."

—Vivek Wadhwa, Columnist, BusinessWeek, Fellow, Harvard Law School and Executive in Residence, Duke University, former Tech Entrepreneur

"Richard Herman and Robert Smith paint a compelling and accurate portrait of the powerful role immigrants play in our economy, and remind us that new people, ideas, and entrepreneurial energy is the American Dream story. Required reading for all policymakers and practitioners working to help America keep its competitive edge in the 21st century."

—John Austin, Non-Resident Senior Fellow, The Brookings Institution, Director, Great Lakes Economic Initiative, Vice President, Michigan State Board of Education

"This is a fascinating chronicle of what can be one of the most powerful economic development forces in our country in the coming years. Richard Herman was able to write it because he has lived, researched, and practiced immigrant entrepreneurship for the past 15 years."

—Alan R. Schonberg, Founder, Management Recruiters International

"In today's turbulent economic times, *Immigrant, Inc.* highlights the true secret to America's past economic success and the key for future growth. America's competitiveness rests on an entrepreneurial culture that is inextricably intertwined and dependent upon immigrants. Let's hope this book's captivating stories and meaningful insights move policymakers to re-light Lady Liberty's beacon and once again welcome immigrants at America's door."

—Baiju R. Shah, President & CEO, BioEnterprise

"A real eye-opener. The book should be required reading for people who believe that immigrants take jobs away from American workers and that most immigrants represent an economic burden for the United States."

—Jan T. Vilcek, MD, Professor, NYU School of Medicine and President, The Vilcek Foundation

"*Immigrant, Inc.* is well researched, wonderfully written, and a fun, fast read. Like *The Millionaire Next Door* (by Stanley & Danko), Robert Smith and Richard Herman wowed readers with stories of extraordinary people doing extraordinary things, and in the process, they are also creating a more diverse, vibrant, and colorful America. A page turner—I couldn't put it down."

—Loung Ung, Author of *First They Killed My Father: A Daughter of Cambodia Remembers* and *Lucky Child*

"A rare and insightful look into the culture of immigrant entrepreneurship. Written with love, sensitivity, and the promise of what immigrants contribute to our great American society, Richard Herman and Robert Smith have shown that immigrants are the lifeline that will keep America from sinking in the global economy."

—Alex Machaskee, Publisher and Chief Executive Officer (retired),
The Plain Dealer, Chairman of International
Orthodox Christian Charities

"The authors' passion comes through in this fantastic book that points to the power and importance of intercultural partnerships in a global economy. I am honored to know Richard and be a part of the forward intercultural movement in Northeast Ohio."

—Connie Atkins, Executive Director, Consortium of African
American Organizations (CAAO)

Immigrant, Inc.

Why Immigrant Entrepreneurs Are Driving the New Economy (and how they will save the American worker)

Richard T. Herman
Robert L. Smith

WILEY

John Wiley & Sons, Inc.

Published by John Wiley & Sons, Inc., Hoboken, New Jersey.
Published simultaneously in Canada.

For general information on our other products and services or for technical support, please contact our Customer Care Department within the United States at (800) 762-2974, outside the United States at (317) 572-3993 or fax (317) 572-4002.

Wiley also publishes its books in a variety of electronic formats. Some content that appears in print may not be available in electronic books. For more information about Wiley products, visit our web site at www.wiley.com.

Library of Congress Cataloging-in-Publication Data:

Herman, Richard T., 1964-
    Immigrant, Inc.: why immigrant entrepreneurs are driving the new economy
(and how they will save the American worker) / Richard T. Herman, Robert L. Smith.
        p.   cm.
    Includes index.
    ISBN 978-0-470-45571-5 (cloth)
        1. Entrepreneurship—United States.   2. Immigrants—United States.
3. Job creation—United States.   4. United States—Emigration and
immigration—Economic aspects.   I. Smith, Robert L., 1959–   II. Title.
HB615.H347 2010
338'.040869120973—dc22

                                                                2009024941

Printed in the United States of America
10 9 8 7 6 5 4 3 2 1

From Richard:
To my beautiful wife, Kimberly, and precious
kids, Nathan and Isabella, for giving me "fresh eyes" to see
and appreciate the abundance. To my mother, Sally, and
dearly departed father, Rich (the engineer-entrepreneur), for
showing me the way. To my immigrant clients and friends, who
have taught me how to "think and act like an immigrant."

From Robert:
To my darling Chul-In,
my favorite immigrant.

Contents

Preface: My Immigrant Experience   xv
Acknowledgments   xxi
Introduction: Welcome to Immigrant, Inc.   xxiii

Chapter 1   **A Mighty New Idea**   1

Chapter 2   **The Mounting Evidence**   7

Discovering a Phenomenon   10
The Accidental Entrepreneurs   12
Urban Legend?   14
A Skill Grows Lucrative   18
Mother of Invention   19
The VCs' Keen Eye   21
New Seeds, Fertile Soil   23

Chapter 3   **A Land of Opportunity, Still**   27

A True Model Minority   30
An Idea, an Obsession   33
Learning to Persevere   35
Survival, Climbing, and Thriving   38
Where Business Is Business   41

Chapter 4   **Restless Dreamers**   45

Seeing It First   47
A 24-Hour Job   49
Mexico Never Tasted So Good   51
No Room for a Dream   53
The Colors of Palestine   56

Chapter 5   **Earth's Best and Brightest**   61

Attracting the Striver Class   64
An African Way   66
The Reluctant Italian-American   67
Out of Shadows, into Solar   71
Love, Study, and a Start-Up   72
At Home Far Away   75

Chapter 6   **Cowboys of a New Frontier**   79

A New Kind of Entrepreneur   81
A Melting-Pot Dream Team   82
The Super Prof   85
Joining a New England Tradition   87
The Guru   88
New Era of Innovation   91
Made in America?   93
Reviving the Motor City   95
Spirits High, Lights Aglow   97

Chapter 7   **Desperate Achievers: Prequel to Google**   99

Starting from Nothing   101
The Boat People   102
An Artful Niche   103
The Family of Google   106
Anxious Wait for Visas   109

Chapter 8   **Importing Solutions**   115

A Gateway Re-Emerges   117
Tapping the Tide   118
Savvy Pilgrims, Creative Shopkeepers   121
A Wave of Home Restorers   123
A Boost for Everyone   125
The Power of One   127
Pushing Open the Door   129

Contents

Toward a "Shared Prosperity"   131
A Harlem-Like Renaissance   133
Seeds of Progress   135

Chapter 9   The Stimulus We Need   137

An Immigrant Advantage   140
America Losing Ground   145
Suffering an Antiquated System   148
A Better Way   152
The Change We Need—Changing Attitudes   155

Chapter 10   Thinking Like an Immigrant   161

The Dream-Keepers   164
A Nation of Immigrants Indeed   166
Keys to Success   168
The Explorer   169
The Knowledge Advantage   172
For Pride, For Family   174
The Power of Teamwork   175
The Possible Dream   177

Appendix   183
About the Authors   211
Index   213

Preface:
My Immigrant
Experience

I arrived with two suitcases at Moscow's Sheremetyevo Airport in the winter of 1993.

The cold hit my face as I walked past rows of scary looking cabbies, an over eager welcome wagon compared to the dour soldiers in the airport carrying assault rifles.

I had just passed the Ohio bar exam, and I decided to move to a country I had never visited, to try my luck at getting rich in a corner of the collapsed Soviet empire.

My friend, Victor, a lawyer from Belarus whom I met a year earlier during our student days at Case Western Reserve University Law School, motioned for me to join him in his car parked outside the Airport. Victor had a job at the Moscow office of a large American law firm.

I was not so lucky. I didn't have a job. But I had about $800 and was single, so I decided to board an Aeroflot jet, fly 15 hours and drop down in Moscow to look for a job. I was ready for an adventure.

Victor drove me into the frozen city of gray concrete buildings, past row upon row of huge military trucks, and I asked myself, not for the last time, "What have I done?"

After getting an apartment, I placed an ad in a Moscow newspaper. An American opening a law office in Russia's capital offered a job.

Our office was two blocks from the Kremlin. The work mostly involved helping Russia's new business class expand their business to the United States, handling their corporate and immigration matters. We worked a lot with young engineers who were relatively free of the old communist mindset and eager to become capitalists.

It was like helping Sisyphus push rocks up a hill. Phones didn't work. Electricity went on and off. Corruption was rampant. The Russian mob was scary. This was the gun-toting Wild West of the post-perestroika era.

But those new entrepreneurs did not quit. They were so determined to succeed that they usually did. And so did I.

After nearly two years, I came home with a new perspective. For the first time, I had a taste of what it was like to be an immigrant and an entrepreneur. I knew that surge of confidence that comes with being a stranger in a strange land.

I felt like I could go anywhere in the world and make something happen.

My intrigue with immigrants only grew. I launched my own immigration law firm, Richard T. Herman & Associates, with one employee, me. Today, my Cleveland law firm has four attorneys and six support staffers. Between the ten of us, we represent six cultures and speak 13 languages.

I think my colleagues are brilliant. But the people who really astonish me are the immigrant clients we serve. Not a week goes by that I don't meet a man or woman who came to this country with nothing but a dream. They're confused and cold and struggling with the language—just like me in Moscow. But they are determined to make it work here.

A year later, they show up back at my office asking for help licensing a business. Soon, they're enrolling the kids in college. Always, they talk about America as a land of opportunity.

I kept asking myself, OK, what's going on? Most native-born Americans don't achieve like this, not so quickly. Do immigrants know something we don't? I began to collect studies on immigrants and their rates of success. I learned things like:

- Immigrants are almost twice as likely as native-born Americans to start a business.
- Immigrants founded more than half of the high-tech companies in Silicon Valley.
- Immigrants are more likely to earn an advanced degree, invent something, and be awarded a U.S. patent.

A few years ago, I met Robert Smith, a journalist who covers international cultures and immigration for the Cleveland *Plain Dealer*. We began to compare notes and found that we were witnessing the same phenomenon.

Cleveland no longer attracted immigrants like it once did. But those immigrants who did come were doing amazing things. Finding two and three jobs in a lousy economy, sending their kids to college, and starting businesses where no one else did.

Bob used to say to me, "Rich, immigrants have a secret. And if we ever find out what it is, we should write a book."

Bob and I share something else in common. We both married into immigrant families. His wife, Chul-In Park, came from Korea as a child and is now a first violinist for the Cleveland Orchestra. My wife, Kimberly Chen, came with her family from Taiwan and is now a doctor.

Both our wives are ambitious not only in their professions but in the way they raise our children. We watched as our wives inoculated the kids with the immigrant genes of self-discipline, hard work, and dedication to education at the earliest ages.

Both in our personal and professional lives, Bob and I saw the connection between an immigrant background and a spirit of striving.

We agreed that too much of the civic discussion focused upon illegal immigration and the problems with immigrants. Few were talking about legal immigrants, their remarkable achievements, and how they were changing America. Our resolve to write this book intensified as the recession worsened and the country increasingly seemed lost.

The studies were beginning to flow from the think tanks on immigrant contributions to the New Economy and urban development. But we wanted to go *behind* the studies, to meet some of these new immigrants who were creating new technologies and new companies.

We decided to uncover their secrets. We decided to meet the men and women who were driving the New Economy and find out how they did it. What made them push so hard to achieve?

Our research took us from Boston's Route 128 to California's Silicon Valley, from tech clusters in Texas to depressed autoworker communities in the Midwest.

We met Desh Deshpande, the legendary Boston entrepreneur who built billion-dollar companies, and Carmen Castillo, a student from Spain who basically started the high-tech consulting industry in her apartment. We peeked into the labs of Ric Fulop and Yet-Ming Chiang, immigrant entrepreneurs building a better electric car. And we sipped Turkish coffee and shared a limousine with Farouk Shami, a Palestinian immigrant whose company exports his BioSilk shampoo and other hair-care products to over 50 countries.

What we discovered was not a secret but a culture: a culture of entrepreneurship. You could call it Immigrant, Inc.

We found that many of today's immigrants arrive ready-made to perform in a knowledge-based, global economy. They're often the best and brightest from back home, and they are certainly the strivers. They have the risk-taking personalities of entrepreneurs, and they dream big and work smart.

But the powerful message is this: their club is not exclusive. Today's immigrants do not succeed by themselves. They work with the locals. They team up with American companies and with in-the-know American colleagues, and then they do something fantastic, like build a better solar panel or resurrect a neighborhood.

Anyone can join the culture because anyone can learn to think and act like an immigrant.

First of all, immigrant Americans are eager to share what they know. They are proud of their success and grateful to America. Secondly, it's part of who we are. Our ancestors were the torchbearers of *Immigrant, Inc.*, creating jobs, pushing the kids in school, and lifting the whole family toward something better.

We just forgot a lot of what they knew and learned.

The impact of the new immigrants—people who arrived after 1965—is undeniable. The implications for a business person, for a community, and for a nation are profound.

For a budding entrepreneur, the new immigrants offer success traits and trade secrets that can be studied and copied. For a struggling neighborhood or a Rust Belt city, they hold out hope for revival. For a nation resolved to be a leader in a global economy, they offer a pool of world-class talent.

The new immigrants are exhibiting something very old and very American, a can-do spirit borne of the immigrant experience.

With the speed and fearlessness of a race car driver—let's say Mario Andretti, an immigrant from Italy—the new immigrants are creating jobs now and designing the American jobs of the future. In the great race called the global economy, they are the nation's competitive advantage.

With this book of stories, we'll show you how.

RICHARD HERMAN
August 2009

Acknowledgments

T he book is the fruit of many generous and knowledge-able people who have shared their stories and ideas on the power of *Immigrant, Inc.*

The authors would especially like to thank those who gave interviews for this book: Dr. Adedeji Adefuye, Monte Ahuja, Dan Arvizu, John Austin, Generoso Bahena, Angelika Blendstrup, Genia and Michael Brin, Carmen Castillo, Jay Chen, Yet-Ming Chiang, Judy Choi, Xunming Deng, Gururaj "Desh" Deshpande, Yi Ding, Suren Dutia, Ric Fulop, Ellen Gallagher, Sorin Grama, Vartan Gregorian, Alberto Ibargüen, Jeffrey Kimathi, David Lam, Jason Lin, Paul Lo, Richard Longworth, Fatimah Muhammad, Anne O'Callaghan, Ib Olsen, Rob Paral, Linn Patel, Safi Qureshi, Noah Samara, Alberto Sangiovanni-Vincentelli, Carol Sardo, Mohabir Satram, Farouk Shami, Ratanjit Sondhe, Raymond Spencer, Tom Szaky, Quy "Charlie" Ton, Alex Totic, Vi Truong, Jan Vilcek, Vivek Wadhwa, and Liwei Xu.

The authors would also like to thank Sheck Cho, our editor, and his colleagues Andy Wheeler, Helen Cho, Dexter Gasque, and Stacey Rivera, at John Wiley & Sons, who believed in the book and guided us.

The authors would also like to credit the following Midwesterners for welcoming immigrant job-creators and working to build bridges to the world: Raj Aggrawal, Connie Atkins, William Avery, Reka Barabas, Dona Brady, Dan Berry, George Burke, Len Calabrese, Carol Caruso, Jim Craciun, Veronica Isabel Dahlberg, Rafael Reyez Davila, Jorge Delgado, Jim Foster, Mansfield Frazier, Joe Frolik, Nick Gatozzi, Ye-Fan Glavin, Michael Goldberg, Barbara Hawkins, Peter Lawson Jones, Ken Kovach, Ray Leach, David Levey, Alex Machaskee, Halley Marsh, Charles Michener, Ed Morrison, Steve Petras, Dr. Maria Pujana, Albert Ratner, Radhika Reddy, Joe Roman, Eduardo Romero, Thom Ruhe, Dick Russ, Jim Russell, Mark Santo, Alan Schonberg, Baiju Shah, Julia Shearson, Paramjit Singh, Tom Sudow, Steve Tobocman, Hugo Urizar, Harry Weller, Ann Womer-Benjamin, Eddy Zai, Rose Zitiello, and many others too numerous to mention.

Introduction:
Welcome to
Immigrant, Inc.

To immigrate is an entrepreneurial act.
—EDWARD ROBERTS, FOUNDER OF
MIT ENTREPRENEURSHIP CENTER

This is a book for people and communities who want to join the new and exciting age to come. It's for those looking to take advantage of a permanently New Economy, an era that will be defined by innovation, smart technology, and multicultural lifestyles.

We do not pretend to have discovered a magic formula to success. We do believe we can help you, your business, or your family tap one of the most powerful business cultures in the world today.

Let us introduce you to *Immigrant, Inc.*

That's the term we use to describe a culture and a way of life that offers a proven path for success in a knowledge-based, global economy.

Immigrant, Inc. is a very new and a very old phenomenon. At the heart of the culture is a special way of thinking about work, about entrepreneurship, about education, about raising children, and, most of all, about seizing opportunity in America—the greatest country on Earth for those with a dream and willingness to take a chance and work hard.

The ambition of this book is not to dazzle you with the success stories of foreign-born entrepreneurs and innovators. Sure, it's important to know that half of all the high-technology companies in Silicon Valley have an immigrant founder and that immigrants are filing technology patents at double the rate of native-born Americans.

"But what does that do for me?" you might ask.

Plenty.

First, we explain how this imported energy results in new wealth and new jobs. Jobs for Americans. Then we explain how all Americans can join the culture of *Immigrant, Inc.*

In a 2003 interview with Leslie Stahl of CBS News' *60 Minutes*, Vinod Khosla, the billionaire venture capitalist and immigrant co-founder of Sun Microsystems, considered the impact of immigrants from his country, India. "How many jobs have entrepreneurs, Indian entrepreneurs, in Silicon Valley created over the last 15, 20 years? Hundreds of thousands, I would guess," he said.

He's about right. The Indian-born Khosla is part of an immigrant wave that helped to transform northern California into the world's epicenter of high technology. He is part of a larger wave that is building the New Economy and creating jobs for American workers.

Coming from all corners of the globe, immigrant innovation and entrepreneurship is the *real* job-creating stimulus.

In her May 2007 testimony before the House Judiciary Subcommittee on Immigration, Patricia A. Buckley, a senior economic advisor to the U.S. Department of Commerce, explained why any community should strive to attract high-skill immigrants:

An important segment of the foreign-born are not in the United States to find a job—they are here to create jobs. . . . The high rates of entrepreneurship among the immigrant population contribute to the dynamics of the economy, fostering both investment and employment.

Immigrants like Andy Grove and Sergey Brin are the well-known catalysts behind New Economy giants. Grove's Intel employed about 90,000 people in 2009, while Brin's Google employed about 20,000. Half of those jobs were based in the United States. More jobs were coming. In February 2009, Intel announced a $7 billion investment in factories in New Mexico, Oregon, and Arizona to manufacture silicon wafers. Speaking before the Economic Club of Washington, D.C., in 2009, Intel's president, Paul Otellini, said he expected this investment in "industries of the future" to create 7,000 high-wage jobs.

He was talking about the continuation of a powerful trend. As revealed by researchers Vivek Wadhwa and AnnaLee Saxenian, immigrants created 450,000 jobs in America by founding one-fourth of the nation's technology and engineering companies between 1995 and 2005.

The job-creating culture is not restricted to California's Silicon Valley but extends throughout America, particularly around major research universities, like the Massachusetts Institute of Technology. A 2007 study by the Immigrant Learning Center near Boston found that over one-quarter of the biotech companies in New England had at least one immigrant founder and that those companies employed over 4,000 workers and produced over $7 billion in sales in 2006.

The phenomenon extends beyond high-tech industries, spilling into middle America. The U.S. Small Business Administration tells us there were 1.5 million immigrant business owners in America in 2002, comprising much of the high-skill and low-skill sectors, and providing jobs to 2.2 million people.

The seeds for this job-generating trend were planted decades ago by immigrant pioneers who founded proud American companies like Dow Chemical, DuPont, Pfizer, Procter & Gamble, Carnegie Steel (later U.S. Steel), Carnival Cruises, and many others.

That's fine, you may say, but what about the jobs of the future? Who will create the 4 million green jobs identified in a 2008 study commissioned by the U.S. Conference of Mayors? Who will invent and commercialize clean technology so that companies can be launched and blue collar jobs will be created in manufacturing, building, and repairing, so that white collar jobs will spring up in accounting, law, and banking?

The same people who made Silicon Valley shine.

Just as foreign-born engineers and entrepreneurs, in partnership with American-born colleagues, ignited the information technology revolution that created millions of jobs in the 1990s, high-skill immigrants are beginning to drive the emerging green technology and clean-energy industries.

Raymond Spencer, an Australian-born entrepreneur, has a window on that future and a gusto for investing after founding a high-technology consulting company that sold for more than $1 billion in 2006.

"I have investments in maybe 10 start-ups, all of which fall within a broad umbrella of a 'green' theme," he said. "And it's interesting, the vast majority are either led by immigrants or have key technical people who are immigrants."

It should come as no surprise that immigrants will help drive the green revolution. America's young scientists and engineers, especially the ones drawn to emerging industries like alternative energy, tend to speak with an accent.

The 2000 census found that immigrants, while accounting for 12 percent of the population, made up nearly half of all scientists and engineers with doctorate degrees. Their importance will only grow. Nearly 70 percent of the men and women who entered the fields of science and engineering from 1995 to 2006 were immigrants.

Introduction

It's not just immigrant entrepreneurs and innovators who are creating and maintaining jobs for Americans. Drivers of the New Economy include increasing numbers of foreign-born executives hired to lead huge American companies and their workforce.

Indra Nooyi, an immigrant from India, not only plays in a rock band, but leads PepsiCo as its chief executive. Irish-born Neville Isdell ran Coca-Cola until Muhtar Kent, a Turkish-American, assumed the leadership of the company in 2009. Sidney Taurel, born a Spanish citizen in Morocco, retired as CEO and chairman of the pharmaceutical giant Eli Lilly and Company. The German-born Klaus Kleinfeld is the chief executive officer of Alcoa, having taken the baton from Brazilian-born Alain Belda.

A close cousin of immigration is foreign direct investment, which is actively courted by American officials seeking to boost job creation.

U.S.-based affiliates of foreign companies employed more than 5 million U.S. workers in 2006. Between 2003 and 2007, foreign companies in America invested about $184 billion to create 447,000 new jobs, many in struggling states like Ohio, Michigan, and Pennsylvania. In one example, Spanish wind-turbine manufacturer Gamesa began converting abandoned steel mills in Pennsylvania into advanced manufacturing facilities for massive blades for windmills, creating 700 union jobs.

Immigrants and foreign nationals are creating jobs for Americans. But that's not the whole story. Immigrants who are joining the American team are making partnerships stronger and companies mightier.

Katie Liljenquist, a professor of organizational leadership at Brigham Young University, is one of a number of experts who say that American workers innovate and solve problems faster when working with a "socially distinct newcomer"—a person from another culture.

While this book is not an immigration policy book, we do hope that the stories it reveals and the people it introduces will help you to see immigrants in a new light—not as a "them" but as part of "us." We hope it will help you to appreciate the critical roles that immigrants play in the growth of industries and the creation of jobs in an age of innovation. This attitude is critical if the nation is to remain at the cutting edge of the New Economy and create a new generation of American jobs.

Immigrants bring the skills to create those jobs, but they bring something even more valuable. They bring their dreams.

Immigrants are the dream-keepers, reminding us that the American Dream is alive, well, and attainable to all. As the familiar factories and offices close, we need this hope.

By learning their stories, we reacquaint ourselves with the values that built America. The greatest gift that the new immigrants offer America is not their ingenuity and drive, but a value system that worked for our great-grandparents and can work for Americans right now.

In this book, we reveal why and how America's new immigrants perform so well in their adopted home. Our aim is to illuminate success traits that can be studied and copied. While America draws many of the best and brightest from India, China, Israel, Russia, Taiwan, Nigeria, and Brazil, it was not enough that these folks arrived smart and ambitious. They were prepared for excellence, adept at building teams, a bit daring, and often brilliant at discovering opportunities.

Immigrant, Inc. is a culture of entrepreneurship and self-reliance built around a set of simple, powerful concepts: relentless preparation, lifelong learning, constant vigilance and exploration of opportunity (no matter how remote), a willingness to take risks, and a deep love and respect for American ideals like thrift and earnestness.

While many Americans have lost sight of those ideals, immigrants have not. Every day, world-class strivers fly past the Statue of Liberty and land at John F. Kennedy International Airport. They endure the humiliations and frustrations of the immigration process and set about building a new future. They may be poor in dollars, but they are rich in audacity and in dreams.

Their struggle and success is a constant reminder that the American Dream lives for all of us.

While it sounds cliché to say that the United States is a nation of immigrants, it is a fact that no other country in the history of mankind has accepted (although not always welcomed) over 70 million immigrants! Many of us are not far removed from the immigrant experience.

Even if you are not among the 50 percent of Americans with close immigrant lineage, you probably share immigrant ancestry. Regardless of whether you came to America enslaved, or arrived here escaping chains of oppression, you are part of a nation of survivors and strivers. Nearly every one of us has immigrant blood coursing through our veins.

As Johns Hopkins University psychologist John Gartner argues, immigrant traits are built into our DNA. America's genetic trail leads back to a class of energetic strivers, brave and optimistic pioneers who created a new world for themselves and their families.

Today, the New Economy is that new world. This book is intended to help you to take advantage of it. It will show you how to unlock and unleash your inner immigrant by embracing the values, aspirations, and discipline of our ancestors and by welcoming and embracing the wisdom of our new Americans.

Whether we like it or not, we are all free agents now. If you are looking for a new job, or thinking about starting and growing a business, the lessons of successful immigrants will empower you.

Immigrant power is the stimulus the country needs if not craves. As Google vice president Omid Kordestani advised the graduates at San Jose State University in 2007, immigrants know a secret or two. He told his audience:

To keep an edge, I must think and act like an immigrant. There is a special optimism and drive that I benefited from and continue to rely on that *I want all of you* to find. Immigrants are inherently dreamers and fighters.

We hope that this book helps you to "think and act like an immigrant" as you pursue your entrepreneurial and professional goals, and in the process, help secure America's global leadership in the twenty-first century.

Chapter 1

A Mighty New Idea

I think we should welcome all peaceful people to our country. They get to pursue the American dream and we get to benefit from all the wonderful things that immigrants bring to our country—like good old-fashioned soccer.

—DREW CAREY

Y et-Ming Chiang was alone in his office on the campus of the Massachusetts Institute of Technology when Ric Fulop, a college drop-out from Venezuela, walked in and spun his life in a new direction.

Neither man had ever met before, but they shared a few key qualities. Both were immigrants to America. Both had experience as entrepreneurs, people who start businesses from scratch. Both liked to dream big, although they ran at different speeds.

Chiang, who came from Taiwan as a boy, was a career scientist who amiably applied himself to his research, pioneering work in ceramics and, more recently, renewable energy, the emerging clean technology that could replace fossil fuels.

Fulop, a serial entrepreneur, lived life on a treadmill. Restless and bold, he started his first computer company in Caracas at age 16.

1

He launched four more businesses—watched them soar and watched them crash—before he walked in on Chiang, introduced himself as a high-tech rock star, one of *Red Herring* magazine's Top 10 Entrepreneurs, and told him about the idea keeping him up at night.

It was 2001, the dawn of a new millennium. The Internet bubble had popped, gasoline prices were climbing, the climate was warming, and the world would soon desire a clean, powerful source of energy. He had heard there was a professor at MIT doing interesting work with batteries. Was he right?

Chiang, then 42, could have exerted his rank. He was an accomplished scientist at one of the nation's elite universities, the youngest tenured professor in the history of his department. While experimenting with very small lithium battery materials, he had discovered a way to extract double the power from conventional battery cells. He thought that some day he might take his idea to private industry, leave academia, and go into the battery business.

Now here was a brash young man at the door, a stranger nearly 20 years his junior, saying the time was now. Chiang takes pride in the aspect of his personality that allowed him to say, "Okay, what do you propose?"

"Plenty," Fulop replied. He envisioned a battery company that would power the next generation of electric cars and eventually power America. He was prepared to pitch the idea to venture capitalists, investors who bankroll promising start-up companies, usually in exchange for a share of the ownership.

Chiang cared little about the business side of the adventure. What fascinated him was the technology. That, and the inkling that his work could change the world. He agreed to go along for the ride. The ride of his life.

Only a few months into their quest, the pair met and impressed a key catalyst, legendary New England entrepreneur Gururaj Deshpande. Desh, as he's known in technology circles, came from India in 1973 with an engineering degree and parlayed ideas on fiber optics into companies that made him one of the richest men in the world. When Fulop and Chiang came calling, he was chairman of Sycamore Networks and a venture capitalist.

Deshpande not only invested in the new company, he recruited other investors and became chairman of its board of directors. He saw a good idea backed by intriguing technology. More than that, he saw a good team, one he suspected would work wonders to achieve its dreams.

Young Fulop, especially, intrigued him.

"He's a good example of an entrepreneur," Deshpande said one day in his office in suburban Boston. "He quit school. Started five or six companies. Raised $100 million. Blew it all. Nothing worked."

He paused and softly said, "I think this one is going to stick."

Chiang and Fulop teamed up with Bart Riley, an American-born engineer and an old friend of Chiang's, to found A123Systems in late 2001. They named the company after a mathematical equation that is critical in nanotechnology and that begins "A123...."

Chiang needed another breakthrough in the lab to make the technology work as envisioned. More than once, the nimble team had to change its approach, but sooner than anyone expected, the promising start-up was offering a battery that packed 10 times the lifespan of conventional batteries and twice the punch.

By early 2009, A123 batteries were powering Black & Decker's pro-model power tools, having knocked out the Japanese supplier. A prototype car battery had sent a motorcycle rocketing at 160 mph. Under the direction of Chiang, the batteries were being refined to propel the new generation of electric cars that automakers promised at the 2009 North American International Auto Show. The company had attracted more than $250 million from investors. It was employing 1,800 people on three continents.

Still, the dream swelled. Fulop, A123's marketing manager, knew that automakers and government leaders alike wanted America's next-generation power source to be made in America, ensuring that the nation was not again dependent on a foreign supply of energy.

He envisioned manufacturing plants in Michigan employing thousand of workers putting out 200,000 car batteries a year. He was seeking nearly $2 billion in new investment.

"This is happening in an amazingly short amount of time," Chiang observed one day in early 2009. "It's mushrooming."

But the company he co-founded was not in a marathon. It was in a sprint, a death race. A123Systems was one of several companies worldwide vying to create the next essential power source. There was the possibility that Chiang's batteries, for all their promise, could be eclipsed by a better technology or beaten by a company in a nation with a more aggressive energy policy, that it could all fade into a costly sunset.

No one knew this better than Deshpande, who more than once had tasted bitter defeat. But he also knew something else about Chiang and Fulop and the leadership team that had assembled around them, some immigrant, some not. He knew that if they fell, they would get up. If they hit a brick wall, they would find a way around it. If they did not succeed the first time, they would try, try again.

He knew that Chiang would never again be just a lab researcher, not after having launched one of the hottest companies in New England. There was no stopping Fulop from diving head-first into the next audacious idea. All three men belonged to the same exhilarating phenomenon. They belonged to the force driving the new, knowledge-based, global economy.

They were entrepreneurs, but more than that, they were immigrant entrepreneurs—the most remarkable business people of the era.

*   *   *

The personalities behind A123Systems belong to a culture that took root in America with the easing of immigration restrictions in 1965, changes that allowed for a surge of immigrants from non-European nations—many of them highly skilled. This culture fell comfortably into the detail work of advanced technology and restlessly asserted itself in the Internet age. Its members founded Intel, Sun Microsystems, Cirrus Logic, Yahoo, Hotmail, Google, and other marquee companies of the dot-com era.

By early 2009, in the midst of an economic downturn so severe some called it the Great Recession, that immigrant culture stood poised to help create the next wave of innovation—the clean technology that would drive an emerging green economy.

The dreamers at A123 are far from alone. From university laboratories to urban neighborhoods, from high-tech to bio-tech companies, immigrants are playing dominant roles as innovators and job creators. They created more than half the companies to rise in California's Silicon Valley, the heart of the high-technology industry, between 1995 and 2005. Across America, fully one quarter of all new engineering and technology companies created during that span had an immigrant founder.

Researchers have long known that immigrants are more likely to start a business, to strive to be their own boss. But recent studies reveal an astonishing rate of entrepreneurship. America's immigrants are far more likely than non-immigrants to launch a company. They are over-represented as leaders in not only high technology but also in the arts, transportation, and the hospitality industries. They exhibit a knack for innovation and invention that is placing American companies at the cutting edge of their industries. A college-educated immigrant today is twice as likely to obtain a U.S. patent as a college-educated nonimmigrant. What's going on?

"First of all, you believe in the American dream thing," said Fulop, in a rare moment of calm. "You get here and you say, 'OK, I have to make something happen.'"

Historians have long cited immigrants as one of the nation's uncommon strengths, typically noting the people who dug canals or poured steel or opened corner stores and pizzerias. The positive impact of those hard-working immigrants is still being felt. However, a new, more remarkable immigrant has emerged, one uniquely positioned to excel in a fast-changing, global economy driven by innovation.

The young men and women who fly to the United States today with two suitcases and a coveted visa are a self-selected group of dreamers, often well schooled in math and science. They are people courageous enough to leave home and resilient enough to endure the hardships of starting over in a new culture. Often, they are frustrated by the controlled economies and rigid cultures of their native lands.

They fall into capitalist America like seeds into the good earth. And they bloom here, hatching ideas and launching companies at a pace never seen before.

These new immigrants are exhibiting something very old and very American, a can-do spirit borne of the immigrant experience. Once again, immigrants are America's competitive edge, but not as wage workers. Like the immigrant trio charging a mighty new battery, they are the innovators who will create the companies and the jobs of the future—if we let them.

Chapter 2

The Mounting Evidence

Every aspect of the American economy has profited from the contributions of immigrants.

—John F. Kennedy

Vivek Wadhwa never envisioned himself an intellectual working in the ivory tower, certainly not one of America's leading researchers on the competitiveness of immigrant entrepreneurs. Before examining the New Economy for Duke and Harvard universities, Wadhwa excelled at it. The Indian immigrant fostered two successful software companies in North Carolina's Research Triangle and lived the life of a wealthy, innovative, workaholic entrepreneur in the red-hot 1990s. Then a near-death experience sounded a shrill alarm.

He was on a rare vacation, a Caribbean cruise with his wife and two children, when he felt the chest pains. For days, he tried to ignore the discomfort. He was only 45. He worked out regularly. Maybe he had strained a muscle lifting weights. But when he returned home and an arm went numb, his wife, Tavinder, insisted on a ride to the emergency room. And just in time. Wadhwa learned he had suffered a massive heart attack. Doctors said he was likely hours away from death.

It was time to exit the fast lane.

The son of a diplomat from New Delhi, Wadhwa grew up an engaged citizen of a fast-changing world. He lived in Malaysia, Indonesia, and Australia before his father's posting to the United Nations brought him to New York City in 1980 at age 23.

Like many immigrants from South Asia, Wadhwa arrived well educated. He held a degree in computing studies from Australia's Canberra University. He added to that a master's in business administration from New York University and then entered an American business world just growing aware of the power of information technology, or IT.

At Credit Suisse First Boston, Wadhwa grasped the potential of advanced information systems sooner than most. He created computer networks for banking so promising his employer spun off his business unit into its own company, Seer Technologies, in 1990.

Seer relocated to the Research Triangle—an eight-county region of North Carolina anchored by the research universities of the University of North Carolina at Chapel Hill, Duke University, and North Carolina State University. As executive vice president and chief technology officer, Wadhwa helped grow the start-up into a publicly traded company worth more than $100 million in the mid-1990s.

"Entrepreneurship came to me," he would say later. "I invented a technology. Then I got the bug. I did not want to work for anyone anymore. I had to make it on my own."

His next venture was bigger and riskier. He launched Relativity Technologies, Inc., in Raleigh in 1997, with an idea to link old and new technologies, much as he had done with cultures all of his life.

The inspiration came not from the business world but from his two sons. The Internet had entered the Wadhwa household the year before, captivating Vineet, then 15, and Tarun, then 11. Dad watched in dismay as the boys created web sites, downloaded graphics, and made friends all over the world. Intrigued, he began to navigate the emerging World Wide Web. He surmised the new communication system was going to be huge.

"I had to be part of this revolution," he said later.

He drained the college savings accounts of his boys to launch his new company. In lean times, the family went without health insurance and often without seeing dad, who worked 18-hour days.

The start-up soared. Relativity's key product, which translated data from mainframe systems to applications on the World Wide Web, achieved commercial success. Wadhwa came to define the cool IT jobs of the Internet revolution. His company kitchen served free and nutritious foods. He gave out $1,000 bonuses to employees who quit smoking, and offered high salaries and stock options. *Fortune* magazine labeled Relativity one of the 25 coolest companies in the world.

By 2002, Wadhwa was a wealthy entrepreneur and a much quoted Research Triangle superstar. Then the heart attack brought him back down to earth. He did not want to die a young success.

In 2003, he stepped down from the day-to-day leadership of his company. Soon after, he relinquished the chairmanship. A legal battle with investors had soured his taste for the business, but he also knew that he needed to change his lifestyle.

In the fall of 2005, he stood before engineering students at Duke University and offered to share his hard-earned knowledge. He had joined the faculty of the Pratt School of Engineering as an executive in residence, expecting to enlighten young people on the risks and rewards of entrepreneurship and to advise faculty who hoped to take their research from the lab to the market.

Instead, he found himself peppered with questions he could not answer.

"What is the global economy? How does it work?" his students demanded to know.

"What courses should we take to get jobs that cannot be outsourced?" they asked.

"Why do so many of you Indians start companies?"

"I was being asked questions that I could not answer," Wadhwa recalled. "That's when I realized the United States had no idea how the New Economy worked, and how its global advantage could be lost."

Intrigued again, he went searching for answers.

Discovering a Phenomenon

Wadhwa built on the work of AnnaLee Saxenian, a professor and later dean of the School of Information at the University of California at Berkeley. She was one of the first researchers to examine the impact of skilled immigrants on the New Economy. Exploring the makeup of the workforce in California's Silicon Valley, the nexus of the nation's burgeoning high-tech industry, Saxenian found that immigrants from India and China ran nearly one-quarter of the valley's start-ups, those companies founded between 1980 and 1998.

Her 1999 report, "Silicon Valley's New Immigrant Entrepreneurs," created a stir. For Wadhwa, it confirmed his suspicion that something astonishing was afoot. Immigrants from China, Taiwan, and India were generating new jobs and wealth on a remarkable scale in northern California. What were they up to elsewhere?

In 2006, Wadhwa put a team of engineering students and graduate assistants to work finding out. Using Dun & Bradstreet's Million Dollar Database, the researchers identified all the small and mid-sized technology and engineering companies that had opened in the United States from 1995 to 2005. In other words, they compiled a database of start-ups at the dawn of the high-tech era. Then they began making thousands of phone calls, contacting the firms and asking where in the world the founder was from.

Wadhwa was startled by the results, which were published in January 2007 in a report written by Wadhwa, Saxenian, and Duke researchers Ben Rissing and Gary Gereffi. Titled "America's New Immigrant Entrepreneurs," it showed that the trend Saxenian documented eight years before had mushroomed to become a nationwide phenomenon.

Across America, immigrants helped to start 25 percent of the new technology and engineering companies of the past decade, the research team found. Where skilled immigrants congregated, the impact was even more profound. During that 10-year span, immigrants helped to launch 39 percent of the new high-tech companies in California, 38 percent of the new companies in New Jersey, and 29 percent of the new companies in Massachusetts.

> *You'll find that immigrants are making a lot more money and achieve a lot more success than the average American. You can learn from those who make it here. There's something special about that group.*
>
> —entrepreneur Vivek Wadhwa

Extrapolating from its sample of 2,054 companies, the researchers estimated that in 2005 immigrant-founded companies were generating $52 billion in sales and employing 450,000 people.

The trend was racing even faster in the Mecca of high technology—Silicon Valley. The immigrant contribution there had ballooned since Saxenian's 1999 report. People born in foreign lands were behind more than half, or 52.4 percent, of the Silicon Valley firms launched from 1995 to 2005. In other words, America's immigrants were driving one of the hottest economies in the world.

Those who were not starting companies were often helping other companies advance into new realms.

In a second part of the study, Wadhwa's team sought insight into who was driving innovation in emerging fields, like information technology, biotechnology, and advanced medicine. To get at that, it analyzed the patent database of the World Intellectual Property Organization (WIPO), a Switzerland-based group that coordinates the filings of international patents.

Here, too, Wadhwa's team found an immigrant innovation explosion. In 1998, people born in foreign lands were listed as the inventor or co-inventor on only about 7 percent of the international patent applications filed from the United States. By 2006, the immigrant share of invention had more than tripled. Immigrants not yet U.S. citizens were behind a remarkable 24 percent of America's international patent applications.

There was now compelling evidence identifying skilled immigrants as the drivers of the New Economy, which most economists agree is no passing fad. The Kauffman Foundation, a leader in the study of entrepreneurship, defines the New Economy as a permanent, global economy powered by technology and innovation.

"The key to maintaining U.S. competitiveness in a global economy is to understand our strengths and to effectively leverage these," Wadhwa's study concluded. "Skilled immigrants are one of our greatest advantages."

The Accidental Entrepreneurs

Some economists caution that the study's findings should not have come as a big surprise. In that era, 13 percent of the U.S. working population was immigrant, after all, and one-quarter of America's scientists and engineers—half at the doctorate level—were born outside of the United States.

Sure, immigrants are more likely to obtain a patent for an invention. "That's because more immigrants than natives have science and engineering degrees," wrote Betty Joyce Nash, an economics writer at the Federal Reserve Bank of Richmond.

Wadhwa and his research team also suspected an education connection. With the support of the Kansas City–based Kauffman Foundation, they went back and surveyed the company founders identified in "America's New Immigrant Entrepreneurs."

The immigrants who launched high-tech companies had indeed arrived smart and eager to get smarter, the surveys found. Ninety-six percent of the founders held bachelor's degrees, and 74 percent held graduate or post-graduate degrees. What's more, their degrees and their expertise were concentrated in the all-important STEM fields—science, technology, engineering, and mathematics—subjects deemed critical to advanced industries.

The researchers learned something else, something wholly unexpected. Almost none of the founders set out to become entrepreneurs—not initially. In fact, the burst of entrepreneurship surprised even the immigrants. Few had come to America with the aim of starting a business. Some came to take a job, and a few came to join family already here, but most came to earn an advanced college degree.

Who but a restless dreamer could leave everything they knew and trusted to start a new life in a strange land? As a nation of immigrants, America became a nation of optimistic risk-takers.

—psychologist John Gartner

They were, in the parlance of the New Economy, high-skilled immigrants intent on sharpening their skills in the best university system in the world.

Once in America, a transformation took place. An average of 13 years after immigrating, the new Americans started a business. Enough of them started enough businesses to power a technology revolution.

Education alone does not account for that kind of drive and achievement, Wadhwa argues. He is convinced something bigger, more powerful, is at work.

First, it's a small group making a mighty big impact. According to the U.S. Census Bureau, there were 38 million immigrants in the United States in 2007, representing 12.6 percent of the population and 15.7 percent of the labor force. Other observers of demographic trends, like researchers at the Pew Hispanic Center, have estimated that as much as one-third of the immigrant population is in the country illegally.

The salient number for entrepreneurship is legal immigrants—immigrants in a position to license and launch a business. That community was about 9 percent of the population in 2007; less than 7 percent in 1990.

As an immigrant and an entrepreneur, Wadhwa knows the hurdles those young scientists and engineers had to clear on their way to starting a company. They showed guts just leaving the familiarity of home. They endured a frustrating and expensive U.S. immigration system. In their new world, they likely faced loneliness and language barriers, and sometimes racism and discrimination. They probably had little access to establishment bankers or traditional sources of capital. They spoke with an accent.

"It's a handicap being a foreigner, whether we admit it or not. That's a reality," Wadhwa said.

Yet many of the immigrants his team surveyed not only became entrepreneurs for the first time in their lives, they started businesses in key new industries. Some went on to set the industry standards.

"Obviously, something is happening," Wadhwa said. "You'll find that immigrants are making a lot more money and achieve a lot more success than the average American. You can learn from those who make it here. There's something special about that group."

Urban Legend?

The image of the immigrant entrepreneur is rooted in American folk wisdom. The Italian cobbler. The Jewish tailor. The Chinese dry cleaner. The Greek restaurant owner. The Korean greengrocer. The Indian hotelier. The Arab store owner. The stories that circulate suggest that immigrants are more prolific entrepreneurs than people born in America. It's no myth. The immigrant small business owner is as common as he or she often appears, though some people do not want to believe it.

"The popular wisdom is that immigrants have the work ethic, gumption, willingness to take risks, and a host of other things that enable them to start businesses at a rate higher than the native-born population," writes a skeptical Scott Shane, a professor of entrepreneurship at Case Western Reserve University, in his 2008 book, *The Illusions of Entrepreneurship: the Costly Myths that Entrepreneurs, Investors and Policy Makers Live By*.

"As a result—the story goes—we can boost start-up activity in this country by bringing in more immigrants," Shane writes. "Once again, the popular wisdom turns out to be an urban legend. A variety of data sources indicate that, since 1980, immigrants have been no more likely than people born in this country to start a business."

The problem with this line of thinking is that it is wrong.

Most scholars agree, and esteemed research groups confirm, that immigrants are not only more likely than native-born Americans to start a business, they are dramatically more likely.

In recent years, the rate of immigrant start-ups surged while start-ups by native-born Americans stagnated. In other words, the culture of immigrant entrepreneurship is growing.

"The resulting gap in the entrepreneurial activity rate between immigrants and natives is large," according to the 2009 Kauffman Index of Entrepreneurial Activity, which measures rates of entrepreneurship across America. The authoritative report found that immigrants have become almost twice as likely as native-born Americans to start their own business. It found that 530 out of every 100,000 immigrant Americans start a business each month, compared to 280 out of every 100,000 native-born Americans.

Updated each year since 1996, the 2009 Kauffman Index demonstrates nearly a 40 percent increase in the immigrant start-up rate over the three previous years, while the native-born rate has remained flat.

While it is true that immigrants also move out of their businesses at a faster rate, it's obvious they are more likely to start a business in the first place. Other institutions that study entrepreneurship are also taking note of the growing industriousness of immigrants.

In 2008, the U.S. Small Business Administration sponsored a broad look at the contributions of immigrants to the U.S economy. Robert Fairlie, an economist at the University of California, Santa

Cruz, examined U.S. Census data and tax records and determined that about 17 percent of all new business owners in America are immigrants, though they make up about 12 percent of the population.

In some states, the immigrant contribution to the general economy is substantial. About 30 percent of all businesses in California are immigrant-owned, as are 25 percent of businesses in New York and 20 percent of businesses in New Jersey and Florida.

Fairlie, perhaps to quash "urban legends," states in his report that "the entrepreneurial success of immigrants is well known. . . . These findings indicate that immigrants make large and important contributions to business ownership, formation and income in the United States."

America is hardly unique in the industriousness of its immigrants. Business ownership is higher among the foreign-born in many developed nations, including the United Kingdom, Canada, and Australia. The phenomenon is so prominent that many nations have created special visas to attract and reward immigrant entrepreneurs.

According to a 1997 report by the International Migration Policy Program at the Carnegie Endowment for International Peace, immigrants are uncommonly entrepreneurial and always have been. In every decennial census from 1880 to 1990, immigrants were significantly more likely to be self-employed than natives, the authors observe.

In his insightful 2005 book, *The Hypomanic Edge: The Link Between (A Little) Craziness and (A Lot of) Success in America* (Simon & Schuster), Johns Hopkins University psychologist John Gartner notes that the single exception to this 110-year-long trend was the roaring 1990s.

"In that decade, when every American college student wanted to found the next Yahoo, native-born Americans increased their level of self-employment to match the immigrant's," he writes. "Both immigrant and native-born Americans were self-employed at a very high rate, just above 11 percent."

Gartner believes that immigrants possess a psychological edge common to entrepreneurs.

In his book, he describes a psychological condition called hypomania, a milder form of the mania associated with bipolar disorder. Hypomanics, as Gartner defines them, experience heightened levels of energy, confidence, and restlessness, but usually none of the draining darkness of depression. This makes them more likely to act boldly and confidently, and maybe dare to start a business, despite the high odds against success.

Gartner contends that America is home to more hypomanics than anywhere else on earth. Thanks to immigrants, it's in our gene pool.

"Who but a restless dreamer could leave everything they knew and trusted to start a new life in a strange land?" he writes. "As a nation of immigrants, America became a nation of optimistic risk-takers."

By accepting the world's strivers and dreamers, Gartner argues, America gained a "hypomanic edge."

The Carnegie report also identified a risk-taking appetite as a key quality shared by immigrants and entrepreneurs. Its authors observe a "self-selection" process that skims strivers from humdrum places around the globe and sends them to the land

> *You basically buy a job (the motel) and staff it with family.*
>
> —hotelier Vinu Patel

of opportunity. They take a less quixotic view of immigrant achievers than others, however. They give a lot of the credit to savvy family back in the old country.

"Households typically make the decision about emigration on a collective basis, determining whom to send and where to send them in ways that they calculate will exact the most success and diminish risk," the authors of the Carnegie report observe. "They are, in a sense, canny portfolio managers."

Not surprisingly, the families send their most likely to succeed, typically, a dynamic son with lots of determination.

Researchers, and immigrants themselves, have revealed other immigrant traits that promote entrepreneurship, like social cohesiveness. The fact that immigrants tend to live near one another leads to niche businesses. Frustration borne from discrimination is a powerful motivator to become one's own boss, interviews reveal. So is an inability to speak English fluently—and thus an inability to apply for many jobs. A ready source of cheap labor can make a family business loom more attractive.

Vinu and Jyodi Patel, Indian-born hoteliers in Cleveland, Ohio, broke into the hospitality industry by putting their three daughters to work changing beds and cleaning rooms until the family business was successful enough to send them to college. The children were all the staff they could afford and they could hardly refuse, the couple explained.

"You basically buy a job (the motel) and staff it with family," Vinu Patel explained. From such constraints and opportunity, an entrepreneurial tradition is born.

"There is even reason to suspect that immigrant self-employment is more of a survival strategy than an indication of socioeconomic success—more, that is, of a lifeboat than a ladder," the Carnegie authors conclude.

For most Americans, it is enough to know that the impact of this entrepreneurial tradition is overwhelmingly positive.

A Skill Grows Lucrative

While many American workers fear that immigrants will take their jobs, be it in a factory or in a laboratory, or seethe to suspect that illegal immigrants are skirting national laws, few disparage the success of the legal immigrant business owner.

Even the humblest mom and pop shop typically provides an essential service, whether it is shoe repair or dry cleaning or a cab ride. Immigrant businesses are widely credited with strengthening the fabric of communities. In clusters, they can revive whole neighborhoods, even cities.

Miami, Florida; Schenectady, New York; Lowell, Massachusetts; and Columbus, Ohio, are four cities that found depressed parts of town revived by the arrival of a sudden, large wave of ambitious immigrants. If the Somali refugees had not shown up unexpected on Columbus's north side, or if Cambodians had not descended upon Lowell, the cities would have been wise to recruit them.

Research by Harvard Business School professor Michael Porter indicates that immigrants not only start businesses in the nation's inner cities, but also are catalysts who inspire more investment. He found that inner cities that attracted immigrants enjoyed the greatest economic growth.

The tradition of immigrant entrepreneurship endures, maybe stronger than ever. Thanks to changes in the immigrant pool, it may also be more potent than ever. Yes, the ethnic restaurants and mom and pop shops remain vital. But today's immigrants bring a whole new set of skills, and immigrant entrepreneurs have ventured far beyond city street corners.

The average annual net income of an Indian-owned business in America is $83,000, Fairlie notes. That's $33,000 higher than the average for a native-born owned business. In fact, many immigrant nationalities, including Taiwanese, Filipinos, Canadians, and Greek business owners, outperform the U.S.-born average.

Meanwhile, the variety of businesses is exploding. Immigrants are overrepresented in industries as diverse as medicine, the arts, entertainment, and recreation.

Most significantly, as Saxenian revealed and Wadhwa elaborated on, immigrants are well represented at the cutting edge. They dominate the so-called sunrise industries expected to create the jobs of tomorrow.

Mother of Invention

There may be no better indicator of transformative creativity than the Nobel Prize. Nearly one-third of U.S. Nobel Laureates are immigrants, including all four U.S. Nobel laureates in 1999.

Immigrant inventiveness has enabled America to lead and transform the world. Levi Strauss, an immigrant from Germany, invented the ultimate symbol of American freedom: blue jeans. Serbian immigrant Nikola Tesla gave us the radio and electrical marvels, and Sergey Brin, a Russian refugee, helped to organize and make accessible the world's knowledge through an Internet search engine called Google.

Patent filings indicate this immigrant tradition in innovation is accelerating.

The U.S. Patent and Trademark Office does not collect the nationality of inventors, which limited Wadhwa's patent research to an international patent database. But Harvard Business School professor William Kerr took another approach, one that he believes further illuminates immigrant innovation.

Kerr examined names on U.S. patent records and made some assumptions, for example, that Chang and Wang were Chinese, while Martinez and Rodriguez were Hispanic. Using name-matching software, he identified the likely ethnicity of everyone who acquired a U.S. patent since 1975, some 7.5 million people.

The results, published in a 2008 report, indicate that foreign-born researchers have become a critical part of America's base of inventors. Most notably, the contributions of Chinese and Indian scientists to U.S. technology spiked in the 1990s, helping to power America's high-tech innovation.

Kerr found that the share of patents awarded to "English-named" scientists fell between 1975 and 2004. However, the share of all patents given to scientists of obvious Chinese and Indian descent more than tripled, from 4.1 percent in the second half of the 1970s to 13.9 percent in the years between 2000 and 2004.

Some of these patents may have been awarded to American-born children of immigrants, but Kerr thinks that immigrants are behind most of the bright new work.

This growth in "ethnic innovation," as Kerr calls it, is concentrated in gateway cities, like San Francisco and New York City, and in high-tech industries like computers and pharmaceuticals. An astonishing 40 percent of patents filed in 2005 by Intel, a silicon-chip maker, were for work done by people of Chinese or Indian origin.

Building on Wadhwa's and Kerr's research, a 2009 study by Jennifer Hunt and Marjolaine Gauthier-Loiselle, professors of McGill University and Princeton University, respectively, found that immigrants obtained patents at double the native rate, due to their disproportionate number of degrees in science and engineering. The study, "How Much Does Immigration Boost Innovation?" concluded that a 1 percent rise in the share of immigrant college graduates in the population increases patents by 6 percent.

People with money to invest do not need any more convincing. The venture capitalists—widely known as VCs—are betting on the New Economy immigrants to build new and better companies, and make them rich along the way.

The VCs' Keen Eye

One of the most prominent venture capital firms in Silicon Valley, Sequoia Capital, makes no secret of the kinds of people it likes to bet on. Sequoia's web site applauds the ambitious immigrant underdogs with "barely a penny to their name."

The firm helped to launch such immigrant-founded companies as Google, Yahoo, PayPal, YouTube, LinkedIn, Nvidia, and A123Systems. Venture capitalist Michael Moritz, a partner at Sequoia Capital and a former board member of Google, explained his affection for new Americans at a business conference in Cardiff, Wales, in 2007.

"It's no coincidence," he said. "You go around most of these companies and . . . all of the founders and very early employees are either an immigrant or a first-generation American. That has been the fuel that has propelled these companies."

In 2006, the National Venture Capital Association, which represents the people and firms that invest in young, risky companies, put hard data to Moritz's observation. It sponsored a deep look at the kinds of people its members were bankrolling and published its findings in a report titled "American Made: The Impact of Immigrant Entrepreneurs and Professionals on U.S. Competitiveness."

And what an impact. Looking at businesses launched between 1990 and 2005 with money from venture capitalists, the researchers concluded that immigrants were behind one-fourth of all public venture-backed companies created in America. Add a high-technology label, and the immigrant share soared to 40 percent. The study showed that the market capitalization of U.S. public companies founded by immigrants and backed by venture capital reached $500 billion.

Some of those immigrants started companies that became icons of the New Economy:

- Sergey Brin, a founder of Google, emigrated from Russia as a child.
- Vinod Khosla, a co-founder of Sun Microsystems, was born in India. His partner, Andreas von Bechtolsheim, came from Germany.
- Pierre Omidyar, the founder of eBay, was born in France to Iranian immigrants.
- Andrew Grove, a founder of Intel, emigrated from Hungary.
- Jerry Yang, co-founder of Yahoo, came to the United States from Taiwan as a teenager.
- Elon Musk came to the United States from South Africa and later co-founded PayPal.

Those are just the rock stars of the New Economy. In companies small and large, some famous and some you've never heard of, immigrants are often the ones pushing the envelope, introducing ideas, defining the state of the art, and earning riches for themselves and their partners.

Researchers found immigrant founders responsible for launching a high percentage of the most innovative American companies. Nearly 90 percent of the venture-backed companies were operating in advanced sectors like high-technology manufacturing, information technology, and life sciences.

VCs like Guy Kawasaki say they like immigrants for their combination of smarts and grit. Kawasaki is the managing director of Garage Technology Ventures, an early-stage venture capital firm, as well as an author and a magazine columnist who writes often about successful entrepreneurship. To boost the economy, he argues, America should encourage immigration.

"If I had a choice between funding someone from a family who moved here from Vietnam whose father and mother run a 7-Eleven versus a descendant of a *Mayflower* passenger with 'IV' in his name, I'll give you half a guess as to my preference," Kawasaki wrote. "You need to encourage smart, hungry, and aggressive people to immigrate from around the world."

Mike Speiser, a managing director of Sutter Hill Ventures, argues immigrants are America's secret innovation weapon.

"If the first benefit of immigration is importing talent, the second is that of importing hunger," he writes in the July 4, 2009, issue of *Salon*. "Many countries lack a way to identify and reward their brightest citizens, while that has been the allure of the U.S. since our inception."

Venture capitalists who happen to be immigrants maybe possess keener insight into the immigrant advantage. On the 2009 Forbes Midas List of the top 100 VCs, six of the top 11 are immigrants, including Michael Moritz at #2, and fellow early Google funders David Cheritan, Andreas von Bechtolsheim, and Ram Shriram.

New Seeds, Fertile Soil

The authors of "American Made," like others examining immigrant entrepreneurship, hint at some kind of alchemy at work. Immigrant plus America often equals super achievement. Is it them or is it America? The answer seems to be that it's both.

Few of the immigrants who attained venture capital funding came to America to start a business, noted Stuart Anderson, a co-author of the report, echoing Wadhwa's findings. Most often, they came as children, college students, or young professionals who had secured a work visa, like the H–1B, designed for foreign workers with special skills. They obviously possessed something special before they arrived here, Anderson observes. But they also found something special here.

"Few of these impressive immigrant entrepreneurs could have started a company immediately upon arriving in the U.S.," he writes. "Many were just children, international students or H–1B professionals. But it's clear that America helped shape them into entrepreneurs as much as they helped shape America."

If America gave immigrants the opportunity to achieve their dreams, the nation grew stronger and more competitive for doing so.

In recent times, public attention and public policy have focused on mass immigration and illegal immigration, two forces that arouse much controversy and anxiety. Far less attention has fallen on immigrants who enter America legally, aim high, and achieve.

> *It's clear that America helped shape them into entrepreneurs as much as they helped shape America.*
>
> —researcher Stuart Anderson

While the small immigrant business is still prevalent and pivotal, today's immigrants often bring degrees from the best universities in India, China, and Africa. They are as likely to invent a better technology as open a bodega. They bring cultural skills that lend themselves to international business and a global economy. They tend to be multilingual, broad-minded, and adventurous. An uncanny number of them possess an ambition that blooms in America's free-market business culture.

This new class of immigrants is as diverse as it is extraordinary.

- Geno Bahena came from Mexico with an eighth-grade education and his mother's recipes. He went on to become one of the most celebrated chefs in Chicago.
- Monte Ahuja arrived with enough money for one semester of college, spied opportunity unimaginable back home, and created Transtar Industries, the most successful auto parts company you never heard of.
- Xunming Deng and Liwei Xu distinguished themselves as two of the top high school students in all of China before college scholarships brought them to America. Now a Midwest community pins its job dreams on Xunlight Corporation, the solar-energy company the couple created here.

Deng and Xu, Ahuja and Bahena, and thousands like them arrived as America was joining a knowledge-based, global economy. They found a market for their food and their science and their passion. A growing body of research attests to the entrepreneurial talent and ideas of this immigrant generation and the phenomenon they represent. But the studies tell only part of the story.

From the immigrants and their odysseys we can learn much more: why they came, what strategies they pursued to achieve their dreams, and what beliefs motivated them to try again and again.

What is it about America that works so well for the new immigrants? What do they bring from the old country that speeds their climb?

As American families and American companies seek to recover from the worst recession since the Great Depression and pursue the jobs of tomorrow, can immigrants point the way?

They already are.

Chapter 3

A Land of Opportunity, Still

To think that a once scrawny boy from Austria could grow up to become Governor of California and stand in Madison Square Garden to speak on behalf of the President of the United States, that is an immigrant's dream. It is the American dream.

—Arnold Schwarzenegger

Monte Ahuja's first memory of the city where he would make his fortune still shines vivid—like a lingering nightmare.

He arrived in Cleveland late on a spring night in 1969. The college semester at Ohio State University was over and he had lined up a summer job 150 miles away with a company that sold the latest backyard appliance, gas grills.

He had little money, no car, and no driver's license anyway. But he caught a ride from Columbus with another student in exchange for some gas money. His first challenge was finding a cheap place to stay.

Back in India, he had heard that his YMCA membership card was good anywhere in the world. He knew there was a YMCA in downtown Cleveland. He considered his options. He did not really have any. He knew not a soul in Cleveland and his new job started the next day.

His ride dropped him off several blocks from the downtown Y and Ahuja began to walk. He carried one small suitcase. It was growing dark. He was on the downscale outskirts of downtown and the streets were empty.

Out of the corner of his eye, he noticed a group of young men. They began to saunter toward him. He quickened his pace. They closed in, peppering him with taunts. Panicked, Ahuja broke into a run. He sprinted across a street and toward a neon Y glowing on a brown-brick building a block away. He reached the doorway unmolested and climbed the stairs and stumbled inside, panting.

A man stood behind the check-in desk in an empty lobby. Ahuja stepped forward and offered his membership card from the YMCA of Chandigarh, India.

"Is this good here?" he asked.

The man studied the card through glasses, looked up at Ahuja, and looked back at the card.

"Yes, it is," he said.

Ahuja let out a breath and smiled. It was his first bit of good news all day.

"But we're full," the man added. "Sorry."

Forty years later, you'll find Monte Ahuja at a far different address. Suburban neighborhoods give way to country roads and bridle trails as you approach his 11-acre estate in the Cleveland suburb of Hunting Valley, one of the most affluent communities in the United States. A driveway winds up a hill past electronic gates to a massive brick house surrounded by serene gardens and tall trees. It represents a remarkable ascent for an immigrant who spent his first night in town on a couch in the lobby of the YMCA.

If you've never heard of Monte Ahuja, your car mechanic has, and that's what matters to him. Ahuja (pronounced a-HOO-ja) is the founder and chief executive of Transtar Industries Inc., the largest seller of transmission parts in the world, a company active in about 70 countries in 2009.

Ahuja wrote the business plan as part of a class project at Cleveland State University. His professor awarded him an A and encouraged him to get started. With meager capital and a powerful resolve, Ahuja did just that. Today, Transtar employs nearly 2,000 people and the business school building at his alma mater is named after him.

> *Most immigrants that I know, they don't say, "I'm going to America to find a job." It's bigger than that. They come here because they see this as a land of opportunity, where you can achieve anything you want.*
>
> —entrepreneur Monte Ahuja

An immigrant entrepreneur and a multimillionaire, Ahuja credits hard work and the magic of America for his success. He insists he could not have scaled such heights in India.

"In many ways, my life is an example of the great American dream," he likes to say.

It's clear, however, that Ahuja brought some key qualities with him from half a world away: a mechanical engineering degree, a restless energy, and self-discipline instilled by strong parents in a traditional Hindu home.

Ahuja, both a driven and a pensive man, acknowledges some of this. He wonders if his blind drive to get to America and to accomplish something big was a sign of self-confidence or an indication of entrepreneurial instinct.

"Nobody could deter me. I was just so determined to make it work," he said. "I was going to go there and find the right idea—and I did."

He's not the only one.

A True Model Minority

Monte Ahuja is part of a wave of immigrants from South Asia in general and India in particular who came to America in recent times and achieved remarkable things. So successful are people from his ethnic background that some call them the model minority. Demographers call them the most successful immigrant wave in history.

Many Americans are aware of Indian immigrants in their midst because of the clerk at the corner store, the one with the lilting Hindi accent. People of Indian descent operate about one-third of the nation's convenience stores, according to the Asian American Convenience Stores Association.

Perhaps they noticed it was an Indian child who again won the school spelling bee. The children of Indian immigrants have come to dominate many of the nation's academic competitions, most notably spelling bees.

The two distinct settings illustrate two uncommonly strong pursuits of Asian Indians—entrepreneurship and education.

If you do any traveling, chances are you have stayed at a Patel Hotel. Indian Americans—almost all tracing their roots to the state of Gujarat in west India, and most bearing the surname Patel—owned more than 40 percent of the nation's hotels and motels in 2008, according to their trade association, the Asian American Hotel Owners Association. It's an astonishing business niche when you consider that, before 1970, Indian Americans barely existed in America, let alone in the hospitality industry.

While mom and dad are making beds or stocking store shelves, the kids are studying to do something better. Indian success at spelling bees, the stuff of legend, is no myth. In 2008, the top two finishers in the Scripps National Spelling Bee were Indian Americans. That was a bit of a letdown from 2005, when the top four finishers were all of Indian descent. Spelling bee workshops draw hundreds of children to Hindu temples in cities with large Indian immigrant communities. So do geography bees, math circles, and science fairs.

It's not a fascination with etymology that finds Indian parents poring over word lists with their children. It's a reverence for learning. People of Indian descent are the most educated ethnic group in America. Nearly 75 percent of Asian Indians older than 24 years of age hold a four-year college degree, which dwarfs the national average of 28 percent.

The schoolwork pays off. In 2007, the median household income for Americans born in India was $91,195, the highest of any identifiable group, according to the U.S. Census Bureau. That's because their success at spelling bees is mirrored in more important fields. While comprising less than 1 percent of America's population, Indian Americans constitute 3 percent of the nation's engineers. They are overrepresented among technology workers, college professors, and doctors. Between 10 and 12 percent of all medical school students in America are Indian, according to the American Association of Physicians of Indian Origin, the largest physicians group in America after the American Medical Association.

Indian success in America is vast and varied. The community now boasts Hollywood filmmakers like M. Night Shyamalan, whose 1999 movie, *The Sixth Sense,* earned more than $325 million at the box office. It includes celebrity doctors like Sanjay Gupta, CNN's medical correspondent and a former candidate for U.S. Surgeon General; and even a few nationally known politicians, like Bobby Jindal, the governor of Louisiana.

Above all, it boasts high-tech entrepreneurs who are creating jobs in the New Economy. The Indian Institute of Technology (IIT), one of India's elite engineering colleges, found that its graduates created more than 20 million jobs around the world, according to a 2008 study.

Silicon Valley and much of the American tech world is awash with South Asian names, many of them IIT graduates like Vinod Khosla, co-founder of Sun Microsystems, Arun Netravali, former president of Bell Labs, and Suhas Patil, founder of Cirrus Logic.

The superior educational attainment, academic culture and likely high IQ of Indian Americans has already made them an economic force in the U.S., and that strength can only grow.

—researcher Jason Richwine

The influence of the Indian immigrant community in the New Economy astonished the National Venture Capital Association, which in 2006 commissioned a study to examine the competitiveness of immigrant entrepreneurs.

Between 1990 and 2005, researchers concluded, immigrants founded 25 percent of the public companies created with venture capital funding. That figure is even higher in high tech, where immigrants founded 40 percent of such businesses. And in the private sector, nearly half of all venture-backed start-ups surveyed were founded by immigrants.

Within that industrious group of immigrant founders, Asian Indians stood tallest. People born in India started 22 percent of the immigrant-founded companies, far more than any other ethnic group and double the share of the next highest ownership group, Israelis.

Why do Indian Americans perform so well? What's their secret? For one thing, they arrive with a natural advantage over many other immigrants—they speak and write English. They also hail from a culture that values education, which tends to propel them to earn advanced degrees. Some argue they are simply smarter than most everyone else, thanks to the self-selection process that sent them here.

America's immigration system favors family reunification. So most immigrants gain entry by virtue of a relative already here. That's not much help to the new immigrants from Asia, Africa and Latin America, who are less likely to have American family who can sponsor their immigration.

A much smaller number of immigrants, about 15 percent, gain entry because of a job offer and a work visa. Many of those tend to be Indians, notes Jason Richwine, a National Research Institute fellow for the American Enterprise Institute.

"The proportion of Indian immigrants given an employment-related green card is one of the highest of any nationality," Richwine wrote in the February 24, 2009, edition of *Forbes* magazine. "Consequently, it is mainly India's educated elite and their families who come to the U.S."

He argues that the selection process skims the best and brightest from a nation of a billion people, obviously.

"To be a great speller—or, more importantly, a great doctor or IT manager—you have to be smart," he writes. "The superior educational attainment, academic culture and likely high IQ of Indian Americans has already made them an economic force in the U.S., and that strength can only grow."

To really understand why Indian Americans achieve such success in America, we need to see the world as they do. The odyssey of a young man from northern India lends some insight into a powerful culture of entrepreneurship.

An Idea, an Obsession

In 1967, when Monte Ahuja graduated from Punjab Engineering College in his hometown of Chandigarh, a provincial city north of New Delhi, America was just opening up to skilled workers from around the world. The Immigration and Nationality Act of 1965 had abolished the decades-old national-origin quotas, removing many of the barriers to immigrants from Asia. The new opportunity caused a sensation on India's college campuses.

Thirty to 35 of the young men from Ahuja's graduating class were going to America, including several of his teammates from the cricket team. Ahuja was intrigued. He had never left India. He had never been on a plane. But he was a good student. Going on to America "seemed like the thing to do." He started reading up on American universities and applying to schools. Delicately, he approached his first hurdle.

When he told his parents of his goal, to go on to graduate school in America, they expressed shock. He was the oldest son in a middle-class family of 11. It was expected he would begin to help support a family that could not afford college abroad. He was about to graduate with an engineering degree, which meant good job prospects in India.

"My parents said, 'How are you going to do it? We can't afford this. You are the oldest son. We are a big family. We're looking for your support,'" he recalls.

His father, an accountant for the government, had always pushed schooling. From fifth grade on, he told his eldest son, "You're going to be an engineer," considered a top profession in India.

"Education is stressed in every home in India," Ahuja said. "Really, it is the only thing that is stressed."

Ahuja kept pushing back, politely but firmly. This could be a great opportunity, he argued. He promised to be gone only a year or two. He assured his parents he would find a job and make money and come home.

Finally, his father relented. And once he gave his blessing, he gave his full support.

"Once he was convinced that I was going to go, Dad offered to sell the house. He told me, 'I'll give you the shirt off my back,'" Ahuja recalls.

> No matter what happened, how miserable, how depressed I felt, the next morning I got up and said, "You know what? I gotta go on."
>
> —Monte Ahuja

His father did not have to sell the house. The family scraped together enough money for two quarters of graduate school at Ohio State University, where Ahuja was accepted for the winter semester starting in January 1969. The whole family saw him off at the airport.

At the time, India allowed émigrés to leave with no more than about $15 in cash. So that's what Ahuja carried in his wallet, $15, and a $1,200 bank draft note for tuition.

"In my obsession," Ahuja says, he overlooked a few details. Like winter. He had no warm coat. He had no extra money, either, should the journey not go smoothly.

The trip was a nightmare. Mechanical problems and weather delays stretched a two-day airplane journey into five days. He arrived in Columbus on December 28, 1968, three days after Christmas.

"It was the coldest, most furious winter I could have imagined," Ahuja recalls. He had about $2 left in his pocket.

At a near-empty airport, he bummed a ride to campus from a long-haired man who turned out to be a professor. He found his rooming house, collapsed on a couch, and two days later started classes. There was no orientation. There was no one to approach for help or advice. For the first time in his life, he realized, he was on his own. He was 21 years old.

"I felt very lonely, especially after just leaving a large family of seven sisters and a brother who all catered to me," he said.

But there was no turning back. His family had shown too much faith for him to fail them.

"I vowed never to ask my father or my family for another dime," Ahuja said. "I would make my own way."

The semester sped by and another tuition payment loomed. On a job board in the engineering school, he saw a posting for a laborer position with Gas Light Ohio, a company in a Cleveland suburb. That's how he came to be sprinting toward the downtown Cleveland YMCA on a spring night in 1969.

Learning to Persevere

That summer, as he dug ditches in the hot sun and installed gas grills and collapsed on his cot at the Y, Ahuja often wondered what his engineering degree was for. More than once, he questioned if he had made a mistake coming to America. But always, he pushed the thought from his mind.

"At so many points I thought, 'Why am I doing this? I could go home and have a good job. Here I'm digging ditches and taking showers with 10 other guys.'"

But quitting was not an option. It was too shameful to contemplate. Forty years later, Ahuja's voice gains a raspy strength just thinking about it.

"No, I am not going to go back to India and say, 'I failed, I failed, I couldn't survive. I couldn't make it.'"

So he worked and worried and wrote letters home that said all was well. His brief, expensive phone calls betrayed no regrets.

"I never, ever shared my miseries with my parents, with my family," he said. "All they ever heard me say was, 'Things are tough but things are fine.' No matter what happened, how miserable, how depressed I felt, the next morning I got up and said, 'You know what? I gotta go on.'"

Ahuja said he thinks a lot of people lack that kind of perseverance, which he describes as essential to success in business. Many times, he said, he beat someone to the job or to the client because he tried harder. He won because he would not give up.

A focus on survival segued into some stability, friendships, and steady part-time jobs. There was another young man from India in his rooming house, and he introduced Ahuja to his sister, Usha. She was a pretty mathematics star in India who had come to the United States to complete her Ph.D., in mathematics. Ahuja was enchanted.

In 1971, he graduated with a master's degree in mechanical engineering and married Usha. A visa issue loomed for the young couple. If they were to stay in the country, he needed to be a student or working.

By now, he had a contact, someone of whom he might ask a favor. The year before, Ahuja had responded to an ad for a job opening at a Cleveland car parts supplier called Lemco Industries. The job was in the catalogue department and the hiring manager told Ahuja he wasn't qualified. But after Ahuja argued for a chance, the manager threw down a challenge. He handed him a car parts catalogue as thick as a phone book and told him to find 10 specific parts in 10 minutes.

Ahuja examined the book, absorbed the logic of its 1,500 pages, and found the parts in 9 minutes. He got the job.

Little was expected of him, the summer help, but he worked hard and smart. He pored over trade manuals in the shop. After a day of work, he walked to the library to read about transmissions. "I had nothing else to do," he explained.

He made himself an expert on car parts. He finished projects early and stayed late. More important, he caught the attention of company president Robert Neitzel.

When the summer ended, Neitzel told Ahuja that if he ever needed another job, he should call him. A year later, holding a master's degree and needing an employer to sponsor a work visa, Ahuja made that phone call.

He was put through to the president, who told him to come on in. Ahuja savored the moment. For the first time in his immigrant odyssey, he thought, "Wow, I'm going to make it."

As a moviemaker might say, it was the beginning of a beautiful relationship. Neitzel became Ahuja's mentor. He pulled him into executive meetings, called him the "whiz kid," and often sought his advice. Ahuja found himself involved in every facet of the company, from purchasing to sales and distribution to personnel and strategic planning. "It was phenomenal training," he said.

The young engineer embraced the business side of the operation. He decided to go to night school for a master's degree in business administration. He enrolled at Cleveland State University, a commuter school not far from his first home at the Y.

For three years, he commuted from work to school to home in Hudson, a Cleveland suburb on the highway to Kent State University, where Usha taught mathematics. The two daughters would come later. For now, the young couple focused solely on work and careers.

The "A" earned in an entrepreneurship course helped Ahuja score near the top of his class. Basically, he had taken what he learned at his day job and designed a better system, one based on just-in-time delivery.

"I acted like I was running Lemco. I asked myself, 'How would I do it the right way?'"

He resolved to solve a supply problem pervasive in the car repair business. Repair shops waited days for parts needed to repair cars and trucks, meaning customers had to wait for days for their vehicles. No one was happy. Ahuja designed a model of fast delivery to restless mechanics. Using UPS, he would deliver parts the next day to repair shops large and small, something never done before.

"Everyone just did it the same way—three or four day delivery," he said. "No one thought to change."

His professor pulled him aside and asked him if he were serious about starting the company. Ahuja said he was. "Then I have someone for you to meet," the professor said. He introduced Ahuja to a banker, who offered a $10,000 loan. Ahuja borrowed another $5,000 from his brother-in-law and found a partner to invest $25,000 more.

On April 1, 1975, four weeks after graduation, he launched Transtar Industries. He was 29 years old.

In the beginning, Ahuja and his partner stocked the warehouse and packaged parts themselves, often working late into the night. Ahuja eventually bought out his partner and soldiered on. The business grew slowly but steadily, from a two-person operation to a staff of 100, to a worldwide company with 2,000 employees and $500 million in annual revenues. By 2008, Transtar was the largest supplier of transmission repair parts in the world.

Survival, Climbing, and Thriving

On a fall morning in 2008, Monte Ahuja sat in a home office bedecked with civic awards and golf trophies and reflected on a marathon. His 61st year found him proud but restless, still quick to take a work call at home. He had sold his majority stake in Transtar in 2005 but retained a substantial ownership position and continued as the company's chairman and chief executive.

> *Education is stressed in every home in India. Really, it is the only thing that is stressed.*
>
> —Monte Ahuja

More than a business success, Ahuja was now an admired civic leader and a philanthropist, the first graduate of Cleveland State University to serve as chairman of the university board of trustees. Business students at CSU filed into the gleaming brick and glass Monte Ahuja Hall. In 2007, he and Usha donated $30 million to University Hospitals of Cleveland, one of the largest philanthropic gifts in America that year.

Despite his wealth and his three college degrees, Ahuja resembles the mechanics whose work he makes easier. He's a plain-spoken, square-jawed man with a ruddy, weathered face topped by a thick head of dark hair. He addresses a subject simply and directly and often at length. He likes to begin with a system and break it down into key parts, much like a vehicle.

He sees three stages of the immigrant experience: survival, climbing, and thriving. Survival is enhanced by the desire to climb and the expectation that, eventually, you will probably thrive, he said.

"Most immigrants that I know, they don't say, 'I'm going to America to find a job.' It's bigger than that," he said. "They come here because they see this as a land of opportunity, where you can achieve anything you want. So they come here motivated to succeed. And they feel the system allows them to succeed."

He thinks a lot of immigrants' success can be attributed not only to high hopes, but also to sacrifice and persistence, and much of that comes from upbringing.

His family's focus on education helped immensely, Ahuja said. He arrived in the United States an educated man eager to learn more. He had a reserve of self-discipline and a strong sense of fairness and loyalty, which he credits to his parents and to his Hindu culture.

"My father used to say, 'Reach for the stars but keep your feet on the ground.' I consider my basic values of family and friends and loyalty intact."

Ahuja believes the harshness of the immigrant experience lent him insight and fortitude that many native-born Americans lack. "They haven't seen the other side of the world. People from Mexico, India, China, they see how difficult life can be. People who are born here, they take America for granted," he said.

"It never occurred to me that I could go to an agency and say, 'I need some money for food.' That was never a choice. If I had to buy food, I had to find a way to make that five bucks. If I was going to go to school here, I had to work here. And if I was going to work here, I knew I had to be better than everybody else. I admired the lifestyle and I was motivated to be a part of it."

He even thinks that discrimination propelled him. Early in his career, Ahuja quickly became aware of the reactions raised by his dark complexion and foreign accent. Some of the racism was blatant. Some was subtle. Always, it reinforced his desire to become his own boss and to overachieve.

A self-taught golfer with an enviable 10 handicap, he's a member of eight country clubs. But he remembers that he was rejected from the first golf club he sought to join because his last name was judged unacceptable.

To grow his business, he had to make cold calls, unsolicited phone calls to potential customers. "I speak different. I have an accent. Some people asked, 'Who the hell are you, coming here from a foreign country?'"

But they also remembered him, which is what he needed them to do.

Ahuja stood out. He was the foreigner, that Indian with the new ideas. He had to explain quickly who he was and how his company was different. He became good at it. "I actually was able to transform that weakness, or deficiency, into my strength," he said. "Even to this day, after nearly 40 years in this business, I'm the only Indian in the industry."

But Ahuja credits most of his success to his adopted home. Compared to the rest of the planet, he insists, America is just a great place to achieve dreams.

Where Business Is Business

The 29,000-square-foot home, with an elevator, a gym, and an indoor pool, attests to the owner's financial success but also to his acceptance in the region's civic leadership. The walk-out basement is large enough to serve dinners to 140 guests when Monte and Usha hold fundraisers for the governor, or for U.S. Senator George Voinovich, an immigrant's grandson.

Reflecting upon his success, Ahuja remarked upon something that still astonishes him about America. As he created a multimillion-dollar business, government officials never hindered him. Tax collectors never harassed him. No one ever demanded of him a bribe.

"You do an honest job and you succeed and nobody bothers you," he said, a trace of marvel in his voice.

It's not like that everywhere in the world, immigrants say again and again.

Ahuja is not the only immigrant entrepreneur to praise the American business environment.

Tom Szaky, the 26-year-old wunderkind who created what *Inc.* magazine called "The coolest little start-up in America," knows he never could have launched TerraCycle, Inc., in his native Hungary or even in Canada, his first immigrant destination.

"I just raised 15 million dollars in my early twenties, and, like, here you can pull that off," he said in early 2009. "What is amazing is that people will support you and it wouldn't happen anywhere else."

TerraCycle's flagship product is a liquid plant food made from worm excrement. It's packaged in recycled plastic soda bottles. Szaky calls himself "an eco-capitalist" and he offers a bevy of green household products in a style all his own. To pitch his product to his first corporate customer, Home Depot, he arrived unshaven, in jeans, and wearing a John Deere baseball cap.

"There is an identification of rags to riches in the underlying culture," Szaky said of America. "In other countries, the dream doesn't exist. You couldn't just start a business."

Ib Olsen echoes those sentiments. The immigrant from Denmark is co-founder of Gaia Power Technologies, which he founded with his wife, an immigrant from Turkey. The New York–based company designs and builds large-scale batteries to store electricity for power companies and businesses. Olsen expresses amazement at the openness of the American market.

"It's the easiest place to start a company, at least compared to the European countries," he said. "The fact is that I can go on the Internet and the next day I can have a company tax identification number."

He's equally impressed that he can hire and fire whom he wishes. "The labor law in the U.S. is very company friendly," he said. "I am not afraid of hiring a couple of people. In Europe, there is much less flexibility for the business owner to react to changing market conditions."

Ahuja shares a common immigrant lament when he says that, back home, he would have run into a thicket of regulations and licensing requirements to start Transtar Industries.

There are other impediments. In many parts of the world, entrepreneurs face cultural constraints that discourage upward mobility and individualism. Corruption is pervasive in many developing countries. In 2008, Transparency International ranked India the 22nd most corrupt nation in the world.

In much of Africa and Latin America, meanwhile, entrepreneurs worry about political and economic instability. In China and Vietnam, the threat of political repression is ever present.

"Success in business in the United States is a lot easier than any other country in the world," Ahuja is convinced. He and other immigrants describe aspects of America that native-born citizens likely overlook or take for granted. They see an upwardly mobile society that newcomers can join rather quickly, especially if they speak English. They see a pro-business environment with institutions that support entrepreneurship, like an independent court system, efficient capital markets, good highways, and a reliable power grid.

They see a need for workers with math and science skills.

The word spreads among the strivers of the world, the people who want more out of life. People not just in India, but in Africa, Russia, Latin America, and the Pacific Rim.

Immigrants time and again talk about landing in America and feeling unshackled, suddenly free to discover all they can be.

As Ahuja describes it: "An immigrant comes here with a pre-determined motivation to succeed. They see other people succeed, and they say, 'I can do that.'"

Chapter 4

Restless Dreamers

Every great dream begins with a dreamer.

—Harriet Tubman

The Spanish island of Mallorca in the Mediterranean Sea offers an idyllic setting. Sandy beaches. Charming, butter-colored villages. Sailing from deep blue bays. But that was not the world Carmen Castillo knew. She was crew class. Her parents moved the family from Granada to Mallorca to work the tourist trade when she was a little girl. In a poor, hardworking Catholic family of 11, little Carmen, the "blond sheep" of the family, stood out.

Her hair color was different from everyone else and so was she. As she washed dishes and peeled potatoes, she dreamed of owning the restaurant. She was a bright student, but even as she earned A's in Spanish language and history, she asked about life in other places.

"I grew up different," Castillo struggles to explain. "At 6, I knew I would own my own company. At 12, I'm already a young woman planning my future."

Spain felt confining to her. A democracy with a modern economy, Spain is also a traditional, patriarchal society, Castillo said. The prospects are limited for people from lower classes, especially a woman, she argues. By the time she graduated from high school, she had resolved to leave.

"I just knew, to own my own business—which is what I always wanted—I had to come to America," she said.

Single, alone, and 22, she came to the United States in 1990 with a temporary visa and a high school diploma. The Internet age was dawning and Castillo sensed the potential. She knew nothing about technology. She did not even own a computer. But she knew something about seizing opportunity.

Within three years of her arrival, she launched Superior Design International from her one-bedroom apartment. Corporate America hoped to tap information technology, and Castillo promised to help find them the staff to do it. She went on to pioneer the consulting edge of the high-tech era.

By early 2009, Castillo was running one of the largest Hispanic-owned businesses in America and one of the largest woman-owned businesses in the world. SDI had offices in a dozen cities and six foreign countries. Company revenues exceeded $200 million a year.

Castillo, now 44 years old and still restless, sits perched at the edge of a seat in her office north of Ft. Lauderdale as if ready to leap. She credits her success to a mentor who still offers advice and support. But she also credits her own vision and derring-do.

"I saw the opportunity. A great opportunity," Castillo reflects. "You have to have that vision. And you have to have guts."

From time to time, she meets others like herself—usually when she meets another immigrant. That should hardly be surprising, she says.

"They had the courage to leave and be new. That right there tells you something," she insists.

The immigrants she knows are often innovators, typically techies but also scientists, chefs, musicians, tour guides, and teachers. They tend to be restless souls who exude energy and optimism during even the bleakest of times.

They are, Castillo believes, born entrepreneurs. Just like her.

Her first visit to the United States, as a tourist in 1989, sealed her decision. She arranged to visit friends she had met while working and cooking in Mallorca. She stayed for three months.

"It was exactly what I expected. I thought I was in heaven," she said.

Castillo returned to America the next year on a student visa, intent on somehow starting a business and making her stay permanent. She's a friendly woman with a quiet confidence, and she tends to connect with people quickly. At culinary school in Palm Beach, Florida, she befriended a couple from Buffalo, New York. When her friend became sick with cancer, Castillo offered to come north for a few months and help care for her three children. In Buffalo, she took a part-time job at a trendy restaurant just opening downtown.

As the word Internet entered the vocabulary, she was running a kitchen and living on high anxiety. Her two-year student visa was about to expire. The thought of going home distressed her mightily.

Her options were limited. She did not want to marry her way into the country, as she knew other women had done. She needed an employer who could sponsor a work visa. Or, better yet, she needed an opportunity to become her own employer.

Seeing It First

After only a few months in Buffalo, Castillo had impressed many with her cooking skills and with her energy, a cheerful passion that rallied a kitchen crew. One of her admirers was Richard Stenclik, a graphic designer who founded a successful recruitment firm called the Superior Group of Companies.

Stenclik and his son walked into the restaurant one day, enjoyed what they considered a marvelous meal, and asked to give their regards to the chef. They met a dynamo with a Spanish accent.

Castillo recalls the elder Stenclik's prediction like he made it yesterday. "He said, 'Oh, you're a superstar and you don't know it yet.'"

With the meter running down on her visa, Castillo told Stenclik of her dream of starting her own business. "Pitch me an idea," he said.

Castillo leveled her gaze. "The Internet," she said. "It's going to make a lot of companies need a lot of people."

That was music to the ears of a personnel recruiter. He wanted to hear more.

"I told him, with all this new technology, all the Fortune 500 companies are going to need to update," she recalled. "They're going to want to be ready for this great movement called high tech. They're going to need talent fast."

They were going to need engineers, computer programmers, program managers, Castillo reasoned. Temporary technical people. Consultants, you might call them.

A person who could connect them to such talent would be very valuable, Castillo argued, seeking to convince herself as much as her backer.

"The time was crushing for me," she explained. "I wanted to stay in America."

Stenclik was sold. The pair talked several more times before he handed Castillo a check for $70,000. Castillo moved back to Florida and into a small apartment. Armed with a telephone and the Yellow Pages, she launched Superior Design International in 1992.

Her quest to come to America became a quest to succeed at that most American of endeavors—entrepreneurship.

*　*　*

Castillo burned quickly through Richard Stenclik's $70,000 loan. A hurricane swamped Florida and set her schedule back three months. She persevered, forcing herself to make cold calls. She pursued business with the same drive and tenacity she pursued coming to America. Potential clients who ignored her phone calls sometimes found her in the lobby, willing to wait all day to make her pitch.

She enjoys sales and considers herself good at it. She believes being a woman makes her a better listener, a better salesperson. Also, it did not hurt to be different, a minority, when selling something brand new. Her customers were seeking innovation. Castillo, a multilingual woman from a foreign land, personified that.

"The challenge was mostly to learn the culture of America and the culture of business," she said. "I'm a very good listener, that's what customers loved. I would listen to them and," she snapped her fingers, "come back with a solution. If they needed an IT worker who spoke six languages, I'd find one."

Small successes led to a small office. Dade County hired her to find the talent to upgrade its information systems. Soon after, Broward County sought the same service. She paid the Superior Group, back in Buffalo, to handle her accounting, legal work and other back office operations, freeing her to focus on sales.

Castillo's big break came when Big Blue returned a call. In 1993, IBM had a large technology center near Castillo's home in Boca Raton. They asked her to help find technical talent. A local contract led to a regional contract, and finally a national contract.

She was in the offices of corporate America now. Delta Airlines, Motorola, United Parcel Service, and Unisys followed. She had learned the secret of the consulting boom in the high-tech age, the source of eternal demand for her services.

"They can never recruit the best of the best, because the best of the best don't want to be employees," she said.

A 24-Hour Job

January 2009 found Castillo at the top of her game, though a visitor to her headquarters might never guess. SDI's modest, uncluttered offices in a suburban office park reveal little of the company's global

We immigrants, we work very, very hard. And I hate to think of Americans lying on the couch watching Lou Dobbs tell them that immigrants are getting all the jobs.

—entrepreneur Carmen Castillo

reach. Castillo had recently opened offices in Shanghai, Beijing, and Bratislava, yet there was not so much as a map on a wall. No photos of family or children, either.

She's still friends with her ex-husband, but Castillo acknowledges that she did not devote enough time to her brief marriage for it to last. "I'm married to my work," she said.

Castillo said she understands why men dominate the ranks of entrepreneurship. She thinks it might be impossible for a woman to raise children while raising a company. She travels constantly. She sleeps with her BlackBerry.

"When you run your own business, it's 24 hours a day, non-stop," she said. "Scuba diving, I'm 120 feet below the surface and I'm thinking of business. At the top of Mt. Rainier, I'm thinking of my business. Once you start, there's no way out."

Still, she relishes the game. She said she sees her company worldwide in five years, ready to staff a "reverse globalization" that will find American companies bringing jobs home from India and China as workers there become less desperate, less loyal.

She suspects every nation is going to specialize in the years ahead. She sees China in advanced manufacturing, India in technology, and Vietnam and the Philippines in call centers.

America could be the center of innovation, "the latest and the greatest," Castillo said. But she also worries her adopted country might be letting go of its advantage.

Like many high-achieving immigrants, Castillo is both perplexed and distressed by the anti-immigrant sentiments that gained currency in the new century. She understands the heightened security concerns after the terrorist attacks of September 11, 2001, and the public's frustration with illegal immigration. But she believes too many people overlook legal immigrants and their remarkable achievements.

"We immigrants, we work very, very hard," she said. "And I hate to think of Americans lying on the couch watching Lou Dobbs tell them that immigrants are getting all the jobs."

She fears America is moving toward walling itself from the world's most likely to succeed—its restless dreamers—people like herself.

"I knew nothing about technology, and I think that's a reason I was successful," she said. "When you know too much, you'll never take a risk. You're too cautious. In my case, I had nothing to lose. I thought, 'If I fail, I'll just go back to Spain.'"

She could not have accomplished in Spain what she did in America, "Not in a million years," she insists. And she is not alone. All over the world are people whose nations do not have room for their ambition.

"The lazy ones, they stay home," Castillo said. "You have to have that spirit, that desire, that passion to accomplish something. You have to be born with it."

The Carmen Castillos of the world look to America: the land where dreams still come true.

Mexico Never Tasted So Good

In 2008, at age 42, Generoso "Geno" Bahena launched his fourth successful Chicago restaurant. The people of the Windy City knew his name and loved his food. He was a celebrity chef on local television. He taught in Chicago area cooking schools and consulted to national restaurant chains, like Taco Bell. The city's food critics credited him with raising Mexican cuisine to its highest standards— far from Mexico.

As much as Chicago loved Chef Geno, as he's widely known, the garrulous chef loved his adopted hometown even more.

Twenty-five years after immigrating, he still laments that he could not have achieved such acclaim back home.

Mexico's macho culture did not embrace a boy who dreamed of becoming a chef. So he brought his mother's recipes north, introduced regional Mexican meals to a Midwestern American city, and became a sensation.

"People were thrilled to have these dishes," Bahena said one day in his restaurant, a trace of wonder in his voice. "Here in the U.S., I was able to play a little bit more with Mexican food. I could try new things, but still keep the old ways. It was very freeing for me."

He became more than a successful restaurateur. In greater Chicago, a region of more than 1 million Mexican Americans, he became a catalyst for cultural fusion. Bahena illustrates a quality found often among the new immigrant achievers. He brings old ideas to new times. Like the immigrants of old, Bahena blends practices from different cultures to create new wonders.

On a weekday night in December 2008, Bahena's restaurant, Real Tenochtitlán, glowed fiesta-bright in a multi-ethnic neighborhood on the city's north side. Mexican artwork and cheerful, Caribbean colors adorned the walls of a contemporary cantina spiced with the aromas of the old country. Bahena moved through the small kitchen like a matador, both hard charging and graceful.

He's a stocky man with a broad, square face and he walks with a bit of a limp, the result of a gout-stricken leg he's been meaning to take better care of. He has a tendency to start talking and not stop. Or to start cooking and not stop.

He peered over the brim of a huge steel pot on a stovetop and gave the brew a delicate stir with a big wooden spoon. Purple hibiscus flowers simmered in water—the base for "flower water," a refreshing soft drink native to a region of Mexico.

Nearby, a woman patted out and shaped some of the hundreds of tortillas made fresh daily. Everything arises from natural ingredients in the kitchen of Chef Geno. He insists his staff prepare food by his exacting standards, which often means cooking the way he learned as a boy on a cattle ranch in the south of Mexico. That poses challenges at a trendsetting American restaurant.

More than 30 ingredients go into one of Bahena's famed moles, including chile peppers ground with mortar and pestle. Once, one of his new assistants asked why they did not simply buy a food processor, plug it in, and whir away.

Recalling the question makes Bahena sigh. For the same reason the restaurant uses only free-range poultry and natural foods, he said. For the same reason all his sauces, pastries, and tortillas are built from scratch.

"It's like food from a ranch in Mexico," he said. "There was no electricity. There was no blender."

An impatient man with many irons in the fire, Bahena is not a purist out of habit. He believes that hand-ground ingredients make tastier sauces and salsas. He believes that some of the old customs can create excitement in a new place. His career trajectory attests to the power of his strategy.

No Room for a Dream

Born in 1965, Bahena grew up in a family of six on a mountain ranch in the Pacific state of Guerrero. His late father raised dairy and beef cattle and tended tropical fruit orchards. As a rancher's son, young Geno worked the fields, milked cows, made cheese, and picked fruits and vegetables. But he also watched, transfixed, as his mother and grandmother prepared meals in the ranch house kitchen.

From an early age, food was his passion. He was quick to volunteer to ride off on horseback to the village market for garlic, sesame seeds, and chiles that flavored the mole sauces. He displayed a knack for memorizing recipes. Sometimes, when the kitchen was empty, he added his own flourishes. By age 12, he was cooking for the field hands and selling his freshly baked cakes at the village plaza. Neighbors hired him to furnish birthday parties with his creations, rustic torts stuffed with mangos and plums.

With high school came a crushing disappointment. As a boy, he was not allowed to enroll in the cooking courses. Instead, Geno was steered into shop class. He began to wonder if he fit in. A broken heart sealed his decision to leave. When his girlfriend, his first love, left him for another boy, he told his father he wanted to try his luck in America. He begged his father to secure him a passport and a visa.

His father resisted. He warned his son that he would be giving up a good life in Mexico and that he would suffer in a cold new world. But he had also encouraged his children to live boldly and to follow dreams.

* * *

In 1982, a nervous 16-year-old stepped off a plane in Chicago and joined the tide of young Mexican men trying their luck in El Norte. It was gray and cold, and Chicago loomed as lonely and as confusing as his father forewarned. A hoped-for job with an old friend fell through. Bahena summoned a pioneer's courage.

"I found myself in the middle of nowhere," Bahena explained, "and I had to prove to myself that I could do something."

A dishwashing job in a taqueria paid $20 for a 12-hour shift. (In 2008, Bahena observed, that same taqueria was paying $25 for the 12-hour shift.) English as a second language classes led to a high school diploma. At bilingual St. Augustine College, Bahena studied the culinary arts. A teacher brought him to the attention of Rick Bayless, an acclaimed Chicago chef. Bayless hired the young immigrant at his Frontera Grill, which specialized in rustic Mexican cuisine.

With a mentor and a passion, Bahena rose from line cook to sous chef to managing chef. When he struck out on his own, opening his first restaurant at age 32, he was widely known as an innovative chef on the cutting edge. Food critics called him a "master of the moles," the complex sauces that complement many traditional Mexican dishes.

Like many immigrants, Bahena credits hard work and perseverance for his accomplishments. But there is another secret to his success. He skillfully blended cultures to create new sensations. He kept dipping back into the old world and bringing back the best of it: fresh ingredients, natural foods, venerable recipes, and a rare spice.

Through a series of annual treks, Bahena traveled to every one of Mexico's 31 states. He sampled regional specialties and talked with the chefs and the farmers who helped to create them. He collected recipes and brought them back to his home in Chicago, where he and his wife have a test kitchen that covers an entire floor of the house.

What he created was not always Mexican and certainly not American. As an immigrant and as an entrepreneur, Bahena says, he was free to innovate like he never could back home. He could take traditional dishes and experiment. Taboos did not exist.

"I tapped my heritage, but did not stop there," he said excitedly. "I kept taking dishes to the next level. I became alert to what Americans liked and did not like."

Today, when he addresses aspiring chefs and would-be restaurant owners at cooking classes and demonstrations, Bahena typically asks them where they are from and what the farmers grow there. He asks them what they love to eat and what they would love to cook.

He advises them to plot a goal and to imagine different avenues of reaching it. Then, think like an immigrant, he preaches. Think as he does each time he opens a new restaurant or invents a new dish or takes a new risk.

That's when he tells himself, "I'm going to do something no one's ever done."

I found myself in the middle of nowhere and I had to prove to myself that I could do something.

—chef Generoso Bahena

The Colors of Palestine

You might never have heard of Farouk Shami, but be assured your hair stylist knows the name. Shami is the founder and chairman of Farouk Systems, which created BioSilk shampoos and conditioners, CHI nail polish, and SunGlitz hair dye, three of the most popular brands in the hair-care market.

Shami, a Palestinian immigrant, also gave the trade ammonia-free hair dyes, environmentally friendly blow dryers, and space-age curling irons. His shampoos and hair tools have earned him more than celebrity status. He is one of the most successful and influential people in the American hair-care industry.

In 2008, Shami's Houston-based company generated about $1 billion in revenues, exported products to over 50 nations, and employed more than 2,000 people. Shami's personal clients have included movie stars and Miss Universe contestants. He's a sought-after speaker at hair shows and in cosmetology schools. But anyone wishing to learn the secrets to the man who invented modern hair styling needs to look beyond his Houston mansion and celebrity cachet to the chaotic village whence he came.

Shami was once the most successful hairdresser in the West Bank village of Ramallah, and that may be his most incredible accomplishment of all. At the time, it was extraordinary just to own a salon. It was 1967. The Six Day War had sealed Palestinian lands under Israeli military occupation. No nonessential products, including shampoo and hair dye, could get in or out of the area. So Shami innovated. As a boy, he had helped his mother pick the wildflowers and vegetables she used to create dyes that brought her embroideries to life. He helped her to mix vibrant, lasting colors.

"So I knew how to do hair color, how to make it last," he said.

Coloring hair with natural dyes became an art form to Shami, art on a living canvas. He slipped into the library at Hebrew University and read books about cosmetics and chemistry. He tapped skills gleaned as a teenaged pharmacist's assistant to concoct his own shampoos and conditioners.

Before long, he was the most famous stylist in the occupied territories and the top choice of brides needing a wedding day makeover. He sometimes worked more than a dozen weddings a day.

Despite commercial success and local acclaim, Shami chafed under both military and cultural constraints. His father, a Palestinian political leader, never accepted the idea of his son as a hairdresser. He flatly accused Farouk of shaming the family. In fact, one of the reasons Shami opened the Ramallah salon was to prove to his father that his chosen profession could be lucrative.

Shami had tasted a more liberating life. Three years earlier, he was accepted to the University of Arkansas. He attended both college and cosmetology school in America before his disappointed father ordered him home. Now he had the confidence for a permanent move.

"I thought, 'Why should I live under occupation when I can live in freedom and democracy in the United States of America?'"

In 1972, he said goodbye to his family and flew to America. He chose Lafayette, Louisiana, because he knew someone there, and opened a small salon. Over the next 35 years, Shami basically repeated the pattern set in his boyhood home—this time in the world's largest beauty market.

After moving to Houston, he became known as an innovator and a trendsetter. He created shampoos, gels, and styling irons. When doctors told him he had developed a severe allergy to the ammonia in hair-care products and that he should quit the business, Shami invented an ammonia-free hair coloring system, today marketed as SunGlitz.

His start-up possessed all the humble trappings of entrepreneurship. Shami concocted the ammonia-free formula in the back of his salon and sold it to other stylists. As he tells the story, Shami repeats the slogan of NASA's Mission Control in Houston: "Failure is not an option."

When demand for the product rose, he set up shop in his garage and put his son to work.

"We became a manufacturer now," Shami recalled. "We would put the powders in a barrel and I would sit on one side and he would sit on the other side and we rolled the barrel back and forth and that was our mixer."

Eventually, he upgraded to a pizza mixer and industrial food service blenders. When national distributors came calling, he bought a factory.

In an industry not known for its environmental sensitivity, safe and natural products became a Farouk System hallmark. His company eschews suspect chemicals in favor of natural pigments and ingredients. Most famously, it infused natural silk fibers into shampoo to create silkier, shinier hair.

> *This country gave me an opportunity perhaps no other country would have given me. I want to give something back.*
>
> —entrepreneur Farouk Shami

Ever the tinkerer, Shami stayed just as busy on the appliance side of cosmetics. He collaborated with NASA scientists to create the CHI, an iron that uses ceramic technology to straighten hair and that became a favored tool of high-priced stylists. His company introduced a blow dryer that emitted considerably less electromagnetic field. All of these products made the trade safer and more effective.

"My mission was to save hairdresser's lives," Shami said. "I was able to dry hair in half the time, too."

In late 2008, with son Rami serving as the company's chief executive officer, Farouk Shami considered more innovations and bold steps. He lamented he could not run for president of the United States because he was not born in America. But he could run for governor of Texas, he said, brightening. He envisioned a boost from the stylists who see him as a hero and who, through the nature of their work, wield influence one intimate encounter at a time.

"A typical stylist has 100 clients," Shami noted.

But another vision also consumed his thoughts, a strategy that could affect thousands of American workers. Shami wanted to bring the jobs back home. Like many American companies, Farouk Systems had turned to foreign manufacturers to build its appliances cheaply. But in 2008, Shami announced a reversal. He vowed that all Farouk products would soon carry a "Made in the USA" label.

Toward that goal, the privately held company began moving jobs from China and Korea back to the United States. In the summer of 2009, Farouk Systems opened a new 190,000-square-foot factory in Houston and planned other new facilities to manufacture hair dryers, clippers, and irons.

The strategy created more than 1,000 jobs initially and prospects for 1,000 more. It drew the interest of economic development experts and the praise of union officials.

"I say, more power to him," the *Houston Chronicle* quoted Richard Shaw, the secretary-treasurer of the Harris County, Texas, AFL-CIO. "Welcome to Houston."

Ever the businessman, Shami said his strategy was motivated by rising shipping costs and concerns over quality control, especially after Chinese-made toys were found laced with lead-based paint. He said he hoped the attractiveness of an American-made product would help to offset higher labor costs and maybe entice other American companies to follow his lead.

Ever the immigrant, he said he was also inspired by patriotism.

"I am an American citizen by choice," Shami said. "This country gave me an opportunity perhaps no other country would have given me. I want to give something back. I want to do my part."

"How can I do that?" he asked. "By creating jobs. Somebody has to start."

Chapter 5

Earth's Best
and Brightest

When the student is ready, the teacher appears.

—CHINESE PROVERB

W hen they decided to plant roots in Northwest Ohio, in America's Midwest, Xunming Deng and Liwei Xu went looking at houses in the suburbs of Toledo. There were plenty to choose from in 2008. A region that long relied on traditional manufacturing jobs was suffering the decline of the American auto industry, based an hour up Interstate 75 in Detroit, Michigan.

The real estate agent who greeted them at an open house one day told them it was a good time to buy. Local property values could soon be rising, she said. There was a new company in the area doing big things.

"It's a solar energy company," she confided. "That's the future." Liwei smiled and said, "Yes, we've heard of it."

> We came here with empty pockets. All we had was a desire to work.
>
> —Xunming Deng

Soon after, she and her husband resolved to get extra busy at work, fast. They were the creators of that company, Xunlight Corp., a clean-tech start-up that the real estate agent—and much of the region—seemed to be looking toward with hopeful eyes.

A scholarship brought Xunming Deng from China to the University of Chicago to study physics in 1985. His future wife followed one year later with a scholarship to study chemistry. Both had graduated at the very top of their high school classes in Nanchang, China. In addition, both scored near the top of national exams designed to identify China's brightest college students.

They were, in other words, two of the sharpest young minds in a nation of more than 1 billion people. Now they were the hope of Toledo.

Working in photovoltaics—the conversion of light into energy—at the University of Toledo (UT), Xunming designed a new means of capturing sunlight. His lightweight, flexible solar modules offered greater versatility than conventional glass solar panels, which are heavy and bulky and often require reinforcing a roof. Xunming's thin-film solar sheets could be rolled out across rooftops like hallway runners, allowing a factory or retail center below to generate clean electricity from the sun.

To bring the idea to market, Xunming and Liwei became entrepreneurs. In the fall of 2007, they moved their start-up from a UT innovation lab to a vacant warehouse in an industrial park one mile from campus. Venture capitalists flew in from the West Coast and from Europe to see the works. Multimillion-dollar investments followed. By early 2009, a newly trained workforce stood ready to roll out next-generation solar panels in the heartland of the American auto industry.

Xunming Deng, a cheerful man restless with energy, beamed to see it.

"We came here with empty pockets," he said. "All we had was a desire to work."

That, and some world-class brilliance. Xunming Deng and Liwei Xu are part of an elite immigrant wave, one that seems to be guided by an invisible hand. It's as if a global jet stream

> *Skilled foreign-born workers contribute to the global technological leadership of the United States.*
>
> —Migration Policy Institute

lifts the best and brightest from hometowns around the developing world and flies them toward America, often for advanced degrees. Once exposed to American life, many of the stellar students decide to stay.

The impact of gifted immigrants is profound. In recent decades, immigrants have become a commanding presence in some of America's most high-skilled professions. While making up about 15 percent of the American workforce, immigrants represent 20 percent of the nation's doctors, 17 percent of the nation's scientists and engineers. Among scientists and engineers with doctorate degrees, fully one-half are immigrants.

In Silicon Valley, half the engineers were born overseas, up from 10 percent in 1970.

World-class talent produces world-class innovation. Immigrants are disproportionately represented in the ranks of Americans who have won Nobel Prizes or who have been elected to the National Academy of Sciences. In 2009, 40 percent of the inventors inducted into the National Inventors Hall of Fame were immigrants.

As a knowledge-based economy has grown, so too has the share of immigrants in high-skill jobs. Part of the reason is that immigrants keep getting smarter. According to an analysis of census data by the Migration Policy Institute, a nonpartisan think tank, about one-quarter of immigrants arriving in the 1980s held college degrees. In the 1990s, 27 percent arrived college educated, and after 2000 it was nearly 35 percent.

"Skilled foreign-born workers contribute to the global techno-logical leadership of the United States," the Institute concluded in a 2006 study.

Attracting the Striver Class

Not all immigrants come with college degrees or even with col-lege prospects, of course. As a group, immigrants tend to be slightly less educated than the native-born population. In 2007, about 28 percent of native-born adults held a college degree, compared to 27 percent of all foreign-born adults. How can that be, when so many immigrants hold advanced degrees?

Imported knowledge comes in great variety, and in extremes. As the 2007 American Community Survey of the U.S. Census Bureau shows, immigrants tend to be clustered at the high and low ends of educational attainment. To illustrate immigrant education levels, demographers draw an hourglass.

Concentrated at the bottom of the hourglass are immigrants from Latin America, especially Mexico. In 2007, only 5 percent of Mexican-born Americans held a college degree and 60 percent had never graduated from high school. As Mexicans are the nation's largest immigrant group, they form a large share of the striver class. Joining them near the bottom of the hourglass are immigrants from some Asian nations like Vietnam and Cambodia and from some African nations like Somalia.

A college degree or technical skill is not the only harbinger of success. There are thousands of immigrants—like Mexico's Geno Bahena or Spain's Carmen Castillo—who arrived with limited education but with other stand-out qualities and who went on to achieve great things. Plenty of America's business pioneers grad-uated only from the school of hard knocks. Many a high-tech superstar, like Microsoft's Bill Gates, dropped out of college to put their ideas into action.

However, most experts agree that a college degree is one of the strongest indicators of future success. Many would also agree that graduates of elite international colleges enjoy even stronger chances of high achievement. That describes many of the men and women swelling the top of the hourglass—highly skilled, highly educated people trained at some of the best colleges in the world.

In 2007, an astonishing 74 percent of Indian-born Americans held a college degree. That's the highest education level of any identifiable ethnic group. The immigrants from India did not stop there. More than 40 percent went on to earn a master's degree.

Many of those immigrants are graduates of an India Institute of Technology (IIT). The IITs, sometimes called the MITs of India, are designed to prepare the top Indian high school students for careers as scientists and engineers. Their impact is spreading around the globe with Indian immigrants.

Not far behind India in the class rankings are Taiwanese. Seventy-one percent of Americans born in Taiwan held a bachelor's degree in 2007, and 37 percent of those went on to obtain a graduate or a professional degree, according to the U.S. Census Bureau. By comparison, about 10 percent of native-born Americans have attained a master's level of education, the census bureau reported.

Meanwhile, 61 percent of Russian-born Americans held a bachelor's degree in 2007, as did 50 percent of Chinese-born immigrants and 47 percent of immigrants from Israel.

When the world's cream rises to the top, it rises in America.

While the nations of Africa are among the poorest in the world, that continent sends America an impressive class of immigrants. In 2007, 40 percent of African-born Americans held a bachelor's degree, only slightly less than the percentage of Asian-born immigrants with a bachelor's degree and significantly higher than the percentage of European-born immigrants. Quietly, often working beneath the civic radar, African-born immigrants illustrate the power of high-skill immigration.

An African Way

Adedeji Adefuye, a Nigerian-born doctor, came to Chicago for advanced training and fell into American life. Now he applies some Old World strategies to a health crisis affecting minority populations. Adefuye is director of the HIV/AIDS Research and Policy Institute at Chicago State University.

He's a tall, handsome man with graying, close-cropped hair, and a doctor with a burning desire to know the causes of the diseases he fights.

Upon arriving at the campus on the city's south side in 2007, Adefuye was surprised at how many other African professors he met. He also understood. Most, like him, had come to America for training they could not get at home.

"When you're a specialist, one of the most frustrating things for you is not to have the resources to do your trade," he explained.

Nigerian medical students typically go abroad for their hospital residency, to gain experience and to see the state of the art. Adefuye went to England. "You're like, 'Oh my God, look what I can do here!'"

Intent on helping his people, he brought his skills back to Lagos, Nigeria, where he opened a medical clinic and pioneered programs to confront preventable diseases. He had seen too many Nigerian children die from the lack of 75-cent measles shots.

> *It's not so easy to pack your bags and go back home.*
>
> —Dr. Adedeji Adefuye

"For me, that kind of work gives me the most fulfillment, fighting malaria, salmonella, diseases that have no business occurring," he said. "I saw them every day in Lagos."

His efforts impressed the U.S. Agency for International Development (USAID), which offered a slot in a prestigious fellowship program at the University of Illinois at Chicago. Adefuye was going to decline the offer, but his community organizing efforts had aroused the ire of Nigeria's military government, which responded with intimidation tactics. His wife, living in England with the couple's two children, said, "Maybe it's time to go."

In 1997, at age 37, Adefuye brought his family to Chicago. He earned a master's degree in public health, which led to a position with the university's School of Public Health.

By 2007, when Chicago State University asked him to direct its efforts to research and prevent the spread of HIV/AIDS in the city, Adefuye had learned something else about the international student experience. A lot of life happens on the way to an advanced degree.

He had three children now, the oldest starting college. His wife was teaching elementary school and the family lived comfortably in the Chicago suburb of Oak Park.

"It's not so easy to pack your bags and go back home," Adefuye said.

He decided America was now their home. Chicago gained a public health doctor who brought high skills and African customs to an urban American problem. As he collected information on HIV/AIDS in black and Latino communities of Chicago, Adefuye ventured into the field, just as he had done in Africa. He walked some of Chicago's worst streets at all hours to know the work of his outreach workers, to witness addicts sharing needles, and to see the high-risk behavior he needed to change. As in Nigeria, he again saw the ignorance that causes terrible disease. And he began to strategize how to stop it.

"I'm not a moralist," he says. "I'm a scientist."

The Reluctant Italian-American

There is more than anecdotal evidence that highly educated, highly skilled immigrants get things done. After documenting the immigrant influence in the growth of America's high-tech industry,

Duke University's Vivek Wadhwa and his colleagues took a closer look at the people behind the company names.

The researchers found a close correlation between immigration, advanced degrees, and innovation. A whopping 74 percent of the immigrant founders of high-tech companies held graduate or postgraduate degrees. The majority had their highest degree in one of the so-called STEM fields: science, technology, engineering, and mathematics.

Wadhwa argues that educated immigrants create jobs.

Alberto Sangiovanni-Vincentelli, a high-tech superstar from Italy, sees a slightly different formula. He believes a culturally diverse mix of smart people—given space and time—produce the kinds of ideas that create wonders. What's more, they're also a lot of fun to work with.

Sangiovanni-Vincentelli's vantage point is a relaxed but cutting-edge idea lab on the edge of UC Berkeley, the flagship campus of the University of California system.

Berkeley is, to many, the epicenter of the information technology revolution that manifests itself in nearby Silicon Valley. Observers may argue whether Berkeley or Stanford has had the greater impact on California's smart economy, but Berkeley can certainly claim to being a wellspring of modern innovation. No other American university has so many graduate programs ranked in the top 10 in their fields. The faculty in 2009 included 74 Fulbright scholars, 28 MacArthur fellows, and 7 Nobel laureates. The student body represents one of the brightest mixes in the world: 64 percent of Berkeley students in 2006 had at least one parent born outside of the United States.

In 2007, the Cadence Research Laboratory@Berkeley opened with window views of campus and San Francisco Bay. Sangiovanni-Vincentelli is the co-founder of its corporate parent, Cadence Design Systems, a world leader in electronics design that employed more than 5,000 people in 2008. While serving as chief technology advisor at Cadence, he took equal enjoyment from another job, as a highly regarded Berkeley professor.

The design center illustrates where he's most comfortable—in the creative space between the corporate offices and the college laboratories. It's a setting both intellectual and multicultural, a milieu he says exists only in America. That's why he's here.

Sangiovanni-Vincentelli arrived in 1975 as a visiting professor. He was a reluctant immigrant who expected to teach for six months and go home to his beloved Italy, where he was one of the youngest professors ever at Politecnico di Milano University.

A classically trained scholar, Sangiovanni-Vincentelli grew up in an aristocratic Italian family. He studied classic literature, philosophy, and art. By high school, he was fluent in Latin and Greek. He earned his doctorate in engineering, he said, because that's what well-off Italian young men were expected to do.

When UC Berkeley offered a temporary teaching post in its Department of Electrical Engineering and Computer Sciences, Sangiovanni-Vincentelli was busy and happy in Italy. But he was also curious about America. He wondered if the Hollywood image were true. Six months in California might just be fun.

It was.

When Sangiovanni-Vincentelli says, "To me, Berkeley is the most beautiful place on Earth," he's not talking about the weather or the view of San Francisco Bay. He's talking about the intellectual diversity, the international students and professors, and the devoted scientists and visiting scholars bringing ideas from around the world.

The atmosphere ignited his imagination and his entrepreneurial skills. Within a decade, Sangiovanni-Vincentelli had helped to found two highly successful microchip design companies: Cadence in 1983 and Synopsys in 1987. He inspired and mentored hundreds of future scientists as well. In 1981, he received the Distinguished Teaching Award of the University of California, the highest honor that students and faculty can bestow upon a professor.

Cadence's newest research lab reflected a Renaissance man's view of science—right from the start. Transparent glass panes rise to the ceiling along one side of the spacious reception area. Etched

> *In the U.S., it does not matter where you are from, only that you have a good idea.*
>
> —Alberto Sangiovanni-Vincentelli

upon the glass are engineering diagrams and mathematical formulas that helped to create Cadence products.

Sangiovanni-Vincentelli greets a visitor enthusiastically. He's a small man with bright eyes and a hurried but gracious demeanor.

"I have to get an espresso. Do you want one? Follow me," he says, and he leads on to the cafeteria, where he brews Italian coffees at a cappuccino machine. His sixtieth year finds him reflective, restless, and excited about the future, provided that America continues to be a land of immigrants.

Sangiovanni-Vincentelli argues that intellectual diversity—the mix of very smart people from around the world—is what makes Berkeley a center of innovation, a setting that offers entrepreneurs a greater chance of success.

"It is not so much the university. It is the ecosystem," Sangiovanni-Vincentelli argues. "The more diverse the original soup, the more combinations you can get, and the more chance you have to be the big player."

Hard work and persistence play key roles, too.

"In some sense, you can say the immigrants are more willing to sacrifice their life to do something," he continued. "That is an important characteristic of an immigrant."

But America makes that sacrifice meaningful. "You look at Italian society, it is very stable, meaning moving for one social class to another is extremely difficult. You're born one way and you stay that way the rest of your life."

England and France also foster rigid social classes, like much of the rest of the world, Sangiovanni-Vincentelli said.

"In the U.S., it does not matter where you are from, only that you have a good idea," he said. "That is why immigrants are in such a good position, because if you have an idea, you can bring it to the table."

70

Sangiovanni-Vincentelli sees a model to be emulated. Just as high-skill immigrants stoked the creative fires in northern California, he argues, they can do so in other parts of America and in other industries.

"What is the most important factor in successful companies?" he asks. "People, people, people."

> *What is the most important factor in successful companies? People, people, people.*
>
> —Alberto Sangiovanni-Vincentelli

Attract enough of the right kind, he argues, and wonders happen.

Out of Shadows, into Solar

Motorists traveling the Ohio Turnpike south of Toledo are accustomed to driving past the huge Chrysler Machining plant in Perrysburg and feeling a surge of pride. The massive complex looms like an emblem of American industrial might. Or long did. By early 2009, the highway view no longer inspired confidence, only questions about layoffs and when and whether the plant might close.

It was the huge factory next door that raised hopes, the one with "First Solar" scripted across its facade. The busy plant had more than 700 workers producing solar-energy components for world export in early 2009. It had a demoralized region hoping for a fresh start.

Legendary glass pioneer Harold McMaster co-founded the company with technology invented in his lab at the University of Toledo (UT), a world leader in glass technology. Most solar panels are made of glass coated with chemical semiconductors, like silicon. For years, civic leaders and union workers alike held out hope that Toledo's glassmaking expertise, long valued by the auto industry for windshields and car windows, could lead to jobs in the growing solar industry.

Suddenly, things seemed to be happening. As First Solar rolled out solar panels for overseas markets, a German solar giant talked of expanding its research and design operations in the area. In a demonstration project, the federal government helped a solar-energy entrepreneur install a solar field at an Air National Guard base near Toledo Express Airport. In the spring of 2009, a Toledo-based solar company announced plans for a new, 400-job plant.

However, it was the newest solar company to spin out of UT that created the biggest stir. In April 2008, Xunlight announced it had received a $22 million shot of confidence from a group of venture capitalists led by Trident Capital, a leading clean-tech venture capital firm. It was the start-up's third large infusion of private cash and it would launch a production line. A Trident executive told Toledo's newspaper, *The Blade,* that he expected Xunlight to become a world leader in the blossoming photovoltaic industry.

More encouraging to local residents were statements coming from Xunlight founders, an immigrant couple from China. Xunming Deng and Liwei Xu said that their company would be based in Toledo, would build its products in Toledo, and that they, too, would settle in the area, which they had come to call home.

A region weary of unstable jobs in auto plants and smokestack industries dared to dream. Xunlight became a must-see stop on any economic development tour. Chamber of commerce officers, county commissioners, the governor, and a U.S. senator and congresswoman stopped by to greet the founders and to offer encouragement.

Probably few of the well-wishers had a clear idea of how the couple came to be in Toledo or fathomed the forces that brought them from the top of the class in China to a struggling Midwest community in need of their skills.

Love, Study, and a Start-Up

After 23 years of marriage, Xunming and Liwei still blush to recall their meeting in college in China. It was a time and a culture when dating was taboo. But China was changing in ways that would tip the trajectory of their lives.

Xunming Deng knew a humble childhood. His father was a tax clerk, and his mother labored in a textile plant.

> *We thought we'd go back, to help. But now it was clear it was better to stay.*
> —Liwei Xu

The family lived on about $10 a month. But their son posted one of the top scores on a national collegiate entrance exam. Destiny called.

It was 1980 and reformist leader Deng Xiaoping was trying to modernize China by sending top college students abroad for advanced training in science and engineering, hoping they would return to enlighten the nation. American universities, eager to host bright international students, cooperated with scholarships. What resulted was a process that skimmed elite students from Chinese colleges and sent them to graduate schools in America.

When Xunming was accepted to the University of Chicago in 1985, he and his secret fiancée, Liwei, plotted their strategy. She would try to follow his path. Astonishingly, Liwei also scored near the top on the national exam. She also was offered a scholarship to study at the University of Chicago. Xunming loaned her the $70 application fee.

The daughter of engineers, Liwei grew up in a happy family that lived better than many. But her parents urged her to seize the opportunity. China was poor, and the world was opening up.

"By that time we realized that, 'Wow, America is prosperous,'" Liwei explained.

The young couple reconnected at the University of Chicago, where Xunming, then 22, pursued a doctorate in physics. Liwei, then 21, pursued her doctorate in chemistry. China had been sending students abroad for a few years now, and a small expatriate community welcomed the newcomers. With their fellow Chinese students looking on, the couple exchanged vows at a simple wedding on Christmas Eve 1986.

All but the foreign students had gone home for the holidays, "And we had the campus to ourselves," Liwei said, laughing at the memory. "Our total wedding budget was one hundred dollars."

Their plans to return home changed abruptly in 1989, as they did for thousands of Chinese students abroad. The People's Army fired on students in Tiananmen Square, killing scores.

"We thought we'd go back, to help," said Liwei, in a voice that still carries the weight of that conflicted decision. "But now it was clear it was better to stay."

The pair now focused solely on succeeding in America. Xunming earned his doctorate in physics in 1990 and went to work for a suburban Detroit company pursuing alternative energy systems. He became a senior scientist and a project manager specializing in solar energy, a focus of his research in college.

"I envisioned that alternative energy would grow more and more important," he said.

Liwei gave birth to the couple's son in 1990 and the next year achieved her doctorate in chemistry. After post-graduate research at the University of Michigan-Ann Arbor, she joined her husband at Energy Conversion Devices, working on batteries for electric cars.

The couple's daughter was born in 1993. They had steady jobs and a young family to support. But Xunming was just getting started. In 1996, to the dismay of his colleagues, he quit his job to join the department of physics and astronomy at the University of Toledo.

The new position meant accepting about a 50 percent salary cut, but it also opened up new horizons. The university offered Xunming the chance to assemble a research team and build his own program in alternative energy. Soon, Liwei quit her job in Michigan and moved with the two children to Toledo to join him.

In 2002, two years after they took the oath of citizenship, the couple launched their solar-energy company.

Family savings and state grants saw them through small successes and failures as they sought to use solar energy to create hydrogen for fuel cells and to generate electricity.

In 2006, they changed the company name to Xunlight, reflecting a sharpened focus on transforming sunlight into electricity.

Working with paper-thin stainless steel, Xunming had designed a solar panel far lighter and more flexible than traditional modules. He also designed machinery that could manufacture it more efficiently than the competition.

The result, he hoped, was a product simpler to build and cheaper to buy.

"That's the innovation," he said. "We cut the equipment cost."

In 2007, they moved the company off campus and into a warehouse big enough to hold their dream, becoming the brightest light in Toledo.

At Home Far Away

On a winter's morning in early 2009, a quiet factory exuded energy. Only exhaust fans sounded in an open, 120,000-square-foot plant bathed in bright lights. Computer-controlled machines the size of semi-trailer trucks were not yet rolling out solar film. The shipping dock was still. But deadlines and anticipation charged the air. Eighty-five employees—10 with doctorate degrees—were nearly ready to commence production.

Xunming and Liwei, surveying the scene in suits and safety glasses, could hardly believe it.

"We went through some pretty tough stages in our life," Xunming explained.

Falling back on a comfortable position in academia at times looked tempting, but the couple never seriously considered quitting this venture.

"Usually, immigrants do not mind putting in effort, a lot of effort, to find success," Xunming said. "And you do not give up hope. That green card might take five years to come. You do not give up hope."

Xunming describes two components of working hard: working smart and pooling resources to achieve a vision.

His company is pursuing a solar niche. Its thin-film sheets are meant not for homes but for factories and retail centers. They will carpet large, flat roofs that cannot sustain the weight of traditional glass solar panels, as most houses can.

Xunming, Xunlight's president and CEO, and Liwei, its vice president of finance and administration, initially expect to export most of their product to Europe, until solar energy takes hold in America. They envision manufacturing more than $200 million worth of solar cells each year. That will require more physicists and chemists, but also traditional business people and rank-and-file factory workers.

They also plan to stay in Toledo, and not only because their daughter likes her high school. Xunming and Liwei said they were surprised by some of the advantages the Midwest offers to manufacturing start-ups, like cheap and available factory space. They found a huge pool of talent from the auto industry, and universities and cities eager to support their ideas.

"There's a whole community that has a new hope because of Xunlight," Xunming said he realizes.

> *Usually, immigrants do not mind putting in effort, a lot of effort, to find success. And you do not give up hope. That green card might take five years to come. You do not give up hope.*
>
> —Xunming Deng

They wonder if their neighbors realize how they came to be here, and why there may not be many more following their lead.

Twenty years ago, they rose to the top of a process that singled out China's bright strivers and flew them to America.

"The United States is very unique in the way it is open to foreigners," Liwei said, and she is grateful.

But the immigration process she navigated—from student visa to green card to citizenship—was far easier than the one facing international students today. As China is expanding opportunities at home, America offers a chillier welcome.

Liwei suspects that young educated Chinese probably feel less compelled to emigrate. As she stood at the cusp of a new industry, one she is helping to propel, Liwei observed that, today, she and her husband could probably launch Xunlight in China.

Chapter 6

Cowboys of a
New Frontier

Occasionally an immigrant can see things which escape the attention of the native.

—MICHAEL PUPIN, SERBIAN-AMERICAN SCIENTIST

On a cold New England night in early 2009, the windows glowed bright in a red-brick building that stood like a lighthouse on a bluff overlooking the Charles River. Its brick smokestack, wreathed in blinking red lights, towered high into the winter sky.

This was the old powerhouse of what was once a mammoth munitions complex in Watertown, a working-class suburb a few miles upriver from Boston. Today, the Arsenal on the Charles, as it's been renamed, is a smart park owned by nearby Harvard University. Fiber optic cables course through old cannon factories that are home to software developers, business consultants, and engineering design firms. In an intriguing re-use, the historic powerhouse hosts the research and development lab of A123Systems Inc., a start-up striving to power the car of tomorrow.

The lab was still busy at 7 P.M. on a Thursday, but the air was more charged in a renovated warehouse just up the block, where A123Systems keeps its corporate offices. In a bright, open, barn-like warren of cubicles and conference rooms, a mix of native-born and immigrant Americans were hard at work. Much of the office staff had gone home for the day, but company executives and their top engineers sweated to make a deadline.

Behind a glass door, casually dressed men and women slapped equations onto a white board as others fired questions and suggestions. Near a display of cordless power tools, a designer bent over a drawing table as a colleague juggled conversations on two cell phones. A relaxed energy permeated the scene, allowing for deep breaths and occasional smiles, despite the hour and frenetic pace.

Probably no one was under more pressure this night than Ric Fulop, a boyish-looking 34-year-old from Venezuela. The science of his Taiwan-born partner, Yet-Ming Chiang, had brought them far in their quest to build a battery more powerful than anyone thought possible. The third co-founder, New England native Bart Riley, provided the engineering expertise. Boston venture capitalist Gururaj "Desh" Deshpande, an immigrant from India, offered advice and key support.

Now the researchers and advisors could relax a bit while Fulop, the company's marketing director, strived to sell their product to the industry and to a major new investor.

An apple-cheeked young man with disheveled black hair, Fulop this night wore jeans and a blue A123 polo shirt. He and his wife had just welcomed their first child, and the new father was parenting via phone calls home. But another responsibility consumed his attention. He was to catch a flight to Washington, D.C., in two hours. In the morning, he would walk into the U.S. Department of Energy and deliver A123's application for a share of federal stimulus money designed to jump-start a new American battery industry.

His colleagues were helping him to put the finishing touches on an audacious request: $1.8 billion to build battery cell factories in America's Midwest.

A humble start-up was poised to take a giant leap forward. Having recharged Black & Decker power tools, the people behind A123Systems were ready to propel all-electric cars. They represented not only a provocative idea—clean, powerful, renewable energy—but also a new kind of team, a crew uniquely qualified to exploit the opportunities of the New Economy.

A New Kind of Entrepreneur

The word *entrepreneur* conjures many images, not all of them flattering. Labels assigned to people who launch their own businesses include self-promoting and obsessive.

On the positive side, the men and women who launch their own businesses are widely seen as hardworking, persistent, daring, and smart.

Both of those typecasts miss some of the characteristics that shape entrepreneurs succeeding in today's knowledge-based, global economy, research and interviews with successful entrepreneurs show.

The captains of team A123 exhibit most of the traditional traits of entrepreneurship. They are bold and energetic people, highly skilled, and prone to optimism. They share a thirst for adventure and an ability to work under pressure.

But the founders also display traits borne of their immigrant experience or their understanding of immigrants. Most speak more than one language. All are well traveled. They bring different ethnic perspectives to a task and an ability to work across cultures.

As their quest unfolded, they proved to be flexible and adaptable, as strangers in a strange land learn to be. When Chiang's initial battery formula failed to work as expected, the team scrambled and found a better one.

Experts say nimbleness and resiliency are crucial qualities when banking upon unproven technology. As mathematician James York observed, "The most successful people are those who are good at Plan B."

Finally, the founders were good at working as a team, that is, realizing their personal strengths and weaknesses and those of their colleagues. Some experts say the ability to size up a challenge and select the right partners to take it on may be the most critical quality of all among the era's successful entrepreneurs.

"The key to success is selection," writes Bill Wagner, author of the book *The Entrepreneur Next Door*. "You must select an opportunity that suits your personality, then hire or select the right people to surround yourself with."

With a blend of new and traditional skills, the founders of A123 trekked confidently into the unmapped terrain of clean technology. They could speak the language of Chinese scientists and of West Coast venture capitalists. They could push the scientific envelope and do the engineering. They were a new kind of entrepreneur, bold but tech savvy: Cowboys of a new frontier.

They, and others like them, are driving the New Economy and pulling companies and industries along with them. It is no small motivation that they believe they can change the world. Along the way, they just might save the American worker.

A Melting-Pot Dream Team

The next time Ric Fulop caught his breath it was late February 2009. He had just returned from a three-week trip to Japan and China, where A123 manufactures battery cells. He would be leaving the next day for a trip that would take him to South America, Los Angeles, and Detroit, where A123 hoped to soon be doing more business. He was a catalyst for a young company on the rise.

In 2009, at the start of its eighth year, A123's high-energy, lithium-ion batteries powered Black & Decker's DeWalt line of cordless power tools. They started airplane engines and propelled hybrid buses.

A company that spun out of a lab at the Massachusetts Institute of Technology (MIT) had recruited an experienced CEO, David Vieau, a veteran of successful high-tech start-ups. It now had more than 2,000 employees, about two-thirds of them overseas, and big plans in America.

You get started on something and it just becomes more and more real. And before you know it, it's all you're doing.

—entrepreneur Ric Fulop

A123 was involved in 18 separate projects with nine auto companies. Its researchers were trying to design a mega-battery to store excess energy from electric grids. They were racing against other advanced battery makers, most of them overseas, to power the future.

As vice president of business development and marketing, Fulop stood hip deep in every aspect of the venture: planning, plotting, engineering, and selling. The work was all consuming, so much so that he rarely, if ever, paused to consider how he does what he does—and why.

"I'm very hungry. I have always been hungry," Fulop finally said, after thinking for a long moment. His appetite is not for food but for the next new thing, which he wants a role in inventing.

"You get started on something and it just becomes more and more real," he said. "And before you know it, it's all you're doing."

In fact, the soft-spoken immigrant has made a career of hatching bold ideas and rallying a team to pursue them. Known for his infectious enthusiasm and his ability to work across cultures, Fulop, who speaks five languages, played a role in five start-ups before age 27. He's credited with pioneering the broadband Internet industry before charging into renewable energy.

Born in 1974 in Caracas, Venezuela, Ricardo Fulop used his bar mitzvah savings to launch his first company at age 16, when he finished high school. His software distributorship was soon earning nearly $1 million a year.

He came to America in 1994 to attend Babson College but never finished. The high-tech industry was exploding in and around Boston and its world-class universities. Fulop wanted in on the action. He started Arepa in his dorm room in 1996. It survived as Into Networks, whose software is used in the Windows Vista operating system.

He dropped out of college and became a full-time entrepreneur. He burned through tens of millions of dollars with Chinook Communications and Broadband2Wireless, promising companies that soared and crashed in spectacular fashion. He picked himself up and looked ahead. *Red Herring*, a magazine that covers the technology industry, named him one of America's Top 10 Entrepreneurs in 1999. He was 24 years old.

In 2001, Fulop was thinking of clean energy and concepts like fuel cells and battery storage, years before Al Gore warned of an inconvenient truth. He still had only a high school diploma, but he's a quick study, a voracious reader. Before he came scouting the halls of the Massachusetts Institute of Technology for battery experts, he had read the latest research reports and mined MIT databases to read the unpublished research. He knew a cathode from an anode particle. He knew the Arctic ice was turning to slush and that fossil fuel supplies had peaked. He suspected the internal-combustion engine would soon give way to electric motors powered by batteries—which burn no petroleum and spew no harmful gases.

"You don't buy market research reports," he said with genial disdain. "You do your own. You have to figure it out."

Armed with expert knowledge, Fulop was willing to present himself to key people, strangers with no idea who he was or how he found them.

"You have to be scrappy and street-smart," Fulop said. "I think an important part of being an immigrant is desperation. Failure is not an option. You've landed here, you're alone, you have to make a new life for yourself."

In fact, one of the reasons Fulop became an entrepreneur, he said, is because he feared no one would hire him in Boston, a class-conscious city not known for its warm welcome to strangers.

"I didn't have a platinum background. All the rubber stamps on my passport," he explained. "I didn't have a Harvard-like degree."

> *"I think an important part of being an immigrant is desperation. Failure is not an option. You've landed here, you're alone, you have to make a new life for yourself."*
>
> —Ric Fulop

He does now. In an uncommon gesture, MIT offered him a scholarship to its graduate business school despite his lack of a bachelor's degree. In 2006, Fulop earned his MBA from one of the world's elite universities.

That's also where he found his teammate.

The Super Prof

Yet-Ming Chiang, the calm to Fulop's storm, was 41 years old and an esteemed professor when Fulop knocked on his door and said he wanted to talk about battery power. He presented himself as *Red Herring* magazine's Entrepreneur of the Year, Chiang recalled, laughing at the memory.

Fulop told Chiang about his interest in starting a company that would tap alternative energy, perhaps using carbon nanotubes. Chiang told him a little about his research with materials that seemed to imbue conventional batteries with remarkable power. He suspected he had achieved a breakthrough, really.

So what are you waiting for? Fulop asked.

Chiang looked at the young man in sneakered feet and weighed his response. A career MIT professor, he was happy in academia. He's a cheerful scientist who enjoys fishing with his three children and tinkering with machines.

"I love engineering. I was always a gearhead," he explained.

But he also possesses a sense of adventure. He owns three motorcycles. In the late 1980s, he took MIT technology and helped to create American Superconductor, which built high-temperature wires to deliver electric power.

He said he saw in Fulop not just energy but talent, "A skill set I didn't have." He takes pride in the aspect of his personality that allowed him to defer to the young entrepreneur, a trait he attributes to the meritocracy that is America.

"If you had a hierarchical mindset, you'd be asking yourself, 'Who is this kid? Why should I be working for *him*?'"

Instead he wondered, "Could this be the time?"

* * *

Chiang is a hybrid, a man of dual cultures. Born in 1958 in Kaohsiung, Taiwan, he was raised in America by parents who instilled in their children the best of both worlds. He grew up disciplined but inquisitive, smart but playful. He does not think his relaxed personality would have been rewarded in the rigid academic systems of Asia.

"All my life, I've felt fortunate to grow up in America," he said.

He arrived at age six with his parents and his three siblings. His father, a mechanical engineer who fled mainland China after the communist revolution, had visited America on business and liked it. He brought his family to Brooklyn, where he earned his master's degree at Brooklyn Polytechnic. The children were raised to revere learning.

> *You could get away with a lot in my family, but you couldn't get away with not doing well in school.*
>
> —Yet-Ming Chiang

"You could get away with a lot in my family, but you couldn't get away with not doing well in school," Chiang said.

At age 18, he followed a sister to MIT, a crucible of entrepreneurship on the banks of the Charles River in Cambridge.

Joining a New England Tradition

The French political writer Alexis de Tocqueville, in his mid-nineteenth-century classic, *Democracy in America*, observed that the English government considered "New England as a land given over to the fantasy of dreamers, where innovators should be allowed to try out experiments in freedom." Freedom is the driver of prosperity, and "nowhere was this principle of liberty applied more completely than in the states of New England," Tocqueville wrote.

Within this growing community of innovators and dreamers, an idea for a university was discussed and founded shortly after Tocqueville's book was published.

The Massachusetts Institute of Technology, considered by many to be the most productive university in the world, is a beehive of entrepreneurism and innovation. It leads the nation's universities in the licensing of technology to start-up firms. From its Cambridge campus, MIT virtually spins out jobs in advanced manufacturing, software, and biotechnology. In 2008, nearly 100 biotech companies stirred in the Kendall Square neighborhood adjacent to campus, according to a census by the Kauffman Foundation.

If companies founded by MIT graduates formed their own country, MIT nation would possess the 17th largest economy in the world, the Kauffman researchers concluded. Immigrants play a key role in that entrepreneurial ecosystem. About 30 percent of MIT's international students start companies, researchers found, and half of those companies take root in America. In 2008, immigrant alumni of MIT employed about 100,000 people in 2,300 American companies, generating $16 billion in sales.

Yet-Ming Chiang walked into that tradition a wide-eyed freshman in 1976. A stellar engineering student, he became a research assistant to W. David Kingery, the father of modern ceramics and 1999 winner of the Kyoto Prize for advanced technology. Chiang joined the faculty upon earning his master's degree. In 1990, he became the youngest tenured professor in the history of the Department of Material Science and Engineering.

When Fulop appeared in 2001, Chiang was applying nanotechnology to battery chemistry. Lithium-ion batteries were starting to power small electronics, like cell phones and laptop computers. But they were expensive and hobbled by power limitations. By adding trace amounts of metals to the formula, Chiang found he was able to generate exceptional bursts of power.

He had, he suspected, found a path to a stable, long-life battery—the Holy Grail of clean-tech. Chiang shared his discoveries with Bart Riley, a friend from his days at American Superconductor. An engineer with a Cornell University doctorate and more than 40 patents, Riley thought they should maybe start a battery company, but neither knew how to go about it.

Enter Fulop, the missing ingredient. In July 2001, the trio sat down to dinner and mulled their potential roles: Chiang, the professor with the key technology; Riley, the experienced engineer; and Fulop, the money-raiser and start-up wizard. The chemistry seemed right. Handshakes ensued, and dreams soared. Within weeks, they had chosen a name, A123Systems, which sounds casual but refers to an important equation in nanotechnology.

"We all thought it was an appropriately geeky name for an MIT spin-off," Chiang observed. "Early on, I ran into a fellow at a Harvard networking event who ran a PR firm, and he said that when we got serious about our company, he would be happy to help us come up with a real name."

That name soon become one of the most respected in the industry.

The Guru

With a team, a promising technology, and a PowerPoint presentation, the trio went looking for investors. They needed tens of millions of dollars to fund research into Chiang's technology, which they had licensed from MIT, and to develop a product.

Fulop mapped out visits to 30 different venture capitalists on the east and west coasts. Early into what Chiang called "the road trip," the founders took their idea to the mountaintop. They visited Gururaj "Desh" Deshpande in Chelmsford, Massachusetts, where he was running his latest successful start-up.

Deshpande is legendary in high-tech circles. To South Asians, he is known as a "karma yogi," a man who follows a path of action to ultimate success. To American venture capitalists, he is a big thinker with a Midas touch. He left India at age 22 for college in Canada, moved down to Boston, and pioneered the architecture of optical fiber networks, super-fast communications systems. He founded two hugely successful companies on his way to becoming one of the richest men in America.

When the A123 founders sat before him in 2001, he was president and chairman of his latest start-up, Sycamore Networks. He was also a venture capitalist and a mentor to hungry young entrepreneurs who hoped to follow his path.

Deshpande liked what he heard and liked what he saw in Chiang, Fulop, and Riley. He agreed to invest in their battery quest and help them to find other backers. Later, he agreed to chair their company's board of directors. The promising trio became a quartet anchored by a seasoned talent.

"He was sort of the grown-up guy," Fulop said later. "He validated the idea."

A123 soon attracted a Who's Who of investors that included the U.S. Department of Energy, fabled Silicon Valley venture capital firm Sequoia Capital, General Electric, Procter & Gamble, Motorola, and Qualcomm.

Deshpande's endorsement, like the king's imprimatur, did not come casually. He is both a practitioner and a student of entrepreneurship, which came to him unexpectedly. The craft fascinates him, partly because he never saw himself as a natural.

Born in 1952, Gururaj Deshpande was raised in small towns in the southern Indian state of Karnataka. Dad worked for the government. There was no business history in the family.

After graduating from the Indian Institute of Technology (IIT) Madras with a bachelor's degree in electrical engineering in 1973, Deshpande considered job offers with Indian firms. But when the University of New Brunswick offered a full scholarship, he left for Canada. His father borrowed the money for his plane ticket.

Deshpande earned his master's degree in electrical engineering and went on to earn a doctorate in data communications at Queens University. In 1980, he married Jaishree, a physicist and a fellow graduate of IIT Madras. He had found his life partner and he believed he had found his vocation. He liked teaching and he was good at it. He envisioned a career as a university professor and a researcher. Then he experienced the riskier side of his craft.

He was teaching college in 1984 when, as a favor to a friend, he joined "a little start-up in Toronto" which had just lost its head engineer. Deshpande assumed control of Codex Corporation and took it to new heights. Everyone made money. He still relishes the memory.

"Once I had a taste of that," he said, "I knew I was going to work for myself."

He decided he did not want to build other people's companies. He would go to America and build his own. He joined Motorola's headquarters in Boston in 1984 and worked for three years waiting for his green card, which provided status as a lawful permanent resident. (The card proving that status is no longer green, but the nickname endures.) While working for Motorola, Deshpande launched his first business, a communications company that he nurtured in the pre-dawn hours. The venture failed and he and his partner lost their small but dear investment.

In 1988, he and Jaishree launched Coral Networks with the family savings. The technology succeeded but a conflict with a partner forced the Deshpandes to quit the venture. It was another bitter defeat.

He rebounded with Cascade Communications, a public computer network and a one-man start-up that hit the jackpot. The company sold in 1997 for $3.7 billion.

Soon after, Deshpande co-founded Sycamore Networks, a maker of advanced optical networking products. Its public stock offering caused a sensation in 1999. The next year, *Forbes* magazine ranked him the 32nd richest person in America.

New Era of Innovation

By early 2009, Deshpande had stepped down from the presidency of Sycamore. He still chaired the board but he no longer went into the office daily. His passions were philanthropy and mentoring, efforts channeled through the Deshpande Foundation, which supports entrepreneurship and innovation in America and in India, and the Deshpande Center for Technological Innovation, which helps MIT professors make the leap from research to commercialization. As a venture capitalist, he likes to help launch one start-up a year.

In his 58th year, Deshpande lived discreetly despite his wealth and success. His work environment reflected his modesty. The Deshpande Foundation, housed in an unremarkable office building off a freeway interchange near his home, lacked even a receptionist. Visitors walk in and start looking for someone.

> *Entrepreneurship is always about changing the game. The magnitude of the change depends on where you are.*
>
> —Gururaj Deshpande

Deshpande arrived on a Friday afternoon in slacks and an open-collared shirt, cordially introduced himself, and led the way to a conference room. He's a compact man with a wide, kind face and a professorial bearing. He nods as he listens, and he pauses in thought before delivering his opinion.

He is firm in his views but he does not push them. Instead, he serenely shares lessons learned from some of the greatest runs in the game.

"Entrepreneurship is always about changing the game," Deshpande said. "The magnitude of the change depends on where you are."

He advises aspiring entrepreneurs to consider the field of play. In smaller places, small changes can lead to big success. In big, technologically advanced cities and nations, big changes are required to make an impact.

He also advises them to break tradition, to deviate from established patterns habitually, and to adopt the concept of entrepreneurship as a career.

"There's no lack of problems to be solved," Deshpande said. "There's plenty of things to do."

He said he sees a new era of innovation emerging, thanks in part to the deep recession of 2008 and 2009 and the humbling of Wall Street. Over the last 10 to 15 years, some of America's best young talent was drawn to investment houses and the stock market, "where creators became gamblers," Deshpande said. Now, bright minds were returning to meaningful work.

"The thrust is coming back to actually creating new things—products, services, technology," he said.

He believes innovation springs from hard times. In 2000, Deshpande told students at his IIT alma mater in India that one of his early failures, with Coral Networks, made him a better entrepreneur. It showed him he could survive defeat.

"I am now more comfortable taking on bigger challenges, because I am not afraid of failure," he said.

He advised the students to make no small plans.

"People do not do more than what they can dream of. So I dream big," he declared.

*　*　*

When the A123 team came calling in 2001, the phrase "alternative energy" was just entering the national lexicon. Deshpande liked the idea of a super battery but, more than that, he liked the people behind it. Fulop, Chiang, and Riley struck him as smart, openminded leaders who would change course if a path were blocked.

"Perseverance can go too far," he counsels. "Just because you have a conviction doesn't mean your conviction is right. It's usually the second or third idea that works."

Also, he liked that two of the three founders were immigrants, and not out of any feelings of kinship. With less to lose, he thinks immigrants are bolder players. With a fresh look at the landscape, he thinks they are better at spying opportunity.

"It always takes an outsider to see the advantage," he said.

He also believes immigrants are better equipped to persevere the rigors of entrepreneurship, having endured a pilgrim's journey. Launching a business always takes more time, money, and sacrifice than anyone imagines, Deshpande said.

> *Just because you have a conviction doesn't mean your conviction is right. It's usually the second or third idea that works.*
>
> —Gururaj Deshpande

He agrees with legendary venture capitalist and Sequoia Capital partner Michael Moritz, who in 2000 wrote, "Force a venture capitalist to choose between a well-heeled Ivy League student and a smart and impoverished immigrant, and we'll pick the latter every time."

Deshpande liked the immigrant personality of the A123 team. But mostly, he thought the team was onto something big. Power storage was the unanswered challenge of renewable energy. Electric cars could not eclipse gas guzzlers until they could run long and steady. Solar fields and wind farms could not dependably power a city until energy could be stored in the calm and in the dark. The world needed a better battery.

"The need for this technology is absolutely obvious," Deshpande said. "It's a good play."

Made in America?

The ensuing years proved Deshpande right. Chiang's lithium-ion battery generated 10 times the power of a conventional battery, ran cool and constant, and recharged quickly. As cordless power tools whirred with A123 batteries—and with more power than plug-in tools—investment grew and the product line broadened.

General Motors delivered a blow in late 2008, when it disclosed it had chosen a Korean company to build battery cells for its much-anticipated plug-in hybrid, the Chevrolet Volt, due to debut in 2010. Fulop shrugged off the setback. A123 remained a partner with GM as it sought a domestic battery source and the entire auto industry was coming its way.

All-electric vehicles were perhaps decades away from mass popularity, but most every automaker was working on a hybrid—cars and trucks powered by a mix of electric and gasoline power. His company was one of the major players in a $2 billion market projected to grow to $20 billion by 2020.

"Just like the PC (personal computer), it could explode," Fulop said.

The question that nagged Fulop and other members of the team was one scarcely raised by established American companies: where would the batteries be made?

At the dawn of the renewable energy era, battery makers in Japan, Korea, and China dominated the technology and the manufacturing. Most American companies that needed advanced batteries turned to foreign suppliers. A123Systems and Johnson Controls were two of only a handful of advanced U.S. battery companies, and even they were making a lot of their product overseas.

That pattern needed to change, the founders agreed.

Their belief in American jobs rested in part on a common immigrant sentiment—patriotism. Like generations of immigrants before them, Fulop, Chiang, and Deshpande all felt indebted to a nation they say gave them an opportunity to flourish.

"There's not too many places in the world where a person can show up with nothing in his pockets and start to do things. The United States is special," Deshpande said.

"Why do it in the USA?" Fulop asked. "We're American, and we're going to kick butt."

Yet-Ming Chiang put it more academically. If America was going to avoid trading dependence on foreign oil for dependence on foreign batteries, it needed to produce its own supply.

"You have to have a domestic source for key components," he said. "You don't want your supplier having higher priorities in their own country."

An advanced American battery industry needs the support of the federal government, Chiang argues, because Asian battery companies are supported by their national governments, which helped them to come to dominate the consumer electronics industry.

Deshpande said America holds a technological advantage, thanks to A123, but could lose the lead if it does not invest quickly in manufacturing.

The idea of such a loss incenses Fulop. He said with increased automation in modern factories, American-made batteries can compete with Asia.

"There's no reason we have to build batteries overseas," he insisted, "especially when the technology was created in North America."

Reviving the Motor City

In April 2009, the news out of Detroit buzzed through a troubled American auto industry. Chrysler had chosen a new American battery company to power its next generation of electric cars.

In selecting A123Systems Inc., Chrysler bypassed the foreign battery makers that controlled nearly 90 percent of the market. The partnership not only endorsed an American battery company, but a battery made in America.

Addressing the media at the New York Auto Show, Chrysler president James Press emphasized the salient point.

"In our tradition of being the quintessential American company, we're partnering with A123Systems, which is Massachusetts based, and we're going to build a factory in Michigan, and build all-American batteries for our cars," he said.

A123 planned to build the first lithium-ion battery cell plants in North America in southeastern Michigan, the heart of the American auto industry. The batteries would propel hybrid Jeep Wranglers and Chrysler vans.

Two months deeper into a brutal recession, a bankrupt Chrysler announced a life-saving alliance with the Italian car maker Fiat. The Michigan battery plant remained on the drawing board of the new car company, raising the prospects that A123 batteries could also power some of the smaller, lighter vehicles built by Fiat. In addition, A123 was preparing to power the electric vehicles of Volvo and the products of other manufactures in an increasingly battery-driven world.

The advanced American battery industry had begun, A123Systems president and CEO David Vieau declared. His company was still counting upon a nearly $2 billion stimulus loan from the Advanced Technology Vehicles Manufacturing Incentive Program to build battery plants. Regardless of the decision by the U.S. Department of Energy, it planned to build battery cells in Michigan and tap Detroit tradition and expertise. Vieau projected more than 14,000 people working in more than 7 million square feet of factory space in the years ahead.

Throughout Michigan and the Midwest, civic and union leaders cheered the made-in-America strategy.

U.S. Senator Debbie Stabenow of Michigan told the national media that a company founded by immigrants was moving the country in the right direction.

"We need a twenty-first-century manufacturing strategy in this country," she said. "Companies like A1234 are not only creating quality, good-paying jobs in Michigan, but are ensuring that we do not move from a dependence on foreign oil to a dependence on foreign technology."

John Dingell, a member of Congress from Michigan, called the A123-Chrysler partnership momentous on two levels. "The future of this country is dependent upon addressing two vital challenges— stopping the spread of global warming, and creating the next generation of manufacturing jobs here in the United States," he said. "This project gets us closer to achieving both of those goals."

Spirits High, Lights Aglow

Back on the banks of the Charles River, the lights continued to burn bright into the night in brawny buildings where scientists once designed armaments and now experimented with battery chemistries.

Yet-Ming Chiang shuttled between labs at A123 and at MIT as if on air. When he realized he had the formula for a better battery, he envisioned cheaper energy, a cleaner environment, less dependence on foreign oil. Now he eyed the prospects of thousands of new jobs in his adopted country.

It's almost an unimaginable opportunity, to be in a position to make this kind of impact.

—Yet-Ming Chiang

"It's almost an unimaginable opportunity, to be in a position to make this kind of impact," he said.

After allowing its lead in computer battery technology to slip away, America had a do-over, a lead in a crucial new industry.

"You could almost say high-energy lithium batteries give us a second chance," Chiang said. "We're part of that second chance. We have world-class technology."

His BlackBerry vibrated on the tabletop. He excused himself for a call from China. The race was on.

Chapter 7

Desperate Achievers: Prequel to Google

Every migration is an opportunity and a kind of death.
—Writer Rob Nixon

Soon after she started work at the National Aeronautic Space Administration (NASA), Eugenia Brin noticed something in the hallways of the Goddard Space Flight Center that made her pause and almost made her weep.

On the doors to the offices were placards with names, some of them obvious Jewish names. Brin, a scientist recently arrived from the former Soviet Union, could not believe what she was seeing. In Moscow, Jewish names would never have appeared in an important government building. Jews would not have been allowed in such prestigious positions.

It was a watershed moment. "For the first time in my life," she said, "I felt free to be who I am."

She took walks down the long hallways of her new employer just to read the names on the doors, marveling again at the bright new world to which she had come.

There was nothing casual about Eugenia and Michael Brin's decision to seek to emigrate from the Soviet Union. Simply by requesting exit visas, they would lose their jobs and maybe ruin the careers of friends and associates. They might be refused and forced to live out their lives as refuseniks, Jews whom the Soviet Union refused to allow to leave. It was 1978. The Cold War had yet to thaw. The concepts of glasnost and perestroika were a decade away.

Anti-Semitism loomed pervasive and endless. It was not so bad for Eugenia, a civil engineer with a low-profile job with the national oil institute. But Michael Brin, a mathematics scholar, chafed at slights and restrictions that stalled his career. The couple's biggest concern was their 5-year-old son, Sergey. His birth certificate labeled him "Jewish." He would grow up with all the prejudice and the limits that imposed.

For the boy, they decided, they must try to leave.

After waiting nine anxious months for exit visas, the family was allowed to leave for Austria. The Hebrew Immigrant Aid Society helped them to apply for admission to the United States as refugees. Eugenia and Michael and little Sergey arrived in College Park, Maryland, outside of Washington, D.C., and moved into a small apartment. With some help from the local Jewish community, they began new lives.

Michael Brin found a teaching position at the University of Maryland and went on to become an esteemed professor of mathematics. NASA hired Eugenia Brin as a research scientist, and she specialized in satellite weather forecasting. And Sergey, who began life in America at age six, grew up and started a little company named Google.

"You know, it truly is the land of opportunity," his mother observed.

The company her son launched in a garage with Stanford University classmate Larry Page in 1998 mushroomed into a worldwide cultural icon, a mighty driver of the New Economy. While making multibillionaires of its founders, Google and its innovative search engine eventually employed more than 20,000 people. It helped the United States to become the world leader in Internet-based technology.

You could say the most successful company of the dot-com era started with a simple welcome to a desperate family.

Starting from Nothing

The United Nations defines a refugee as someone who has been forced to flee his or her country because of persecution, war, or violence and who cannot safely return. Refugee workers and resettlement counselors offer a simpler definition. A refugee, they say, is someone who has lost everything.

The United States typically accepts a little more than 1 million immigrants a year and a much smaller number of refugees. The refugee quota in 2009 was set at 80,000 people. These are immigrants for whom the door to the past is shut. They left their homes because of death threats, religious persecution, civil war, or starvation. Often, their flight was sudden and frightening. They begin new lives knowing there is no going back.

From such desperate straits emerge world-class strivers.

The ranks of high-achieving refugees include Albert Einstein, stateswoman Madeleine Albright, billionaire George Soros, and Congressman Thomas Lantos, as well as General John Shalikashvili, the former chairman of the Joint Chiefs of Staff, and writer Loung Ung, a survivor of the Killing Fields of Cambodia whose books and activism now inspire millions.

Refugee immigrants have been some of the most ambitious entrepreneurs of the New Economy. Sergey Brin has said his goal in starting Google was no less than to try to organize all of the world's knowledge. Andy Grove, who escaped to the West after witnessing the Hungarian Revolution of 1956, powered the technology revolution by starting Intel Corporation.

Quy "Charlie" Ton simply wanted to make sure his mother had not suffered in vain. His success in an immigrant niche industry illustrates the drive and the strategic vision often forged during a refugee ordeal.

The Boat People

Ton was 14 years old in 1985 when his mother told him it was time to leave. He did not like what she had in mind. The fishing boat loomed simple and shaky on the dark shore. Rough hewn, it was little more than an open husk with a diesel engine. It was the only hope, his mother whispered.

Vengeful communists had ruled Vietnam since the American forces pulled out in 1975. Quy's father, who had fought with the Americans as an officer in the Army of South Vietnam, was confined to one of the harsh jungle prisons called re-education camps. Quy's older brother had fled by boat two years before.

Now it was Quy's turn. While raising four children, his mother had saved enough money to buy him a spot on a smuggler's vessel. There was no future for him in Vietnam, she explained. He needed to sail away and to try to reach America.

Quy told her he did not want to leave. When she insisted, he obeyed. With 66 others, he climbed aboard the humble craft. But as it sailed off, and as he looked back at his mother where she stood crying, he did not think of America. He prayed that a big storm would blow them all back to shore.

The desperate boat did not get blown back. It chugged for hundreds of miles across the open waters of the South China Sea. Two weeks into the journey, a Philippine fishing boat spied the craft and towed it into Subic Bay, from where Quy was steered to a refugee camp.

An aunt sponsored his immigration to America, and he joined her and his brother in New Orleans, becoming one of the more than 800,000 Vietnamese refugees widely known as boat people who made it to America and were allowed to stay.

Quy finished high school and went on to college. He studied chemical engineering at Louisiana State University, but he had no patience for it. He felt compelled to establish himself quickly in business, to leap ahead. It was a miracle he was even here. By some estimates, one-third of the boat people died at sea. There was a whole family back home that needed whatever help he could send.

When a friend at college, an immigrant from India, asked him what he wanted to be, Quy replied, "A millionaire." He set about that task with a refugee's zeal.

An Artful Niche

By late 2008, Quy "Charlie" Ton was a millionaire many times over. His Regal Nails salons were ubiquitous, numbering more than 1,000 across America, with many of them found in Wal-Mart stores. He had pioneered an immigrant niche and built it into an empire, America's largest chain of nail salons.

His mother, who cried for days after sending her child to sea, saw her prayers answered and her courage rewarded. Ton supported family on both sides of the world, as well as a growing army of employees and franchisees.

At age 38, he remained restless and ambitious. He was pushing beyond the discount end of the market with a chain of posh day spas. From his factories and warehouses in Baton Rouge, Ton manufactured and supplied most everything his industry needed, from emery boards to pedicure thrones. Meanwhile, his chain continued to grow.

"Every day is a learning day for me," said Ton, a polite and measured man. "That's how I operate my companies."

He's a self-taught entrepreneur whose business acumen comes from how-to books, leadership classes, and experience. His seriousness and sense of responsibility spring from a harsh and unsure life.

"It's all how hard and how smart you work," Ton said. "I do not believe in lucky."

Vietnamese immigrants like Ton all but created an economic niche that carried them into the middle class. There's nothing like a Vietnamese nail salon in Vietnam and, once upon a time, there was nothing like it in America, either.

> *It's all how hard and how smart you work. I do not believe in lucky.*
>
> —Quy "Charlie" Ton

Vietnamese women began carving out the niche in the late 1970s in California, home to the largest concentration of Vietnamese outside of Vietnam. Some credit a refugee program that offered cosmetology classes and produced a class of manicurists. Once started in the trade, the Vietnamese immigrants greatly expanded the market, making commonplace a service once considered a posh indulgence.

Vietnamese salon owners say the nail trade works for them because it requires little training, little investment, and limited English skills. It also taps a cultural skill.

A customer might walk into a salon and ask to have her nails done, but to a Vietnamese nail technician, she is asking for "mau ve" (pronounced MOW-vay), nail art. With whisker-thin brushes, they draw sunsets and fireworks and starry nights on a thumbnail-sized canvas.

Mau ve resembles traditional Vietnamese embroidery and lacquer art, where artisans might arrange thousands of tiny eggshell fragments with toothpicks to create inlays. Known for careful and precise craftsmanship, Vietnamese immigrants are also sought-after employees at high-end furniture makers such as L. & J.G. Stickley near Syracuse, New York.

Le Su, a nail-salon owner who plays the organ at a Vietnamese Catholic Church in Cleveland, said he loses himself in nail work.

"You do a beautiful nail, it's like you're playing a song," he said.

But Thuong Nguyen, a young nail technician who emigrated from Vietnam in 2002, said it's just a job, one that she was able to land with little training and not much English.

By 2008, Vietnamese Americans were running 80 percent of the nail salons in California and 44 percent of the nail salons nationwide, according to California-based *NAILS Magazine*.

Ton joined the phenomenon in the mid-1990s, when he began importing supplies for a nail salon that his Vietnamese-born wife worked for in New Orleans. The industry was mushrooming, and Ton rode the wave. His Alfalfa Nail Supply, based in Baton Rouge, became a wholesaler to nail shops across the country.

As he imported the products that salons needed and ran his own nail salon, Ton looked for an opportunity to expand the market. In 1997, he achieved his breakthrough. He convinced Wal-Mart to test in-store salons in a few locations. Ton noted that 70 percent of Wal-Mart shoppers were women. He suspected they might indulge in an "affordable luxury," and he was right. Business soared and the chain grew from year to year. In late 2008, Ton licensed his 1,000th franchise.

Though a proud U.S. citizen, Ton remains very much an immigrant businessman in a niche industry. Almost all of his franchises are owned by fellow Vietnamese immigrants, whom he prefers to deal with. He believes a refugee ordeal shapes devoted workers.

"They work very hard, 10 to 12 hours a day," he said. "They save money. They don't spend money, they save so that their children can go to good schools."

He and his wife, Phuong Le, practice the same strategy. They push their two young daughters to achieve A's in the classroom. They occupy their after-school time with piano lessons, gymnastics, ballet, and swimming.

"It's important. It gives them a sense of responsibility," Ton said. "When it's time for them to go to music, they just get ready to go, without asking why. They just do it."

Such obedience and self-discipline propelled him to walk onto a boat to exile in 1985. Because of his mother's courage, his daughters will not face such a trial. But when they are tested in life, their father expects them to be ready. When they venture out on their own, he expects them to accomplish something great. This is, after all, America.

The Family of Google

Charlie Ton's immersion in a successful immigrant niche, while still common, is not so typical anymore. The jobs and industries of the New Economy are more likely to find immigrants and native-born Americans working together. Immigrant entrepreneurs typically blend two or more cultures to form versatile teams. High-achieving immigrants likely live in two worlds at once, presenting a dynamic new version of the American family.

One such family lives happily in suburban Washington, D.C.

* * *

With a cold Moscow-like rain falling, Richard Herman and Olga Sonis pulled up to the modest older home on a cul-de-sac near the University of Maryland. The door opened and Eugenia "Genia" Brin, a youngish-looking 60-year-old woman, smiled warmly. She motioned for them to enter and to disregard the friendly advances of the large family dog, Toby.

The visitors came with gifts of Russian chocolates and champagne. Richard Herman is an immigration lawyer in Cleveland. His co-worker, Olga Sonis, is a refugee from Uzbekistan.

Like the Brins, Sonis is a Jew who fled the former Soviet Union. She has worked for more than 15 years as a caseworker for the Jewish Family Service Association of Cleveland, which resettled nearly 7,000 Russian Jews in Greater Cleveland in the 1990s and early 2000s.

Hearing the visitors in the foyer, Michael Brin came down the stairs. He was wearing a smart black pullover with the colorful Google logo scripted above the pocket. He happily eyed the chocolates and champagne and waved everyone inside the simply decorated home.

Genia Brin guided them to a dining table laden with cheese, grapes, crackers, juice, and bottled water. She began the story of why her family left home in 1979.

> *Of course we were identified as Jews in our passports, the main identification document in the Soviet Union. So there was not much prospect for a normal career . . . . We had a young child, about five at the time, and his future was very dim in terms of career and environment.*
>
> —Genia Brin

It was a tale punctuated with sighs and laughter and back-and-forth bantering. The Brins interrupted one another, corrected memories, and flashed endearing smiles.

Sergey Brin is known to be funny, inventive, competitive, and wicked smart. An afternoon with his parents suggests where he might have acquired those traits.

"We felt we had to leave," Eugenia Brin began. "Of course we were identified as Jews in our passports, the main identification document in the Soviet Union. So there was not much prospect for a normal career . . . . We had a young child, about 5 at the time, and his future was very dim in terms of career and environment."

Michael pulled up a seat at the table. He began to insert his side of the story in a playful but competitive manner.

"So, more or less, I was the main initiator of leaving Russia?" he asked, looking at his wife.

"That is right," Genia replied with a smile.

Olga Sonis beamed to witness the interplay between the immigrant couple, who were like so many other Russian Jewish couples she knew.

"It was Michael's initiative," Genia continued. "He had already experienced much rejection in the academic world because of being Jewish. I was a good student. He was an excellent student."

Michael had dreamed of becoming an astronomer. But astronomy was taught within the physics departments in Soviet universities, and government officials did not trust Jews so close to nuclear rocket research. So Michael abandoned that dream, and through a family friend, gained entrance to the math program at Moscow State University, one of the most prestigious math institutions in the world.

Discrimination was commonplace in the academic world there, too. Jews were tested separately and more harshly than other students during entrance exams.

"I graduated with a degree in fluid mechanics, and Michael graduated with a degree in math," Genia explained.

"With honors," Michael said, referring to himself.

"With honors," Genia conceded.

"Actually high honors," Michael finished.

With that, Genia ordered her husband into the kitchen to prepare more food. When he came back, she told him he had brought the wrong cheese.

Michael Brin shrugged and smiled, as if acknowledging there is always a higher authority.

"A typical Jewish couple," Olga Sonis said, and she burst out laughing.

Genia resumed her story. Denied graduate school, Michael continued to study mathematics on his own and to publish research papers. He received his doctorate in math by working around the system that tried to shut him out. At that time, a student could defend a doctoral thesis, even without attending graduate school, as long as a university agreed to consider his thesis and he passed certain exams.

So that's what he did. He recruited an ethnic Russian professor who helped him to successfully defend his thesis in Ukraine.

Even with the advanced degree, life did not change much. Michael continued laboring as an economist for Gosplan, the Soviet central planning agency. The couple reached a fateful decision. If Michael was to be able to pursue his passion and talent in math and, more importantly, if little Sergey was to have any kind of future, they would have to leave.

Anxious Wait for Visas

Michael Brin had been outside of Russia once in his life. In 1977, he visited Poland for a mathematics conference, and there he met some American mathematicians.

"We got to talking, and they looked like nice people. It was kind of clear to me that I belonged to that community," he said.

Additionally, his grandmother had lived in America many years before, as a student at the University of Chicago. It was decided the family would try to emigrate to the United States. As a result of international pressure, the Soviet Union was allowing thousands of Jews to leave. But the process was fraught with peril. Simply requesting the visas brought scrutiny and often persecution from authorities, and there was no guarantee the visas would be granted.

"It was like a game of roulette whether you get it or not," Genia Brin said. "So it was a difficult nine months. We were exposed."

Michael was fired from work. Genia left her job, rather than jeopardize the careers of her peers. She knew that her transgression would cast suspicion on the entire office. For some income, Michael started translating Russian and English for technical manuals. Genia kept the family situation a secret to gain a computer programming job in a small institute.

One day in May 1979, the papers saying they could leave arrived, and just in time. The doors were starting to close. Authorities were approving fewer and fewer exit visas. The Brins wasted no time leaving. Michael, Genia, Sergey, and Michael's mother, Maya, boarded an airplane for Austria.

Representatives from the Hebrew Immigrant Aid Society (HIAS), America's oldest immigrant and refugee aid agency, met them at the airport in Vienna and handed them a small amount of local cash. HIAS arranged for transportation to Paris, where a temporary research position awaited Michael, thanks to a friend who had emigrated the year before. While the family waited in Paris, HIAS handled the paperwork and the complex processing for entrance to the United States. The Brin family landed at New York City's John F. Kennedy Airport on October 25, 1979.

Genia Brin holds a deep appreciation for HIAS, which for more than a century has helped Jews escape persecution and establish new lives in free countries. HIAS was instrumental in pressuring the Soviet Union to allow Jews to emigrate from Russia and from Eastern Europe in the 1970s, and in persuading the American government to accept them.

In 2009, Genia served on the board of directors of the non-profit agency. She was the catalyst behind one of its innovative projects, a digital archive of the Russian Jewish experience, which debuted on the agency's web site as myStory.

> *It was amazing to me that all these Jewish people were allowed to work at NASA so freely and they expressed their Jewishness every day, openly celebrating Jewish holidays.*
>
> —Genia Brin

The family's first few years in America were difficult. They lived in a small apartment and walked miles to the nearest grocery store. They knew no one but they benefited from the kindness of strangers. A synagogue helped them to get furniture. A $2,000 loan from a local Jewish agency allowed the couple to buy a used car, Genia explained.

Nodding her head, Olga Sonis whispered, "Very typical . . . walk to grocery store, then buy a cheap car."

The Brins enrolled six-year-old Sergey at a local Montessori-style school, the only private school nearby, and came to appreciate the decision. They credit the Montessori method with instilling in Sergey a habit of independent thinking and a hands-on approach to life.

Genia found work at a small consulting firm that specialized in the oil industry. The next year, she began work at NASA's Goddard Flight Center as a computer programmer. Her job was to improve the use of satellite data for weather prediction. First, however, she allowed herself to enjoy a liberating feeling of tolerance and acceptance.

"I walked down the long hallways and read the name tags on the office doors," she explained. "A good 50 percent of them were Jewish-sounding names. It was amazing to me that all these Jewish people were allowed to work at NASA so freely and they expressed their Jewishness every day, openly celebrating Jewish holidays."

In 2009, Genia Brin was a senior support scientist at NASA, working part time. She was also in the early stages of Parkinson's disease and hoping to spend more time with her infant grandson, Sergey's first-born child. Michael continued to teach advanced mathematics at the University of Maryland. The couple's second child, 21-year-old Samuel, was studying computer science at the University of Maryland.

"Samuel and Sergey are very, very close," Genia Brin said. "When Samuel has a problem, he calls his brother first before talking to us."

Sergey, of course, was one of the most successful entrepreneurs in the world, running a company that seemed to be forever ahead of the curve. Much of what he knew and believed was shaped by immigrant parents from Russia. Observers say he shares his parents' easygoing laugh and sense of humor, their intellectual curiosity, and their tendency to expect a bit more.

In 2003, Sergey Brin and his partner, Larry Page, traveled to Israel, where they addressed the student body at an elite high school. In their book *The Google Story*, David A. Vise and Mark Malseed recall how Sergey Brin received a rock star's welcome in an auditorium crowded with teens whose families escaped persecution in the former Soviet Union.

Sergey congratulated them on their achievements at the technology-oriented high school. Then, to the students' delight, he shared a common bond.

"Similar to here, I have standard Russian-Jewish parents," he said. "My dad is a math professor. They have certain attitudes about studies. And I think I can relate that here, because I was told that your school recently got seven out of the top 10 places in a math competition throughout all of Israel."

With perfect comedic timing, waiting for the applause to die down, Sergey resumed, "What I have to say is, in the words of my father, 'What about the other three?'"

Sergey gained several other rays of insight from his parents, knowledge that he took to California. He was aware that he could disrupt the status quo if it was not to his liking, and pick up and do something completely different. He realized he could move between cultures and gain from the experience. He knew that people from different backgrounds bring different abilities and perspectives to a task.

While high-tech companies in Silicon Valley generally have a high ratio of immigrant founders and key executives, Google's immigrant-led genesis and leadership is higher than most. It's been that way right from the start:

- The late Rajeev Motwani, an immigrant from India and Sergey Brin's Ph.D. advisor at Stanford University, became a company advisor and an early investor in Google.
- David Cheriton, a Stanford professor and an immigrant from Canada, introduced Sergey and Larry to Andreas (Andy) von Bechtolsheim, a German immigrant who had co-founded Sun Microsystems. Bechtolsheim became Google's first major investor.
- Michael Moritz, an immigrant from Wales, led the second round of funding for Google on behalf of his company, Sequoia Capital.

- Google's distinctive logo was designed by Ruth Kedar, an immigrant from Israel.
- Ram Shriram, an immigrant from India, is a founding board member and remained a major shareholder in 2008.
- Omid Kordestani, an immigrant from Iran, was Google's twelfth employee and in 2009 served as senior advisor in the office of the CEO and founders.
- Urs Holzle, an immigrant from Switzerland, was one of Google's first 10 employees and its first vice president of engineering.

Google's current slate of leadership is also immigrant-laden. About 40 percent of the company's 10-member Board of Directors and 50 percent of its 16-member Operating Committee were born abroad.

"There are literally hundreds of examples of immigrants and non-immigrant foreign workers playing a vital role in our company," Pablo Chavez, Google's Washington lobbyist, wrote in a policy statement issued in 2007. "Immigrants from countries like Canada, Iran, and Switzerland now lead our business operations, global marketing, global business development, and data infrastructure operations. Without these talented employees and many others, Google would not be where it is today."

Even Larry Page, while American-born, grew up with immigrant influences. Page was a boyhood admirer of Nikola Tesla, a Serbian immigrant who invented a motor that made alternating current (AC) the premier form of electrical energy. Tesla was a prodigious but largely unappreciated inventor who died poor despite holding more than 100 patents.

In honor of Tesla, Elon Musk, a co-founder of PayPal (and an immigrant from South Africa), founded Tesla Motors. Tesla offers the Tesla Roadster, a super-chic, super-fast, all-electric sports car that sells for more than $100,000.

Both Larry Page and Sergey Brin own a Tesla, as does California Governor Arnold Schwarzenegger, an immigrant from Austria.

Chapter 8

Importing Solutions

The more I traveled, the more I realized that fear makes strangers of people who should be friends.

—SHIRLEY MACLAINE

A dozen people stood expectantly in the chandelier light of the Mayor's Reception Room in Philadelphia City Hall on a gray morning in early 2009. Their earnest faces reflected nine nations of the world. The group included an accountant from India, a nurse from Jamaica, a refugee from Cambodia, a scientist from Mexico, and a florist from Italy.

Immigrants all, they had gathered to take the oath of citizenship at the invitation of Mayor Michael Nutter, who led them in the Pledge of Allegiance while cameras flashed and family members beamed. Philadelphia had never seen anything like it.

No one could remember City Hall ever hosting a naturalization ceremony, the final step to U.S. citizenship. The swearing-in of new citizens usually took place in a federal building several blocks away. But this was no ordinary city and these were no ordinary times.

It's very important that the world knows that Philadelphia is an immigrant-friendly city.

—Philadelphia Mayor Michael Nutter

In January 2008, Michael Nutter took charge of a huge city facing a financial crisis, a frightening murder rate, and a shrinking and anxious middle class. It also was a city with a solution within its grasp.

The mayor vowed to make America's sixth largest city safer, bigger, and more productive. He described plans to replenish declining neighborhoods with newcomers, extend the city's reach into the global economy, and foster a cosmopolitan feel. Essential to all three goals were the people being honored in City Hall—new Americans.

Immigrant welcome efforts by a nonprofit agency, underway for several years, were showing results. Now, the mayor was blessing the crusade. He had hired an Asian business liaison and instructed city departments to prepare to greet people in a world of languages. Such steps represented an unusual endorsement of multiculturalism by an American mayor, and some questioned Nutter's sincerity. But when he hosted the naturalization ceremony that February day, people knew he was serious.

"It's very important that the world knows that Philadelphia is an immigrant-friendly city," Nutter told the *Philadelphia Inquirer* newspaper. "The vast majority of new immigrants have demonstrated that they are tremendously involved in the community, quite entrepreneurial, actively engaged in the neighborhoods, paying attention to what is going on with their children, and a great opportunity to increase population."

Outside of City Hall that day, plenty eyed the newcomers with suspicion and derision. For more than two years, Geno's Steaks, a famous purveyor of Philadelphia's signature dish—the cheesesteak—had posted signs at its iconic restaurant in South Philadelphia declaring, "This is America. When ordering, please speak English."

The formerly Italian neighborhood was changing, drawing thousands of Mexicans and a sprinkling of Vietnamese, Cambodians, and Indonesians. Restaurant owner Joe Vento, a 60-something grandson of Italian immigrants, said he was fed up with customers not knowing the language of their new home. The speak-English signs, which spawned bumper stickers and T-shirts, were not the only signs of tension in a city hearing new voices.

On and around the busy commercial corridor of 52nd Street, black residents charged that the new immigrant shopkeepers were getting ahead with government help. The immigrants, in turn, said they were being harassed and sometimes robbed by their neighbors.

It was clear that hard work and resources would be needed to integrate immigrants into a largely homogeneous city. But that was the plan and Philadelphia was sticking with it. Something remarkable was happening.

A Gateway Re-Emerges

After years of news of rising crime and population decline, Philadelphians in November 2008 learned of an intriguing new trend. The Brookings Institution, a think tank based in Washington, D.C., reported that more than 100,000 immigrants had streamed into the region between 2000 and 2006, creating a foreign-born community of more than a half-million people. It declared that Philadelphia appeared poised to re-emerge as a gateway to America, a status it last knew in the early twentieth century.

In the city, immigrants were opening shops and offsetting losses in the native-born population. In the suburbs, they were launching biotech start-ups and drawing new investment to the pharmaceutical industry. A hopeful region was beginning to see immigrants in a new light.

While Philadelphia was not the first Rust Belt city to experience the transforming power of immigrants, it appeared to be enjoying a bigger boost than others. Chicago grew with an immigrant surge in the 1990s and the Windy City celebrated the 2000 Census, when it posted its first decade-to-decade population gain in 50 years. But Chicago's growth—which emboldened the city to bid for the 2016 Summer Olympics—poses daunting assimilation challenges. The bulk of its newcomers came from a single source, Mexico, and many arrived unskilled and illegal.

The greater Philadelphia area, in contrast, drew a more diverse stream. Its immigrants came from all over the world, with no single nation dominating. The largest group of immigrants, 39 percent, hailed from Asia. Many came bearing college degrees and skills needed in the New Economy.

Those without college diplomas often arrived from entrepreneurial cultures. The Brookings researchers found that the new Philadelphians were more likely to be employed than their native-born neighbors and more likely to open a business.

Little surprise then, that on the eve of a symbolic naturalization ceremony, Mayor Nutter told the city's immigrants: "We want folks to come here. This is your City Hall, and this is where your swearing-in should be."

Tapping the Tide

Philadelphia stands at the forefront of a new economic strategy: immigrant-driven revival. There are many versions of the emerging tactic, but it comes down to attacking blight and reversing decline by enticing industrious newcomers to town, offering them enough support to get started, and allowing capitalism and immigrant dreams to run their course.

The phenomenon appeared to unfold largely unaided in the 1990s, when historic flows of immigrants sparked renewal in many older American cities, including New York, Miami, and

Chicago. The human tide spread out and found new gateways during a decade of record immigration. Immigrants helped to propel cities like Boston, Atlanta, Toronto, and Seattle into international cities. They added population and vitality to once homogeneous places like Portland, Oregon; Columbus, Ohio; and the twin cities of Minneapolis and St. Paul, Minnesota.

In urban areas across the land, immigrants filled empty neighborhoods, opened shops, and pushed their children to the head of the class.

"Perhaps no one factor has more revivified the geography of the American metropolis in recent years than immigration," wrote urban development expert Joel Kotkin in his 1999 report, "The Future of the Center: The Core City in the New Economy."

Meanwhile, the tide bypassed many large and aging industrial cities, like Cleveland, Baltimore, Buffalo, and Pittsburgh, and not entirely by accident.

What looked like a spontaneous phenomenon often had a guiding hand. Cities and states have no control over the nation's immigration policy. The federal government sets quotas, issues visas, and bestows citizenship. The United States typically accepts a little more than 1 million immigrants and refugees each year. The new Americans usually get started in gateway cities, like New York and Los Angeles. However, once they step off the plane, they are free to go wherever they wish.

Several cities experimented with immigrant-attraction efforts in the 1990s and some got good at it. The people of Minneapolis and St. Paul sparked a chain migration when they opened their arms to refugees from South Asia and from Africa. Other refugees followed. By 2000, the Twin Cities of frigid Minnesota supported an improbable mosaic—the largest communities of Hmong and Somalis in North America.

Simpler efforts also proved transformative. In Boston, the Mayor's Office of New Bostonians—one of the first offices of its kind in an American city—helped welcome immigrants and international students, many of whom stoked the region's high-tech economy.

In one of the most focused recruitment efforts, Schenectady, New York, targeted Guyanese families living in a crowded neighborhood of New York City and beckoned them upstate. Guyanese Americans snapped up inner-city houses selling for as little as $1 and painted and rebuilt them at a rate that sparked an urban renaissance.

Some cities are just getting started. Steve Tobocman, the former Majority Leader of Michigan's House of Representatives from Detroit, was busy touring Philadelphia, Toronto, and other rising cities in 2009 and examining the impact of immigrants. He was leading a study for Global Detroit, an initiative that seeks to revive Detroit's economy with international investment and immigration.

The crusade is the brainchild of John Austin, a Brookings Institution researcher, vice president of the Michigan Board of Education, and the descendant of an immigrant entrepreneur.

As he looked at the shuttered auto factories in Detroit, Austin wondered where the culture of entrepreneurship had gone. He concluded that generations of dependable, good-paying factory jobs, requiring only a high school diploma, had bled the region of its innovative spirit and cooled the pursuit of education.

Tobocman and Austin hope immigrants can ignite a new era of innovation and learning. They have a base to build upon. One-third of Michigan's high-tech start-ups were launched by immigrants. They and other civic leaders hope to build upon the Detroit area's large Arab American business community and a growing Mexican American community.

Austin said he understands that it is not always easy to welcome newcomers.

"But the most powerful way culture is changed, I am convinced, is by welcoming an influx of fresh ideas, fresh people, with diverse and different assumptions," he said.

Savvy Pilgrims, Creative Shopkeepers

The tactics employed in Boston, Minneapolis, Schenectady, and now Detroit spring from a new civic philosophy. They rest on the belief that immigration is not simply something that happens to a city but something that can be made to happen. What's more, the philosophy holds that immigration should often be encouraged—for the greater good of all.

It's an old belief finding new life. "The richest regions are those with the highest proportion of immigrants," reads a 1953 report by the President's Commission on Immigration and Naturalization. "Their industry, their skills, and their enterprise were major factors in the economic development that made these regions prosperous ones."

The ability of immigrants to succeed in American cities has been well documented. But a less-publicized body of research illuminates the ability of an immigrant tide to lift every boat in the harbor.

Immigrants do not succeed alone. Along with offering English courses, the non-profit Immigrant Learning Center in the Boston suburb of Malden, Massachusetts, commissions studies that explore the immigrant experience and the impact of New England's newest cultures.

It found that today's pilgrims open more than greengroceries and dry cleaners. A study by Boston University researchers concluded that immigrants were behind 26 percent of New England's biotechnology companies.

The learning center also commissioned a study of the impact of mom and pop shops. Researchers from the University of Massachusetts concluded that immigrant storefronts packed the power to spark commercial revivals on poor and lonely

> *Remarkable creativity and adaptability are common traits in these entrepreneurs.*
>
> —Study by the Immigrant Learning Center

streets. As they sold fresh foods, flowers, and phone cards, the merchants generated foot traffic, enhanced safety, and inspired others to invest.

What's more, the shopkeepers were marvels unto themselves. The researchers discovered an exporter from Asia working as a sushi chef while he opened an herb shop. They interviewed a Vietnamese immigrant who had expanded his grocery into a bookstore and a flower shop. They met a Latino business owner thinking of buying a Chinese restaurant and continuing to serve Chinese food. He judged East Boston had enough taquerias.

"Remarkable creativity and adaptability are common traits in these entrepreneurs," the researchers concluded.

So is self-reliance. The immigrant entrepreneurs rarely, if ever, accessed help or loans available from the city or state, the researchers found. They strove alone, consumed by businesses entwined with their personal lives, succeeding "through a complex combination of hard work, savvy, and creativity."

Not everyone believes that. So successful are immigrant entrepreneurs that myths and mistruths have sprung up to explain the phenomenon. Some people claim that immigrant-owned businesses enjoy unfair, shadowy advantages, like tax breaks or other government help.

Not true. The federal government extends not a single tax advantage to a business based on immigrant roots. Nor does anyone else. Local business development programs, meanwhile, typically target a general audience or a struggling native-born group, seldom immigrants.

Still, the misperception persists. The belief that immigrants enjoy extra help may stem partly from the limited aid the federal government extends to refugees. Refugees, the world's most desperate immigrants, receive a modest living stipend to get them started in America.

The myth may also be fostered by the tendency of immigrant-owned retail businesses—like many other small, cash-based businesses—to be less than diligent about playing by the rules.

Immigration lawyers are well aware that some immigrant shop and restaurant owners under-report their receipts to circumvent the tax collector, fail to abide by health code regulations, or hire undocumented workers.

Some of that behavior is cultural. Many immigrants hail from lands where the government is distrusted and avoided, or where business rules are lax or non-existent. Hiring an undocumented worker from the old country may be seen as a humane gesture.

At times, immigrant business owners are disconnected from the mainstream due to language and cultural barriers.

That's not an excuse, just a fact.

Immigrant advocates believe communities can increase compliance and integrate immigrants more quickly into the establishment system through education and outreach. Some argue this outreach could also be used to welcome immigrant entrepreneurs to town, and to encourage them to grow their businesses and create more jobs.

The ripple effects are what matter to most Americans. Those can be profound.

A Wave of Home Restorers

In the aging factory town of Schenectady, New York, the homes of Guyanese Americans are easy to spot on inner-city streets lined with century-old double-deckers. Theirs are the houses freshly painted in tropical colors and necklaced by flower gardens. Theirs are the houses crowding out the blight.

Most of Schenectady's Guyanese families were crammed into high-priced apartments in the Richmond Hill section of Queens when Mayor Albert Jurczynski discovered them. A grandson of Polish immigrants, the mayor was looking for a way to revive and repopulate his city, which had lost thousands of jobs and one-third of its residents since 1950. Bleak, inner-city neighborhoods had hollowed out as homes were abandoned, and no one was interested in reinvesting.

There are plenty of Guyanese who sit around watching television. But they're back in Guyana. The ones who want to change their life, they're the ones who leave.

—home restorer Mohabir Satram

A Guyanese-American friend told the mayor about his people in Queens. Immigrants from the South American nation of Guyana, most were the descendants of indentured servants from India. They possessed English skills and a Hindu work ethic. More than anything else, they desired to own a house.

"I thought, well, we have plenty of those," Jurczynski recalled. "Maybe these people are the answer."

He struck upon a recruitment strategy. Working with Guyanese realtors in Queens, the mayor began filling buses with Guyanese couples on Saturday mornings and motoring them three-and-a-half hours north for a tour of his struggling city. The bus drove past vacant houses on the city's demolition list. The day usually ended at the home of the mayor's Italian mother-in-law for homemade wine and cookies.

Guyanese-American couples came back with checkbooks. Vacant houses began selling, saws began whirring. New colors joined the urban pallet. A familiar immigrant story unfolded.

Arriving unskilled and often uneducated, the Guyanese took low-wage jobs as dishwashers, janitors, and nursing home aides. Dual-income couples invested in their homes. West Indian restaurants and groceries opened to serve the new market. Some Schenectady employers, mindful of a hungry new workforce in town, began reinvesting.

In less than a decade, Guyanese Americans became about 10 percent of the city of 62,000, and inner-city streets once considered worthless stirred with fussy homeowners. Property values rose countywide, surging in some of Schenectady's worst neighborhoods. Between 2003 and 2008, the median home price in the city of Schenectady climbed by 35 percent, to $118,200. In 2008, the city's housing director credited an industrious immigrant group with insulating the entire county from the worst of the mortgage meltdown.

"They breathed new life into this town," said Jurczynski, who looks back on the recruitment effort as one of the shining moments of his mayoral tenure. "They changed Schenectady. And they never asked for a dime from anyone."

Mohabir Satram, one of the busiest of the Guyanese home restorers, says "Mayor Al" gleaned the cream of the crop.

"There are plenty of Guyanese who sit around watching television," Satram said. "But they're back in Guyana. The ones who want to change their life, they're the ones who leave."

A Boost for Everyone

America's love-hate relationship with immigrants traces to the nation's earliest days. "Is rapid population [growth] by as great importations of foreigners as possible . . . founded in good policy?" Thomas Jefferson asked in 1782.

Fears that immigrants will take local jobs and supplant local culture are not without a grain of truth. Most immigrant-advocacy groups combine assimilation strategies with welcoming efforts, seeking to integrate foreign cultures into the mainstream as quickly as possible. Studies have shown that immigrant waves do depress wages, especially for low-skilled workers with limited job options. But that's only part of a sweeping impact.

More recent studies show that, as an immigrant tide rises, so does the regional economy.

A pair of economists, Giovanni Peri, from the University of California-Davis, and Gianmarco Ottaviano, from the University of Bologna, Italy, examined the effect of immigrant labor on economies in America's 100 largest cities from 1970 to 2003. They found that high-immigrant cities enjoyed more robust economies than low-immigrant cities. As the economy grew, wages for all workers tended to rise with the foreign-born population.

Other scholars found that immigrants also boost home values. An 18-year study of Washington, D.C., by the Alexis de Tocqueville Institute found a positive correlation between the number of immigrants in a neighborhood and increasing property values. Some experts say immigration reform should include a housing component that helps connect foreclosed and abandoned homes to immigrant families looking for a foothold.

In recent years, the urban-renewal power of immigrants has intrigued a growing list of scholars, including Michael Porter, a man people the world over look to for a plan.

Porter, a Harvard business professor, is widely considered the world's leading authority on competitive strategy. He coaches businesses, countries, regions, and even sports teams on how to leverage their advantages to beat the competition, whether it be China or the Yankees. Porter serves as a senior strategy advisor to the Boston Red Sox.

He knows something about world cultures and he knows something about winning. The son of a career Army officer, Porter grew up traveling and living all over the world. He was an all-state football and baseball player in high school in New Jersey. At Princeton University, he played intercollegiate golf and split enough fairways to become New England champion.

His ideas on economic strategy, extolled in his 18 books, are taught at virtually every business school in the world. In recent years, Porter has focused much of his attention on the economies of America's inner cities. He believes that he has found the secret to tapping inner-city potential. Immigrants, Porter argues, provide run-down neighborhoods with a powerful jolt of economic vibrancy, and a city that wants to pull ahead should try to attract them.

Porter examined the economies of 100 distressed inner cities and their fortunes from 1995 to 2003. Time after time, he found that immigrants were catalysts to economic growth. Where immigrants settled, businesses sprang up and jobs appeared. Where immigrants were absent, nothing changed.

Upon releasing his study in 2006, Porter observed that immigrants were capitalizing on slim business prospects but prospects nonetheless.

"Immigrants clearly and more readily identify the unique business conditions and opportunities that inner cities offer and are able to capitalize upon them. There is a direct correlation between immigrant populations and job growth in inner cities," he concluded.

He could have been talking about Jason Lin, a one-man economic engine in the inner city of Cleveland, Ohio.

The Power of One

On a fall morning in 2008, Jason Lin strolled through his masterpiece, an old industrial warehouse he had painstaking renovated into modern offices and storefronts. The past weekend, a large room on the second floor hosted his daughter's wedding reception. She was his youngest, the surprise that followed a life-changing tragedy, and he was still glowing with pride from her wedding day.

Lin walked the halls with a stiff, peculiar gait, pushing himself up steps with a cane. It was remarkable he was walking at all. His legs are hollow. An indomitable spirit propels him.

The son of a Chinese rice merchant, Lin grew up in North Vietnam in an industrious family that fled south with the rise of communism. He was working as a translator for the U.S. Army in 1975, and he and his wife and their two young children barely escaped the Fall of Saigon.

Their refugee odyssey brought them to Cleveland, where Lin found work as a freight handler at the airport. He was, like his father, an entrepreneur at heart. Not all Chinese and Vietnamese immigrants possess an entrepreneurial personality. But those who flee communism, maybe risking their lives on desperate boats, are people with passion, Lin explains.

I know that I need to get up again. I asked the doctor, "When can I walk?" He said, "Well, we can talk about that later." I said, "No, I need to plan."

—Businessman Jason Lin

"The people who left China because of communism, those are the entrepreneurs," he said. "They all want to own their own business."

True to his dream, Lin launched a trucking firm and a travel agency before branching into Chinese and Vietnamese cuisine, at one point owning five restaurants.

He was driving home from one of those restaurants on a winter night in 1982 when he stopped to help one of his employees whose car had broken down. He was straddling two cars, hooking jumper cables to a battery, when a young driver smashed into the stalled car at high speed. Lin was pinned vice-like between the two vehicles. When he awoke in the hospital, both of his legs were gone above the knee.

Through long nights and weeks in a hospital bed staring at swelled stumps, Lin, an obsessive planner, took stock of his situation. He had a wife and two children to support and several businesses to run. He was 31 years old. He ignored doctors who told him he would never walk freely again. He dismissed therapists who warned of a long recovery.

"I know that I need to get up again," he recalled thinking. "The kids are four and five. I asked the doctor, 'When can I walk?' He said, 'Well, we can talk about that later.' I said, 'No, I need to *plan*.'"

He instructed his wife to bring him boards, which he tried to fashion into artificial legs. When hospital officials found out, they had him fitted early for prosthetics but told him to wait for physical therapy.

The effervescent Lin had no intention of waiting. Grasping a long pole for balance, as a stilt-walker might, he practiced walking on his new limbs. He walked right into his first physical therapy session, shocking the therapists. Within eight months of losing his legs, he was walking freely. In 1983, his youngest child, Kathleen, was born.

Lin poured the same planning and tenacity that got him walking into his businesses. He scouted bleak streets for prospects that could be exploited with sweat and diligence. In 2005, he came upon a colossal wreck on Cleveland's near west side, in a one-time Italian immigrant neighborhood now primarily Latino and Appalachian. The surrounding streets were largely poor but Lin saw opportunity. Doctors needed offices. Hair stylists needed shops. Weddings needed halls.

He bought the building and began to renovate, piece by piece. By 2009, the new office building stirred with tenants, including a barber shop and several small businesses. Momentum spilled out of the doors. Lin had bought the industrial building next door and sold it to a Chinese investor and his son, who envisioned a fish farm. A neighborhood activist observed, "With 19 Jason Lins, we could revitalize this whole neighborhood."

But Cleveland did not have 19 Jason Lins. In 2008, it had fewer immigrants than nearly any other big city in America. That was partly by chance and partly by choice.

Pushing Open the Door

When the tides of migration flowed past Greater Cleveland in the 1990s and early 2000s, some civic leaders raised an alarm. They told of what immigrants were doing for other struggling cities and suggested Cleveland try to capture its share. But even modest immigrant-attraction efforts, like posting an international liaison at City Hall, never gained the blessing of people with influence. As Philadelphia welcomed 113,000 immigrants between 2000 and 2006, Cleveland lost another 7 percent of its population and became almost entirely native-born.

The "i" word was seldom raised as a strategy in a city debating recovery strategies, including what to do about thousands of foreclosed and abandoned homes. An aversion to immigrants permeated the region's political leadership and peaked at city hall.

Mayor Frank Jackson dismissed suggestions that the city try to attract immigrants to reverse population decline and to revive inner-city neighborhoods that were mostly black and poor. Jackson, a multiracial mayor who identified most strongly with his African-American roots, told civic groups he did not trust immigrants to help his people.

If someone else wanted to try to draw immigrants to Cleveland, "I will not be against it," Jackson told the Cleveland *Plain Dealer* in early 2009. "However, as we move ahead, I'm always interested in the self-help mode, in taking care of our own."

Six hundred miles away in Philadelphia, Anne O'Callaghan heard those statements and shook her head. It's the same attitude she encountered at Philadelphia City Hall, when she first proposed a center to aid immigrants and to encourage them to stay.

A pleasantly persistent Irish immigrant, O'Callaghan almost single-handedly launched Philadelphia's pro-immigrant course. She is the founder and the executive director of the Welcoming Center for New Pennsylvanians. Her agency is now being copied by cities across America. But when she first pitched the idea in 2002, skepticism ran deep in high places.

O'Callaghan initially envisioned her center inside Philadelphia City Hall. A widely respected fundraiser, she used her contacts in philanthropy circles to gain a face-to-face meeting with former Mayor John Street.

The mayor dismissed her idea of a welcome center by dismissing the potential of immigrants. They took jobs, he said. They needed services.

O'Callaghan reminded the mayor that she too was an immigrant, one who had launched her own business, a software company that serves the home health-care industry. He responded with words she still finds remarkable.

"He said, 'You're not really an immigrant,'" O'Callaghan recalled. "He meant I was educated. I speak English. He saw immigrants as a burden. A lot of politicians, they don't get it."

The belief that immigrants burden the community or take away jobs from native-born Americans, especially minorities, persists despite being more fear than fact. Chicago demographer Rob Paral found that the unemployment rate among African Americans is, on average, lower in states and cities with the most recent immigrants in the labor force. After examining census data, Paral concluded that recent immigrants made up 17 percent of the labor force in Miami and 3 percent of the labor force in Cleveland, yet the unemployment rate of native-born blacks in Cleveland was double that of Miami.

"On the question of race, we find that there's just no connection between immigration and unemployment. The culprit when it comes to unemployment is not immigration," Paral states in a report released by the Immigration Policy Center in 2009.

Nevertheless, there would be no Mayor's Office of New Philadelphians, O'Callaghan realized. Rebuffed, she was not defeated. As a physical therapist, she was accustomed to helping patients realize what was best for their recovery. Plus, she never lost her immigrant's zeal.

Toward a "Shared Prosperity"

In 1970, the former Anne Leahy came to Philadelphia from County Monaghan for advanced training in physical therapy. She was 27 and expecting to stay a year. As often happens with visitors from afar, she met someone. In 1971, she married Sean O'Callaghan, a second-generation Irish American and a Philadelphia lawyer. As she likes to say, "I saved him from a life of ease and comfort."

With the region's immigrant surge growing more visible in the late 1990s, Anne O'Callaghan became active in a small nonprofit agency that helped Irish immigrants, many of them illegal. But she often found herself trying to answer the questions of Chinese, Mexican, and Liberian immigrants who walked in the door.

> *You need to be able to see how your community can be transformed. And we have lots of places in the city where you can walk down the street and see that.*
>
> —Anne O'Callaghan

Many of the newcomers sought services that seemed simple and attainable. They asked where to find English classes, who to talk to about licensing a business, how to apply for a Social Security number.

"I am kind of a problem solver. I guess many therapists are," she said. "I would look at this and say, 'Oh, I should be able to find ESL classes out there.' And I would spend weeks on the phone," listening to recorded messages, getting nowhere.

She decided a system was needed, a central clearinghouse that would collect the kinds of information immigrants needed and make referrals. When City Hall showed no interest, O'Callaghan took her idea to people and groups with a regional view. She approached foundations and state representatives and a few forward-thinking city council members.

In March 2003, the Welcoming Center for New Pennsylvanians opened in temporary offices donated by labor unions. Modest funding came from private foundations and from the state, which remains the center's largest backer. Its primary mission then, as now, was to match immigrants with jobs and to integrate them into the community.

The agency quickly took on the personality of its founder, who pushed the philosophy of shared prosperity. If immigrants came to Philadelphia and did well, O'Callaghan argued, they would pay more taxes, hire more workers, and create more jobs. If immigrants came and flourished, so would the city.

By 2009, she directed a full-time, multilingual staff of 18 in offices above a train station in Center City Philadelphia. Her budget had grown to $1.2 million. The center's job counselors matched talent with employers. Its web site included a searchable database of English classes across the metro area. Its simple, powerful brochures bore titles like "How to Start a Coffee Shop in Philadelphia."

"You need to be able to see how your community can be *transformed*," O'Callaghan preaches. "And we have lots of places in the city where you can walk down the street and see that."

A Harlem–Like Renaissance

Center City is the civic hub of Philadelphia, but the downscale intersection of 52nd and Market streets rivals it for foot traffic. A neighborhood sometimes compared to Harlem for its concentration of African-American business and culture had fallen on hard times by the start of the twenty-first century. Violent crime, job losses, and a debilitating public works project chased out businesses and homeowners.

But in the spring of 2009, there was a hint of renaissance in the air.

A new elevated train station had opened above the intersection, easing commutes to Center City and the suburbs. New shopkeepers had pried the boards off of vacant storefronts and restocked shelves. On a bright April weekday, the sidewalks of 52nd Street stirred with a level of capitalism seldom seen in an American inner city.

Sidewalk tables laden with merchandise stretched for blocks along the noisy avenue. Vendors sold clothing and handbags, watches and jewelry, sunglasses and suitcases. They stood outside of Chinese restaurants and mid-priced men's clothing stores and hawked their wares in lilting West African accents.

By 2009, Philadelphia had the largest Liberian community in America. Seemingly half of it was selling something on 52nd Street.

Through the midday throng strode Fatimah Muhammad, a trim, upbeat, 25-year-old woman from New Jersey. She ran Welcoming Center West, a spin-off from the main office in Center City.

The satellite opened in 2008 after neighborhood leaders and residents called upon the Welcoming Center for New Pennsylvanians to share its insights with both immigrant and native-born residents of West Philadelphia. Anne O'Callaghan readily agreed.

From a South 52nd Street storefront, Muhammad and her small staff offered "English for Entrepreneurs" and classes in business planning and accounting. They counseled immigrant shopkeepers on how to respond to threats and harassment, some of it from gang members. They brought together immigrant and native-born business owners for mutual support and for cultural celebrations. And they worked to quash myths.

Muhammad talked daily with people who had lived 30 or more years in the neighborhood and never saw their prospects change. Suddenly, a Hindi-speaking couple from India owned the corner store and seemed to be making a go of it.

Immigrants, many of them new to the city, owned 65 percent of the corridor's shops, stores, and restaurants, said Muhammad, who visited 175 separate businesses conducting an impact survey. Few were experienced entrepreneurs, she found. Many were simply survivors who could not otherwise find jobs. But their shops and restaurants were succeeding.

"It's a sore spot, because people think immigrants must have some advantage," she said. "It's the only way to explain they can do this. They think, 'Maybe the government's giving them money.'"

It's not. The city, hard-pressed for cash, does not even provide financial support to the Welcoming Center. Muhammad's survey found that most immigrant entrepreneurs did not take advantage of what little help was available from development programs.

However, in their quest to rise in America, immigrants do enjoy some advantages over their native-born neighbors. Immigrant children are more likely to grow up in a two-parent family. Immigrant parents are more likely to hold a college degree. The family might have brought seed money from the old country, or it might be able to tap a revolving loan fund within its ethnic community.

More often, Muhammad found, Mom and Dad worked in a kitchen washing dishes until they saved enough money to buy a restaurant.

She walked into a dollar store beneath the elevated train tracks and said hello to a Pakistani couple that smiled to see her. Their six-year-old daughter stood by her father's knees behind the cash register. Khalid and Rukhsana Chaudary bought the store six years before. They lived outside the city, in Delaware, a source of some resentment. But they also swept the sidewalk and hired workers from the neighborhood.

> *It's a sore spot, because people think immigrants must have some advantage. It's the only way to explain they can do this. They think, "Maybe the government's giving them money."*
>
> —Fatimah Muhammad

"It doesn't matter what the skin color is," Muhammad said later, walking up 52nd Street. "It's more about, 'Are you really trying to be an active part of the community?' A lot of the black residents have told me, 'I don't know where we'd be without these immigrants.'"

Seeds of Progress

With the advent of the Nutter administration, the city's immigrants gained another key ally. By 2009, there were flyers posted around town announcing that City Hall was prepared to speak with people in 20 languages on a walk-in basis. The mayor had hosted a naturalization ceremony. People were using the words "Philadelphia" and "gateway" in the same sentence for the first time in nearly a century.

Hard feelings and opposition lingered, but the seeds of change had been planted. On a spring afternoon, in a pleasant South Philadelphia shopping center occupied almost exclusively by Southeast Asian businesses, Vi Truong worked the counter of his savory shop. He sold preserved plums and apricots and other dried fruits and pushed fresh sugarcane stalks through a press to produce sweet, frosty drinks.

Truong would have trouble ordering at Geno's Steaks, a few blocks away, for he labored to speak English. A builder in Vietnam, he'd been too busy working to attend school since he and his family immigrated in 1999, sponsored by his brother. In 2004, the family moved from Seattle to Philadelphia. He had heard it was a good place for an immigrant to start a business.

Truong introduced new flavors to his new city, but his bigger contribution is not so obvious. He and his wife arrived with a son and a daughter. Both children recently graduated from Philadelphia-area colleges. His daughter is an accountant. His son is an engineer and a chemist. Both decided to live and work in the city, adding to a rising young professional class.

Dad, preparing sugarcane drinks the Old World way, beams with quiet pride.

Sometimes, he even hears, "Welcome to Philadelphia."

Chapter 9

The Stimulus We Need

It is not the strongest of the species that survive, nor the most intelligent, but the ones most responsive to change.

—CHARLES DARWIN

The video makes your blood boil, as it was meant to. We see Hispanic young men drop over a wall one after another, presumably sneaking into the United States from Mexico. Like escaping inmates, they hit the dusty ground and scurry away. An unseen voice warns: "Today, anywhere from 3,000 to 8,000 illegal aliens will cross the border, most disappearing into American society, a wave of illegal immigrants affecting every aspect of American life, undercutting wages and jobs for low skilled Americans and legal immigrants and crowding classrooms, hospitals and prisons."

As CNN reporter Christine Romans reads her script, the screen fills with images of Hispanic men working on a rooftop, dicing vegetables in a kitchen, and milling behind a chain-link fence in orange prison jumpsuits.

Suddenly, Lou Dobbs himself appears, looking grim and staring directly into the camera as he announces: "This is a problem that is not going to go away and a crisis that is only worsening. Thank you."

To a viewer, it's impossible to tell when the news reporting ended and the editorializing began, but the message is chilling and clear. An invasion is underway. A plague is spreading among us.

By April 2009, that November 2006 segment from "Lou Dobbs Tonight," titled "The Cost of Illegal Immigration," had been viewed more than a quarter of a million times on the video sharing web site YouTube. It was part of a "Broken Borders" series of reports promoted by Dobbs and by CNN as an examination of America's immigration issues. Night after night, month after month, the celebrity journalist pounded home the point that illegal immigrants were infesting America.

Against that backdrop, some people tried to discuss comprehensive immigration reform.

If the topic of immigration incites emotional responses and heated conversations in America today, that may be because many people hear "immigrant" and think of illegal immigrants flouting American laws. They hear "immigrant" and envision waves of lower skilled workers scaling the border walls, an image that Lou Dobbs shows them as often as he can.

Less publicized is the fact that at least one-third of the undocumented population came to America legally but overstayed their visas. Some of those with expired visas are surgeons, teachers, and other professionals. Americans have been trained to focus on the most negative images.

Meanwhile, a large, *legal* community of immigrants waits for attention. While illegal immigration commands the spotlight, some of the world's most talented people are turned away from America, or told to go home after earning prized degrees in technology and engineering from American colleges and universities. That is the real unfolding crisis.

Addressing undocumented immigrants is crucial and the nation may be moving closer to consensus. A May 2009 poll by the Pew Research Center found that, by a margin of nearly two to one, Americans support a path to citizenship for undocumented immigrants.

Perhaps more Americans are beginning to understand that comprehensive immigration reform would make the country safer and economically stronger. The Congressional Budget Office estimated that $66 billion in new revenue over 10 years would have been generated if supporters of the 2006 immigration reform bill had succeeded in legalizing most of our undocumented immigrants.

Still, immigration reform raises a host of complex issues.

At the dawn of the twenty-first century, illegal immigration had indeed mushroomed into a demographic challenge with a Latino hue, as the Lou Dobbs video implied. In 2008, about 12 million people were living illegally in America and nearly two-thirds of them had come from Mexico, according to a study by the Pew Hispanic Center. The flow of unauthorized workers slowed as the economy weakened and the recession deepened, but a sizeable unauthorized community remains. It presents daunting challenges to a society asking, "What do we do?"

No immigration expert recommends trying to uproot and forcibly deport 12 million people. However, many also fear that offering illegal immigrants a path to citizenship smacks of amnesty and that could encourage more people to skirt the rules and enter the country any way they can.

Meanwhile, the impact of illegal immigration grows increasingly complicated. Many undocumented immigrants have been in America for years now. They belong to families that demographers awkwardly call "mixed status." Dad might be illegal but mom is a U.S. citizen. Their American-born children are U.S. citizens at birth. Loving families can be shattered, emotionally and economically, when a member is arrested and deported.

In another common scenario, a child who came across the border in her mother's arms suddenly faces a complicated future at age 18. She's likely unable to enroll in college, no matter how stellar her academic record. She is still an illegal immigrant, barred from participating fully in American life. Yet she cannot easily return to a country whose language and customs she never really knew.

Targeted reforms seek to address some of the problems. The DREAM Act (Development, Relief, and Education for Alien Minors Act) would offer some hope to the 65,000 undocumented children graduating from America's high schools each year. Introduced into both houses of Congress in March 2009, the bill would offer conditional permanent residency to undocumented immigrants who entered the country as minors, so that they can enroll in college or serve in the military. But the legislation faces strong opposition and its passage is far from certain.

With such complex issues to address, it should come as no surprise that lawmakers are moving cautiously and at times erratically toward comprehensive immigration reform.

The problem for the United States is that the most controversial side of the drama—illegal immigration—dominates the debate. Lost in the indecision and the rancor are the legal immigrants who make up the largest share of America's foreign-born population. Forgotten are the thousands of people standing in line, waiting to get into the country legally.

In that queue are brilliant engineers, high-technology specialists, talented artists and musicians, investors, and merchants almost certain to become entrepreneurs in whatever part of America they land.

This is a demographic group with the power to transform industries and communities, as we have seen again and again. High-skill immigrants represent a wave of creative energy. In an era of economic uncertainty, they are the stimulus we need.

An Immigrant Advantage

While it may seem counterintuitive to promote immigration during an economic downturn, with millions of Americans looking for work, many academic researchers and economists are doing just that. They are not promoting mass immigration, but smart immigration.

At the same time, they question the wisdom of turning away talented people and expelling stellar international students, in part, because the nation has not decided what to do about illegal immigrants.

By accepting industrious, highly educated immigrants, they argue, the United States can foster a culture of innovation and entrepreneurship, which in turn will build a foundation for creating jobs.

History shows that a recession can be a good time to start a business. Some of America's most successful companies took root during economic doldrums, including Microsoft, Hewlett-Packard, Intel, CNN, FedEx, MTV, and even Burger King. Immigrants nurtured the culture of innovation that built Silicon Valley in the 1980s and 1990s, and they are beginning to do it again, in emerging industries like clean technology.

Research by Vivek Wadhwa, AnnaLee Saxenian, the Kauffman Foundation, and others has documented how high-skill immigrants promote invention and expand the economic pie. They are not competing for jobs with Americans—they are creating jobs that were not here and they are filling jobs that Americans are increasingly unqualified to fill.

More and more observers say that a thoughtful discourse on economic revival must include leveraging our immigrant advantage.

Thomas Friedman, a journalist with a global view and author of the bestselling book *The World is Flat: A Brief History of the 21st Century*, argues that America should frame the discussion of economic stimulus around technological innovation, start-ups, and immigration, not bailouts or protectionism. In the February 10, 2009, edition of *The New York Times*, he asked us to be ourselves again:

Dear America,

Please remember how you got to be the wealthiest country in history. It wasn't through protectionism, or state-owned banks or fearing free trade. No, the formula was very simple: build this really flexible, really open economy, tolerate creative destruction so dead capital is quickly redeployed to better ideas and companies, pour into it the most diverse, smart and energetic immigrants from every corner of the world, and then stir and repeat, stir and repeat, stir and repeat, stir and repeat.

We don't want to come out of this crisis with just inflation, a mountain of debt and more shovel-ready jobs. We want to—*we have to*—come out of it with a new Intel, Google, Microsoft and Apple.

That kind of achievement is going to require imported talent. As President Bill Clinton predicted in 1997, "Where once nations measured their strength by the size of their armies and arsenals, in the world of the future knowledge will matter most."

Unfortunately, America's arsenal lacks native-born firepower.

In 2006, a landmark report by the National Academy of Sciences warned that America's lead in science and technology was "eroding at a time when many other nations are gathering strength." Among its alarming findings were the following:

- Less than one-third of the nation's eighth grade students performed at a proficient level in mathematics.
- American youth spend more time watching television than in school.
- Only 15 percent of U.S. college students earn degrees in a natural science or in engineering, compared to 38 percent of undergraduates in Korea, 47 percent in France, 50 percent in China, and 67 percent in Singapore.
- In 2004, China overtook the United States to become the leading exporter of information technology products.
- The largest employer in the United States was Wal–Mart.

Craig Barrett, the chairman of Intel Corp., warns that America is losing its competitive edge for a lack of savvy in science and engineering. He has testified before Congress, urging lawmakers

142

to invest seriously in science and engineering education. Until we produce the talent we need, Barrett argues, the government should make it as easy as possible for foreign students to stay on after they graduate, instead of expelling them back to their home countries.

In a widely quoted suggestion, Barrett said the government should "staple a green card" to the diplomas of any immigrant graduating from a U.S. university with a degree in math, science, or engineering.

His argument stems from staffing realities. Immigrants have become an essential part of America's research laboratories. In 2008, nearly two-thirds of all science and engineering doctoral candidates in U.S. universities were foreign-born.

In fact, the impact of international students is profound and growing. More than one-third of the students attending Harvard Business School are international. In March 2009, the National Center for Education Statistics reported that 68 percent of Ph.D. economists graduating from U.S. universities were international students.

In 2008, an all-time high of 623,000 international students, 7 percent more than the year before, were studying and researching— and spending money. According to the National Association of Foreign Student Advisors, these students and their dependents contributed over $15.5 billion to the U.S. economy.

The international students create intellectual property in the research labs and imbue the campus with global diversity. Upon graduation, many bring innovation and international skills to their U.S. employers. Some start their own companies.

Carl Schramm, president of the Kauffman Foundation, argues that promoting entrepreneurship is the best stimulus for the struggling U.S. economy. In a 2009 essay entitled "Americans Say, 'Free the Job Creators,'" he writes that a smart entrepreneurial agenda would "encourage the world's brightest students to come here, study, and become entrepreneurs."

Of course, before they can become entrepreneurs, international students need to be able to work in the United States, become permanent U.S. residents, and eventually Americans. If that is discouraged, they will go home or to countries with more flexible immigration policies, Intel's Barrett and others argue. Some of the graduates will start companies that compete against us. Others will go to work for U.S. companies tempted to open research and development centers overseas because of the growing numbers of skilled workers suddenly available—workers educated in America.

"We go where the smart people are," Intel spokesman Howard High said back in 2005. "Now our business operations are two-thirds in the U.S. and one-third overseas. But the ratio will flip over the next 10 years."

It doesn't have to flip. Intel and other innovation-driven companies can continue to innovate right here, many economists say. But only if they can recruit the best people.

In his book *The Accelerating Decline in America's High-Skilled Workforce: Implications for Immigration Policy*, economist Jacob Funk Kirkegaard sees an economic malaise brewing. Kirkegaard argues that poor-quality public education, retiring baby boomers, and increasingly restrictive immigration laws jeopardize America's economic growth.

Clearly, U.S. policymakers cannot do anything to stop baby boomers from aging, nor can they turn a switch and reverse more than 30 years of education stagnation. But they can open the door to bright, industrious newcomers.

"U.S. policymakers can only hope to counter these long-term phenomena in a timely manner by reforming high-skilled immigration," he writes.

Dan Arvizu echoes that sentiment from Golden, Colorado, where he directs the National Renewable Energy Laboratory. Policymakers envision millions of new jobs as the nation pursues renewable energy sources, like wind and solar power, and builds a smart grid to tap it. But Arvizu warns that much of the clean-technology talent lies overseas, in nations that began pursuing alternative energy sources decades ago.

Expanding our own clean-tech industry will require working closely with foreign nations and foreign-born scientists, he said. Immigration restrictions are making collaboration difficult. His lab's efforts to work with a Chinese energy lab, for example, were stalled when a key Chinese scientist could not get a visa to visit.

"We can't get researchers over here," Arvizu said in an interview in March 2009, his voice tinged with dismay. "It makes no sense to me. We need a much more enlightened approach."

Some say we need that enlightenment fast.

America Losing Ground

By 2009, Vivek Wadhwa had studied the role of high-skill immigrants in America's New Economy for five years, working with researchers from Duke and Harvard universities and the University of California at Berkeley. The fourth piece in his revealing immigration series is the one that piques his emotions. It warns of a "reverse brain drain" gathering strength.

In September 2006, more than 1 million people were standing in line waiting for visas to work in America. They were international students and high-skill professionals and their family members. They represented some of the brightest minds in the world. And many of them would soon be leaving.

For America is no longer the only land of opportunity. China and India, with a combined 2.5 billion people—nearly 40 percent of the world's population—are developing rapidly and creating New Economy opportunities at home.

Wadhwa sounded an alarm in the spring 2009 issue of *Issues in Science and Technology*, the journal of the National Academy of Sciences. "The United States is facing a potentially disastrous exodus

> *The United States is facing a potentially disastrous exodus of young scientists and engineers who are likely to be among the world's most productive inventors and engineers.*
>
> —Vivek Wadhwa

of young scientists and engineers who are likely to be among the world's most productive inventors and engineers," he warned.

Wadhwa estimates 50,000 immigrants have left the United States in the last 20 years and returned to India and China, and he expects an additional 100,000 to leave in the next few years, as a trickle becomes a flood. Much of the blame, he argues, rests with a slow and outdated immigration system.

Each year, the U.S. government issues 120,000 permanent resident visas, known as green cards, to skilled workers and their immediate family. Narrowing the path further, no more than 7 percent of those visas can go to people from any one country. So hopeful immigrants from populous nations, like China and India, now face waits measured in years.

After revealing the high-skill visa backlog in 2007, Wadhwa and his researchers began to examine the impact. With the support of the Kauffman Foundation, they surveyed about 1,200 Chinese and Indian professionals who had studied or worked in America and returned home.

The returnees were an impressive bunch, overwhelmingly young, smart, and ambitious, as described in the March 2009 report, "America's Loss is the World's Gain." Nearly 90 percent held master's or doctorate degrees. Many said they expected to start their own companies.

Homesickness was common among the immigrants who went back, and many expressed frustration with the U.S. immigration system. But even more said the home country suddenly offered good jobs and bright career prospects.

That is the new reality that demands a response, Wadhwa argues. Foreign-born mathematicians, engineers, and chemists can now find world-class companies in Bangalore, Beijing, Tel Aviv, Seoul, and Singapore. With high-tech opportunities blossoming elsewhere, and anti-immigrant attitudes hardening in America, Wadhwa said his adopted homeland faces a crisis.

"The United States is no longer the only place where talented people can put their skills to work," he writes. "It can no longer expect them to endure the indignities and inefficiencies of an indifferent immigration system, and it must now actively compete to attract these people with good jobs, security and other amenities."

The competition is heating up. In an earlier study, Wadhwa pointed out that most high-skilled immigrants obtained their primary education before coming to America, meaning that the United States inherited the benefits of schooling that was paid for elsewhere. Some countries are looking to recoup that investment and attract its diaspora back home.

In April 2009, China announced it would begin offering bonuses to executives and academics who came back to help the nation build its New Economy.

Similarly, Alberta, Canada, sensing an opportunity to snatch talent from America, is sending recruiting teams to U.S. cities to lure disgruntled foreign professional workers on temporary H-1B visas. The province is offering expedited permanent residency cards and quicker pathways to entrepreneurship.

Many researchers believe these immigrant-attraction strategies will show results.

"The reality of the global economy is that employers and their capital will follow the talent—wherever that talent is permitted to work and flourish," Stuart Anderson, executive director of the National Foundation for American Policy, wrote in 2007. "While members of Congress often talk about 'protecting' American jobs, those who persist in pursuing restriction on hiring skilled foreign nationals unfortunately are inhibiting creation and innovation in the United States."

In 2007, Microsoft opened up a research and development facility in Vancouver, Canada, just over the border from its Seattle headquarters. Microsoft defended its decision by citing U.S. immigration restrictions on high-skilled talent.

Perhaps no country understands better the role of foreign talent in creating jobs for its people than Singapore.

In July 2008, Singapore's Prime Minister, Lee Hsien Loong, declared that Singapore must be open to foreign talent to achieve a "critical mass" for innovation and entrepreneurship.

Even with the global recession in full swing, Singapore Deputy Prime Minister Wong Kan Seng announced that restricting the entry of high-skill immigrants would be "short sighted" and "could ultimately lead to more job losses for Singaporeans."

America loses more than innovation if newly minted graduates go elsewhere; it loses tax dollars.

A 2009 report by the respected Technology Policy Institute found that immigration restrictions cost billions in lost opportunity, taxes, and wages. The institute concluded that legislation considered by Congress to loosen green card and H-1B visa restrictions could reduce the federal deficit on the order of $100 billion across 10 years.

In short, fantastic opportunities are being lost as high-skill immigrants are steered elsewhere. We need to polish our welcome.

For starters, Wadhwa argues, the United States could reduce the huge backlog of visa requests simply by making more visas available to skilled immigrants and by accelerating the processing times.

His is one voice in a growing chorus that hopes to wrest the spotlight from illegal immigration and illuminate the larger wave, its potential, and the consequences of inaction.

Suffering an Antiquated System

Anyone coming to America from a foreign land experiences the U.S. immigration system. They seldom forget the experience. This vast bureaucracy, with tentacles reaching into myriad federal agencies, wields enormous power over the lives of people trying to follow its directives. Federal immigration authorities decide if a persecuted family can escape Congo, if a prospective college student from Germany will start the school year on time in Bowling Green, or if a Honduran family separated for years will be reunited in Miami.

Basically, U.S. immigration law dictates who can enter America and how long they can stay. Congress can enact new immigration policies as it deems fit—and it did so in 1986 and in 1990. But the foundation of the system remains the Federal Immigration and Nationality Acts of 1965 and 1952. The 1965 act diversified America by opening immigration to new parts of the world, but it also levied restrictions that soon became dated and counterproductive. In a manufacturing era, the act made family reunification an overarching goal while paying relatively little attention to the migration of highly skilled workers. In fact, it imposed rigid nationality quotas on skilled immigrants.

Our immigration laws discriminate pretty heavily against highly talented scientists and engineers who want to come to this country and be part of our technological establishment.

—Federal Reserve Chairman Ben Bernanke

The result, critics say, is a dinosaur of a system ill-equipped to deal with the demands of a fast-changing, global economy.

"Our immigration laws discriminate pretty heavily against highly talented scientists and engineers who want to come to this country and be part of our technological establishment," Federal Reserve Chairman Ben Bernanke told a Congressional panel in May 2009.

Of particular concern to employers and economists are two sets of quotas: one that limits the number of green cards available to skilled workers, and another that limits the green cards available to a nationality.

The U.S. Citizenship and Immigration Service (USCIS) issues about 1 million green cards per year. Also know as immigrant visas, green cards bestow permanent residency, or the right to live and work permanently in America. A green card puts one on the path to citizenship.

In a typical year, the vast majority of green cards go to people sponsored by a family member already here. There is no limit to the numbers of green cards that can be issued to the spouses, parents, and unmarried children of U.S. citizens.

America accepts far fewer people whose main reason for coming is to practice a profession, to pursue science, or to start a company—even if that person possesses extraordinary ability. The government is restricted by law to issuing 140,000 employment or skill-based green cards each year. That's about 15 percent of the immigrant visa pool. A chunk of those green cards are set aside for religious workers and wealthy investors, so the United States actually offers 120,000 employment-based green cards each year.

Within the employment visa categories, known as EB visas, are several subcategories that acknowledge skill levels. For example, 40,000 visas are designated for persons of extraordinary ability—outstanding professors, researchers, and multinational executives. Another 40,000 visas are designated for professionals with advanced academic degrees. And another 10,000 visas are available for wealthy people who commit to investing in a U.S. enterprise and creating jobs.

So, out of 1 million green cards issued in an average year, 90,000, or about 9 percent, are reserved for persons with advanced degrees, exceptional skills, or capital to create jobs.

Put another way, about 9 percent of immigrant visas are reserved for high-skill immigrants—the people driving the New Economy. It's a scant amount in the context of a U.S. labor force of 154 million people.

Should those exceptional immigrants hail from a nation whose workers are in high demand—for example, India and China—they face delays imposed by a nationality quota system.

The 1965 immigration law sets per-country limits on employment green cards. People from any one nation cannot use more than 7 percent of the immigrant visas available that year. This means that workers from large sending countries are forced to wait, sometimes more than 8 years, because their visa allotment has been "oversubscribed" by their fellow citizens.

The 7 percent quota applies equally to every nation on Earth, regardless of its size or the potential number of immigrants it sends to America. For example, Malawi, which has a population of 10.5 million people, is allocated the same number of employment visas as India, which has a population of over 1 billion.

In any given year, only 5,600 green cards reserved for Indians with advanced academic degrees or exceptional ability, the same number available to nationals of Malawi.

Congress has sought to circumvent the quotas and respond to industry demands—especially in high technology—with guest worker visas like the H-1B, a source of some controversy. The H-1B is a temporary visa for a professional offered a job by a U.S. company that agrees to pay the prevailing market wage.

Only 65,000 regular H-1B visas are available each year, a quota set in the early 1990s and temporarily increased to 195,000 from 2001 to 2003. Many employers say the cap is set too low to meet their needs, especially as they seek to staff engineering and software positions.

Some lawmakers would like to help them with a higher quota. These skilled immigrants often come to America as students, then go to work in growing industries. A 2008 study by the National Foundation for American Policy found that for each worker hired on an H-1B visa, at least five new jobs were created.

But many labor groups argue that the cap is already set too high. Only a bachelor's degree is required to qualify for this visa, and critics charge the H-1B visas crowd skilled Americans out of the workplace, suppress wages, and make it easier for employers to outsource jobs to low-cost countries like India.

Even immigrant advocates criticize the H-1B as a second-class visa that produces an anxious life. Tied to their employers, the guest workers cannot switch jobs unless their new employer is willing to sponsor their visa, and their spouses are not allowed to work. The three-year visa can be renewed once. But after six years, the visa holder must go home unless he or she is able to get a green card sponsor.

The national origin quotas, coupled with a limit of 90,000 immigrant visas reserved for highly skilled professionals or investors, helps to explain why so many talented immigrants—many of them H-1B visa holders—wait in vain for permission to live and work in America.

A Better Way

Strong family values rank high among the qualities immigrants bring to America. A smart immigration policy would not pit family reunification dreams against high-skill immigration. Both are crucial for society. But changing times demand a reaction. The days of mass immigration are over, just as a visa system based largely on kinship ties is outdated. America's population now exceeds 300 million. The country no longer needs settlers to tame the West. Immigrant families are no longer forever separated by nineteenth-century modes of travel and communication. It's time the system was brought into balance, with an equal emphasis on family ties and job creation.

There's a new frontier called the global economy, and we need the pioneers who will rush to meet it. The nation is ready.

America has learned many lessons from the terrorist attacks of September 11, 2001, and the government has put in place a state-of-the-art security system. It incorporates global intelligence and criminal database information for background checks on people applying for U.S. visas.

While comprehensive immigration reform looms daunting in the near term, the stimulus of high-skill immigration need not be delayed before consensus is achieved on the host of other issues. High-skill immigration reform is a good place to re-start the national discussion on immigration law reform. The econ-

> *I think it is absolutely normal to resist the kind of change that waves of immigration suddenly thrust on people.*
>
> —Journalist Alberto Ibargüen

omy demands it, and it will help Americans better understand the contributions that *all* immigrants make to this country.

Good proposals on high-skill immigration reform are out there and more are coming all the time.

The Kauffman Foundation drove home that point in a position paper published in April 2009 titled "Knowledge Economy Immigration: A Priority for U.S. Growth Policy." Authors Tim Kane and Robert E. Litan argue it is needless to try to reform the entire immigration system at once.

"Of all the policies that could be changed, probably none would have a greater positive impact on long-term economic growth than removing barriers to the immigration of highly skilled and highly educated individuals," they write.

The pair advises against attempting broad reforms in a contentious political climate. They say moving to a Canada-like point system, which places a premium on high-skill applicants, is probably too ambitious to achieve quickly.

Instead, they suggest eliminating the cap on H–1B visas, which would allow employers to hire all the foreign professionals they feel they need, and granting green cards to any foreign citizen who graduates from an American university with a degree in math, engineering, or science.

A version of this proposal made its way into Congress in March 2009. Arizona Congressman Robert Flake introduced the "Stopping Trained in America Ph.D.s from Leaving the Economy

Act." The so-called "Staple Act" would offer immigrant visas to foreign-born students earning doctorate degrees in science, technology, engineering, or mathematics.

Political commentator and historian George Will proposes what may be one of the simplest and most salient fixes: "add a zero." Will suggests that the government simply "add a zero" to the 140,000 employment green cards offered each year, boosting the total to 1.4 million. That's a whole lot of very smart people.

"Two-thirds of doctoral candidates in science and engineering in U.S. universities are foreign-born," Will wrote in the June 26, 2008, edition of the *Washington Post*. "But only 140,000 employment-based green cards are available annually, and 1 million educated professionals are waiting—often five or more years—for cards. Congress could quickly add a zero to the number available, thereby boosting the U.S. economy and complicating matters for America's competitors."

Richard Herman, an immigration lawyer with a practice in Cleveland, has offered a couple of job-producing alternatives, one with a clean energy focus. He proposes an Energy Scientist Green Card be made available to people with skills that would readily apply to the renewable energy industry.

Herman also proposes expanded use of the EB-5 Foreign Investor green card program that offers 10,000 green cards per year for foreign investors, their spouses, and children, who invest $1 million ($500,000 in economically distressed areas) and who create 10 jobs.

There is no waiting line for this green card—only a fraction of the EB-5 quota is used each year. That may change, as the government promotes the program with clearer guidelines. Soon, it had hoped to be issuing all 10,000 green cards every year—producing a potential of $2 billion in investment and 40,000 new jobs annually.

Working with the Greater Cleveland Partnership and the Great Lakes Chambers of Commerce, Herman, international attorney Mark Santo, venture capitalist Charles Stack, and others have developed a legislative proposal for a High-Skill Immigration Zone. It would lower immigration barriers in Rust Belt cities like Detroit, Cleveland, and Pittsburgh, and allow them to import foreign talent.

Such zones would accelerate the transition to a knowledge-based economy. Without this shock treatment, many of America's older, less-educated cities will not be able to keep up with the likes of Seattle, Boston, and San Francisco, let alone Bangalore and Beijing.

Struggling cities could also benefit from an increase in the annual refugee quota. Many of the 80,000 or so refugees the nation accepts each year become grateful, productive citizens. Providing sanctuary to the persecuted people of the world is not only a proud feature of the American character, it is an economic revitalizer.

Refugees are playing critical roles in revitalizing blighted neighborhoods of St. Paul, Minnesota; Columbus, Ohio; and Lewiston, Maine.

Finally, immigrants and refugees could provide an anecdote to the foreclosure crisis that has emptied so many neighborhoods.

Gregory Crespi, a law professor at Southern Methodist University, proposes the creation of a new visa category for immigrants who purchase a home with at least a $40,000 down payment.

There is no shortage of creative ideas. We just need to be open to the opportunities.

The Change We Need—Changing Attitudes

While tinkering with high-skill visas can show quick results, more substantial immigration reform is going to require more than changes in quotas and visa requirements. It will require changes in attitudes. Some believe the masses of Americans will begin to value the new immigrants and the shared prosperity they represent only as they come to know them. So they work to put faces on the foreign names. They labor to reveal the breadth of immigrant accomplishment and foster a wiser, more welcoming America.

As a former newspaperman, Alberto Ibargüen knows a good story when he hears one. And the story of immigrant Americans is a good one. Sometimes, though, it's how the story is told that matters most. That is where Ibargüen finds reason to be optimistic. He sees President Barack Obama leading the immigration debate in a calmer, more thoughtful direction.

Ibargüen, the son of a Puerto Rican mother and a Cuban father, is the former publisher of the *Miami Herald*. In 2005, he became president and CEO of the John S. and James L. Knight Foundation. As it seeks to rebuild communities and the journalism industry, the foundation also works to speed the assimilation of immigrants as it advocates for enlightened immigration policy. Ibargüen believes in a soft approach that begins with an understanding of human nature.

"I think it is in the nature of the human experience to feel safe and comfortable with what we know," he said. "I think it is absolutely normal to resist the kind of change that waves of immigration suddenly thrust on people."

His goal is to "lower the volume" of the debate so that sensible decisions can be made. Toward that end, the Knight Foundation publicizes the contribution of immigrants and encourages immigrants to fully join their new country as active, voting, naturalized citizens.

Meanwhile, Ibargüen looks to the White House to shape a new dialogue.

"We are all part of one tribe," President Obama writes in his 1995 autobiography, *Dreams from My Father: A Story of Race and Inheritance*. His staff reflects a leader comfortable in a worldly, multicultural milieu.

Within Obama's elite inner circle—himself and the 22 members of his Cabinet—are five children of an immigrant or parent born abroad, five grandchildren of an immigrant, two people married to immigrants, and three people who have lived abroad as a child or as a young adult.

Perhaps President Obama is the right person, at the right moment, to unify the country around immigration, Ibargüen says, daring to dream.

"President Obama is a calm, rational individual," he said, "and frankly that gives me hope that somebody will lead the immigration conversation in a less ideological, less chauvinistic way."

> *We must help our fellow citizens understand that for this great country to thrive and retain its unique characteristics, it must be open to immigrants.*
>
> —Philanthropist Jan Vilcek

In the melting pot of New York City, another, more immigrant-focused foundation wages a welcome campaign.

Jan Vilcek apologizes for having no secretary to provide a greeting, and rushes to open the door to his small office in the massive New York University Medical Center complex where he is a living legend. The 75-year-old microbiology professor quickly sits down behind his desk and begins talking with a slight Czech accent.

Vilcek and his wife, Marica, defected from a communist Czechoslovakia in 1964. Dr. Vilcek landed at NYU's School of Medicine, where he began exploring the frontiers of the immune system. In 1989, he and his Chinese-born research partner, Junming Le, developed an antibody that led to the miracle drug Remicade. The anti-inflammatory medication revolutionized the treatment of rheumatoid arthritis, Crohn's disease, and other inflammatory disorders.

In 2005, Vilcek made the largest donation ever to NYU's School of Medicine, more than $100 million for medical research. By then, he had already turned his attention to another disease: prejudice and ignorance.

In 2000, Jan and Marica established the Vilcek Foundation to raise awareness of the contributions of immigrant scientists and artists. Headquartered in a 1902 carriage house on East 73rd Street in New York City, the foundation presents $25,000 cash prizes to foreign-born scientists and artists who have made extraordinary contributions to society. It also provides a venue for immigrant artists and filmmakers to showcase their work.

Recent winners of Vilcek Foundation Prizes include Mike Nichols, an Oscar and Tony award–winning director from Germany, and Ham Tran, a promising young filmmaker from Vietnam who explores the stories of the Vietnamese boat people.

The first Vilcek Prize in Biomedical Science in 2006 went to Joan Massagué, an immigrant from Spain honored for groundbreaking cancer research. The 2009 prize went to Huda Zoghbi. A Lebanese-born neurologist and molecular biologist, she discovered the gene responsible for Rett syndrome.

"There is xenophobia in America, a prejudice that intensified with 9/11," Jan Vilcek said. "We must help our fellow citizens understand that for this great country to thrive and retain its unique characteristics, it must be open to immigrants."

A short subway ride away, another esteemed immigrant labors to open minds and change attitudes. His foundation is a well-known beacon of knowledge. Vartan Gregorian is president of the Carnegie Corporation of New York, a philanthropic powerhouse on Madison Avenue founded by America's first billionaire.

America was always said to be a land of religious freedom and tolerance. But I don't think that tolerance based on law is enough.

—Educator Vartan Gregorian

Andrew Carnegie, an immigrant from Scotland, built the Carnegie Steel Company, which became U.S. Steel, the largest steel producer in the world. He created hundreds of thousands of American jobs and, while still a young man, began endowing more than 2,000 free public libraries that bear his name. He created the Carnegie Corporation in 1911 to promote "the advancement and diffusion of knowledge and understanding."

Today, Gregorian believes that includes helping people to understand the role of immigrants in America.

An Armenian born in Iran, Gregorian came to the United States in 1956 to attend Stanford University, where he earned his doctorate in history and humanities. Later, he became president of the New York Library System and president of Brown University. Sitting in an easy chair in an office piled with books, he described education as a liberating force.

"America was always said to be a land of religious freedom and tolerance," he said. "But I don't think that tolerance based on law is enough. Tolerance must be based on understanding."

A scholarly man with a twinkle in his eye, Gregorian promotes that tolerance in means subtle, creative, and illuminating.

Every July 4th, Gregorian places a full-page, color advertisement in the *New York Times* titled "IMMIGRANTS: The Pride of America." Circling a picture of Andrew Carnegie, like a galaxy of stars, are the pictures of 39 other famous immigrants: people like Rupert Murdoch, Ted Koppel, Arianna Huffington, Dan Aykroyd, Carlos Santana, Liz Claiborne, Indra Nooyi, Jerry Yang, Mel Martinez, David Ho, and Salma Hayek.

The advertisement reads, in part: "Our national motto, E Pluribus Unum—'out of many, one'—continues to be an ideal we can all aspire to and a true guiding light for our nation."

Chapter 10

Thinking Like an Immigrant

Ah, ah,
We come from the land of the ice and snow,
From the midnight sun where the hot springs blow,
The hammer of the gods
Will our ships to new lands,
To fight the horde, singing and crying:
Valhalla, I am coming!
On we sweep with threshing oar,
Our only goal will be the western shore.
Ah, ah

—IMMIGRANT SONG
LED ZEPPELIN*

Turtles sunned themselves beside the beautiful Guadalupe River on a fall afternoon as butterflies danced overhead. From the bow of a raft, Richard Herman could see fish swimming in the water below.

But there was no time to admire nature. Herman shared the two-man tube with Mansoor Malik, a 60-year-old aeronautical engineer from Pakistan. And Malik wanted to race.

"Let's go. Let's go!" he cried, as other rafts closed in. Herman looked back at the older man, who was paddling and smiling broadly. Malik had flown into Texas from Islamabad, Pakistan, for the gathering of like-minded, smart, competitive people. He was not about to concede anything.

About 20 small rafts glided down the lazy river outside of San Antonio. They held 40 men and women in town for a gathering of The Indus Entrepreneurs, or TiE, a high-tech trade group plugged into the New Economy.

Successful entrepreneurs from the Indus region of South Asia founded TiE in Silicon Valley in 1992. They came together to mentor and to support one another in their strange new surroundings. They went on to foster a mighty culture of entrepreneurship. By the fall of 2009, TiE claimed 12,000 members in 53 chapters in a dozen nations.

Although the group's immigrant roots remained obvious, from the Hindi accents of top officers to the Bollywood dancers at the dinners, the group was open to anyone who believed in its dual ideals. "TiE guys," as some call them, talk of a virtuous cycle of wealth creation and community service. They see their purpose as nurturing the next generation of bold entrepreneurs, who in turn will give back to their communities, achieving both commercial success and spiritual well-being.

The group's letters have come to stand for Talent, Ideas, and Entrepreneurship. The organization welcomes all who believe that entrepreneurship can transform the individual, the community, and the nation.

The believers form an impressive band of brothers and sisters. TiE's marquee event, an annual convention called TiEcon, draws thousands of attendees and speakers like Steve Ballmer, Nicholas Negroponte, Vinod Khosla, and California Governor Arnold Schwarzenegger. Prominent venture capital firms and investment banks line up as sponsors. High-technology heavyweights like Microsoft, IBM, Fujitsu, and Intel make sure they are well represented—and with good reason.

"It's the largest collection of entrepreneurs in the world," venture capitalist John Doerr told the *San Jose Mercury News* after TiEcon 2006. "You look in their eyes and you see the future."

TiE also sponsors regional conferences and networking retreats, like the gathering of charter members in San Antonio in October 2008. Richard Herman, the founder of an immigration law firm in Cleveland, Ohio, flew in with Baiju Shah, the president of a Cleveland biotech incubator called BioEnterprise. The two men had recently helped to organize a Cleveland chapter of TiE, and they looked forward to meeting legends of the New Economy.

What they found was far more inspiring. They stepped into a celebration of entrepreneurship: a multicultural gathering equal parts networking, mentoring, and play. Lectures and workshops that explored topics like niche markets and recession start-ups were leavened with outings that fostered fun and teamwork.

One of those diversions put Herman in a raft on the Guadalupe with Mansoor Malik, who had come to San Antonio representing the National University of Science and Technology in Pakistan. The rafting trip was designed to be a peaceful, beer-sipping float. But the TiE guys turned it into a race.

As Malik screamed that others were passing them, Herman began to match his teammate's excitement. Soon, the two were paddling in furious rhythm.

"Yes, yes, that's the way, my friend," yelled Malik, as the raft began to move in a straight line and gather speed. "This is American-Pakistani teamwork at its finest!"

Drenched in sweat and river water, Malik and Herman finished the four-mile trek near the front of the pack—a respectable showing. They pulled their raft onto the riverbank and fell back on the grass and peeled off soggy shirts and shoes. They laughed as they opened water-logged wallets and laid out paper money on the grass to dry, Pakistani rupees and American dollars.

Time would tell how long their relationship would last, but Herman was struck by how quickly and naturally the unlikely pair achieved camaraderie. The pattern would repeat itself throughout the four-day retreat. He left for home with an iPhone brimming with new names and email addresses, and with invitations to stop in and say hello should he ever be in San Francisco, Chicago, London, or Islamabad.

It was obvious to him that the foreign-born business people valued him being there, maybe as much as he appreciated their willingness to accept him into the tribe. For the price of a hotel room and a convention credential, he had gained a window-view into the mighty culture of immigrant entrepreneurship. He felt a little like one of them, and not for the last time.

The Dream-Keepers

America stared up from the depths of recession in mid-2009, hoping the worst was over. Beginning in December 2007, housing values plunged, banks teetered, and employers cut pay and slashed jobs in what mushroomed into the worst economic downturn since the Great Depression.

Immigrants are those with the starkest sense of how this country differs from all others, and their very belief in that difference makes it—partly— come true.

—Author James Jasper

But the gloom did not seep into the TiE gathering in San Antonio in the fall of 2008, nor did it mar many of the other immigrant business gatherings that year, to hear participants tell it. Many had seen the stock value of their companies plunge and often their personal fortunes, too. But many had also experienced adversity before.

Optimistic by nature, the entrepreneurs tended to talk about possibilities and their next bold venture. It was not ignorance or hubris buoying their spirits. As researchers have documented, immigrant entrepreneurs possess a remarkable record of achievement. To them, the American dream still shined in the darkest days. It was almost as if they knew something the rest of America had forgotten.

Many others have noticed that quiet confidence and its ripple effects.

"Immigrants are those with the starkest sense of how this country differs from all others, and their very belief in that difference makes it—partly—come true," James Jasper wrote in his 2000 book, *Restless Nation: Starting over in America*.

Echoing that observation, author and historian Harold Evans observed in his 2004 book, *They Made America*, "It is commonly said that these later immigrants brought their dreams. In fact, they brought ours."

As Special Liaison Counsel with the United States Citizenship & Immigration Services, Ellen Gallagher is often asked to work immigration cases that present particularly compelling humanitarian circumstances. She sees how hard many immigrants work to reach America, and what they achieve after having arrived.

"I am impressed and often amazed by their determination and strength; they have seen so much, endured difficult challenges and become stronger as a result," she said.

In May 2009, Gallagher attended the graduation ceremony of Hitesh Tolani, an immigrant from Sierra Leone who earned his doctoral degree from the University of Pennsylvania's School of Dentistry.

He and his family overcame tremendous obstacles, including his father's death and his mother's struggle with cancer. They unquestionably epitomize "the American dream," she said.

"If I ever need a top dentist, I'm boarding a plane to find Hitesh," Gallagher said and she laughed.

Back in the 1960s, John F. Kennedy wrote about the remarkable resiliency of immigrants and their unshakable belief in the American ideal, a faith he felt was contagious.

"Immigration is by definition a gesture of faith in social mobility," Kennedy wrote in his book, *A Nation of Immigrants*. "It is the expression in action of a positive belief in the possibility of a better life. It has thus contributed greatly to developing the spirit of personal betterment in American society and to strengthening the national confidence in change and the future. Such confidence, when widely shared, sets the national tone."

If the national tone seems to have soured a bit, immigrants remain believers. They remind us, in word and deed, that America is the destination of choice because America works.

Part myth, part reality, the American dream is essential because it is what unites us. It is the shared belief that, in America, anything is possible, that people starting at the very bottom can catapult to the very top. Immigrants are the dream-keepers.

By the lessons they unconsciously impart, the new immigrants can help Americans re-connect to the American dream and to an awareness of the skills and attitudes required to achieve it. Their survival instincts, their entrepreneurial skills, and their legendary work ethic are not trade secrets. In fact, they represent something of a national skill set.

Traits honed by our immigrant ancestors generations ago are being reintroduced by a new wave of adventurous, clever, indomitable pioneers. From them, we can learn what it takes to regain our optimism, confront today's economic challenges, and achieve our dreams.

Immigrants can teach us how to think and act like immigrants. The leap is shorter than it might appear.

A Nation of Immigrants Indeed

The oft-heard observation "We are a nation of immigrants" is more fact than folklore. Soon after the start of the new millennium, the U.S. Census Bureau reported that the number of foreign-born and first-generation Americans had reached its highest level in history.

About 60 million Americans—or one in every five people—are immigrants or the children of immigrants.

Later examination revealed that about 40 percent of Americans were the grandchildren of immigrants. When you consider native-born Americans married to immigrants, it's apparent well over half the nation has a close familial relationship to immigrants.

Those who don't count at least one immigrant among their friends and business associates are basically missing an era.

There is a less obvious, equally powerful mark of immigration upon the national soul. Johns Hopkins University psychologist John Gartner is one of several scholars who believe that immigrant genes have made us what we are. In his book, *The Hypomanic Edge*, Gartner argues that the genetic material of self-selected, highly motivated immigrants has passed down from generation to generation, creating the "American character" that drives the nation.

He points out that Americans work longer hours than people in any other country, are more entrepreneurial, and are generally more optimistic. It's in our DNA.

In *Restless Nation*, James Jasper notes that Americans move to a new home more often than citizens in any other country: one out of five Americans move each year. Jasper believes this "restlessness" is a product of our immigrant heritage.

"Immigrants are unusual people, with special drive, ambition and talent," Jasper writes. "They come to America in pursuit of economic success and single-mindedly win it—at least the ones we hear about, the ones who stay to raise families. Most of the losers return home."

> *Don't bemoan the way things were. They will never be that way again.*
> —Entrepreneur Andy Grove

If our inner immigrant lies dormant, if the lessons handed down by our immigrant ancestors are forgotten, we are the lesser for it. These immigrant traits lead to achievement in business and in life.

When embarking upon a new ambition, Andy Grove, the Hungarian immigrant who was part of the founding team of Intel, says he tries to think and act like an immigrant.

"Going through a career inflection point is not an easy process … It's a bit like emigrating to a new country," Grove wrote in his 1996 book, *Only the Paranoid Survive*. He continues:

> You pack up and leave an environment you're familiar with, where you know the language, the culture, the people, and where you've been able to predict how things, both good and bad, happen. You move to a new land with new habits, a new language and a new set of dangers and uncertainties.

> At times like this, looking back may be tempting, but it's terribly counterproductive. Don't bemoan the way things were. They will never be that way again. Pour your energy, every bit of it, into adapting to your new world, into learning the skills you need to prosper in it and into shaping it around you.

Keys to Success

Where do we find success strategies in this new world, the practices that will lead to achievement in a multicultural America and in a new, global economy? We can look to *Immigrant, Inc.* and step into a culture of entrepreneurship.

Interviews with dozens of successful immigrant entrepreneurs make clear that an innovative approach to business is part of a larger approach to life. They may hail from myriad cultures and backgrounds, but high-achieving immigrants display a common body of beliefs and personality characteristics. Most, we have found, possess these success traits:

1. A keen sense of adventure
2. A reverence for education
3. Love and respect for family
4. An eagerness to collaborate

5. A tolerance for risk and failure
6. Passion, often borne of desperation
7. A tendency to dream

Not all seven traits are present in all immigrant achievers. Often they are all present at once.

The Explorer

Monte Ahuja, who created Transtar Industries based on his master's thesis, was the first in his family to leave India. He came alone and with little money to a new land where he knew no one. He obviously possessed a sense of adventure and the qualities that trait is built upon—curiosity, self-reliance, a measure of courage.

His MBA undoubtedly helped him to succeed as an entrepreneur. But so, it could be argued, did a sense of desperation. Ahuja convinced skeptical parents to support his move to America. He was determined not to return and tell his family he had failed. In his view, that would dishonor them all. So he worked on, lonely and poor, longer than many people might have, until he achieved his dream.

The first key quality—a sense of adventure—is the universal trait from which all others spring. Immigrants in general and entrepreneurs in particular describe an insatiable curiosity that finds them forever peering around the bend, wondering what people are doing elsewhere.

If this trait is universal, it is also the most easily emulated. Immigrant entrepreneurs talk often about the benefits gleaned from uprooting oneself. They describe the hard-

> *I think it takes an outsider to see the advantage. I think going outside is a great thing. I find that Americans who go outside of America and come back tend to be better entrepreneurs.*
>
> —Venture capitalist Gururaj Deshpande

ships of relocation, but also the advantages that come to a stranger in a strange land. Freed from the constraints of culture and tradition, and maybe judgmental peers, newcomers are free to express themselves. Pioneers see a new landscape and spy opportunity the natives might have missed. With independence, they say, comes self-confidence, resourcefulness, and creativity.

More than a few scholars have observed that the experience of living abroad seems to spark creativity and problem-solving skills, shaping people who are more likely to disrupt the status quo with a new idea or a new business.

Peter Drucker, the distinguished management guru, an immigrant from Austria, defined the entrepreneur as someone who "upsets and disorganizes."

Professor Raj Aggarwal, a professor of international business and finance at the University of Akron, also observes that "immigrants are inherent disrupters."

He could have been talking about Ratanjit Sondhe, a Cleveland polymer chemist from India who founded Poly-Carb, a construction chemicals firm. Sondhe, a Sikh, introduced business practices imbued with spiritualism as he built his company into an industry leader. He sold the start-up in 2007 to Dow Chemical.

Sondhe, a charter member of TiE Ohio, observes that immigrants bring three essential ingredients to American business: speed, technology, and frugality.

"Immigrants see the opportunities in America, and go full blast," he said.

Living abroad lends one "fresh eyes" to see opportunities at home, Intuit Inc. advises business professionals and entrepreneurs in its *Future of Small Business Series*. Thus immigrants often "identify and customize products for new and previously undefined market niches."

While most of us cannot simply pack up and move to another country and become a temporary immigrant, anyone can become a virtual immigrant. We can do this by traveling deliberately, by visiting new places and immersing ourselves in different cultures, if only for a while.

"You'll come back with a new perspective on your own world," said Gururaj "Desh" Deshpande, the New England entrepreneur and venture capitalist. Sitting across his boardroom table, Deshpande recalled the many entrepreneurs he has worked with and advised.

"I think it takes an outsider to see the advantage. I think going outside is a great thing," he said. "I find that Americans who go outside of America and come back tend to be better entrepreneurs."

Others suggest learning a new language, befriending immigrants, or dating someone from another culture.

The goal should be to get out of your comfort zone and experience a new perspective, Deshpande said.

"If you look at the most successful people, they are the people that move from one part of the country to another part of the country," he said. "I think they are able to look at the game differently."

Deshpande's thirst for adventure propelled him through three start-ups, bold ventures that made him rich and famous. Of course, he also armed himself with a doctorate in data communications. That's another universal characteristic of immigrant entrepreneurs. They tend to be highly educated, whether through an elite university or the school of hard knocks.

Malcolm Gladwell, an immigrant from the United Kingdom and author of *Outliers: The Story of Success*, argues that the common scene of Asian students studying late into the night at college libraries is a product of a culture.

"The genius of the culture formed in the rice paddies is that hard work gave those in the fields a way to find meaning in the midst of great uncertainty and poverty," he writes.

Immigrants from Asia and other regions are now applying this lesson in the fields of science and engineering.

Steven Chu, secretary of the U.S. Department of Energy under President Barack Obama, recalls an intense academic focus growing up.

"Education in my family was not merely emphasized, it was our raison d'être," he wrote shortly after receiving the 1997 Nobel Prize in Physics. "When the dust settled, my two brothers and four cousins collected three MDs, four PhDs, and a law degree. I could manage only a single advanced degree."

High-achieving immigrants love learning and they push their children to love learning. Often, they push them right to the head of the class.

The Knowledge Advantage

At 5 P.M. on a cold fall night, flush-faced children push through the door of an unusual tutoring center above a pet shop in a strip mall in suburban Cleveland, Ohio. After a full day of school, they are arriving for more work, and with hardly a shove from the adult who drove them here.

The children cross the room and grab a work packet from a file box. They slip into an adjacent room, sit down at a long table, and bend over worksheets designed to propel them beyond their grade level.

Their parents, meanwhile, settle into the small waiting area and chat about school and math clubs and swimming lessons. This October night, many leave wishing one another "Happy Dawali," best wishes on India's most popular holiday.

Similar scenes were unfolding at Kumon Learning Centers across America. Founded in Japan in the 1950s, the Kumon method seeks to instill in young minds mastery of education fundamentals with daily drills in math and vocabulary. Its classes are often packed with the children of immigrants.

In this suburb south of Cleveland, that means Asian Indians, who make up less than 10 percent of enrollment in the local public school district but more than half of the 100 children who file into the Kumon center for instruction and more homework.

They are the children of parents like Jignesh Amin, an immigrant from India who founded a greeting card business in

Cleveland. Though his two boys attend a quality public school in an affluent suburb, he sought more rigorous academics, the kind he knew back home.

"I really find the math and science instruction here lacking," Amin said.

That refrain is heard often among immigrant parents from not only India, but from Taiwan, Hong Kong, China, Israel, and Africa. They worry that American society, for all its shining qualities, places too little emphasis on elementary education.

So they seek out and find enrichment. They steer their children into math circles and tutoring clubs. They compete at spelling bees and science fairs. They congregate on Kumon nights and share a culture of learning.

The children work quietly and alone for 15 or 20 minutes, then show their work to an instructor, who awards points for excellence. On nights the children do not come to a center, they are expected to spend "Kumon time" at home on daily assignments. Parents are expected to enforce the schedule and grade the homework, even on weekends and holidays. Thus does Kumon demand an extra measure of devotion from both parent and child.

At this Kumon center in suburban Cleveland, Judy and Benjamin Choi, immigrants from Korea, have re-created some of the academic rigors of the old world.

The Chois bought a Kumon franchise after watching the program help shape their two children into academic superstars. To walk into the modest, orderly offices of their Kumon center is to walk into a pep rally for thinking. Pennants of elite colleges, like MIT and Stanford, banner the walls. Beneath them are newspaper stories of Kumon kids who super achieved—including the Chois' son, who was valedictorian of his high school graduating class, and their daughter, who was salutatorian of her class.

A bookshelf holds a small forest of trophies to be handed out to high achievers. The children prize the stars and stickers awarded for flawlessly completed assignments.

Successful immigrants, and Asian immigrants especially, have no qualms treating academics like a marquee sport.

"Stress effort first and foremost, but don't forget about the importance of achievement!" Dr. Soo Kim Abboud and Jane Kim write in their book, *Top of the Class: How Asian Parents Raise High Achievers—And How You Can Too.*

After embarking upon rewarding careers as a doctor and a lawyer, the sisters examined their paths to success and the paths followed by so many Asian Americans. Then they divulged what they learned in an unusual guide book.

"Contrary to what the public may believe, Asian students are no more intellectually gifted than non-Asian students," they write. Yet a racial group that comprises barely 5 percent of America makes up a much higher percentage of the student body at elite universities. Asian adults swell the ranks of high-skill professions.

What's the secret? Immigrant parents who insist that their children value education and strive as they did, the sisters reveal. They share memories of math camp and music recitals, family meetings and high expectations.

Their Korean-born parents instilled a respect for learning and the expectation that the children would perform at a high level, not just for themselves, but for the family honor.

"Our parents always viewed our family as a team working toward a common goal," they write. "If any member of the family was struggling, the entire family would rally behind him or her. There were no individual successes or victories—only family accomplishments."

For Pride, For Family

The mantra "Honor thy father and thy mother" resonates with a guiding force in many immigrant households. It's often because the children have witnessed a great sacrifice.

David Lam, a Chinese immigrant from Vietnam, built Lam Research Corporation into a billion-dollar company that services the semiconductor industry. Venture capitalists and investment banks helped his company to grow, but Lam especially reveres his first investor. Just the thought of her brings tears to his eyes. His mother's investment was an act of loyalty.

Sitting in his office in Silicon Valley, Lam gathers himself to recall his parents. He describes humble people who raised eight children and sent them all to college.

> *My mother was my very first investor in my company. She was just tremendous. She then pushed my brothers to invest as well. She was very good at that.*
>
> —Entrepreneur David Lam

"My mother was my very first investor in my company," he said. "She was just tremendous. She then pushed my brothers to invest as well. She was very good at that. A couple of them stepped up and invested. None of them understood what I was doing. My mother doesn't even read English. They trusted and believed in me."

Achieving success, regardless of the personal costs, was the only way Lam felt he could repay his parents' extraordinary sacrifice and his siblings' support.

They felt duty bound to support him. He felt duty bound to repay them. An immigrant family thrived.

The Power of Teamwork

Back in the 1980s, an American-born college student named Scott McNealy teamed up with two international students, Vinod Khosla and Andy Bechtolsheim, to launch Sun Microsystems. Their humble start-up blossomed into an innovative marvel, one of the most powerful companies in the Internet revolution.

Looking back, McNealy, Sun's chairman, attributes much of his personal success to hanging out with smart immigrants. In a September 2008 interview with San Francisco–based Vator TV, he advised aspiring entrepreneurs to follow his example.

"First of all, I would suggest, when you go to school, hang out with really smart, innovative, super bright, off-the-charts people," he said. "Stay at the party as late as they do. Become their best friends. That's what I did."

His foreign-born business partners valued his friendship as well. For if there is one lesson immigrants learn quickly, it is that native guides can help steer them through new terrain. They may spy opportunity others missed, but they usually have to work with the locals to seize it.

"Ninety percent of the technology companies are founded by teams," said Safi Qureshi, the Pakistani-born CEO of a wireless video technology company called Quartics. He is also a trustee of the Merage Foundation for the American Dream, which honors the contributions of American immigrants.

Qureshi, a successful entrepreneur twice over, said forming companies in today's complicated, hypercompetitive economy requires tremendous amounts of collaboration. Diverse teams provide an edge, and not only through technical expertise.

"This is a very tough business," he said. "When there are down days, you need your partners to pick you up."

He notes that immigrants can offer an added dimension to a partnership, like cultural savvy, multiple languages, and contacts in growing overseas markets.

"We (immigrants) can give you insight," he said. "We know China. We know India. You cannot start a tech company today in the U.S. without Chinese or Indians. We provide a huge advantage—not only technically, but with knowledge of global markets."

To find immigrant partners, he advises, go to where the immigrants are.

Outside of colleges and keg parties, a good place to strike up a relationship with professionals from abroad is within the networking groups that have sprung up in immigrant communities across the land.

The best known, TiE, has an Indian-American flavor and a busy schedule of gatherings nationwide. Taiwanese entrepreneurs welcome newcomers to the Monte Jade Science and Technology Association, named for the highest mountain in Taiwan. Latino entrepreneurs focused on high technology, biotech, and green tech collaborate through Hispanic-Net. Chinese immigrants are trying to build bridges between the American and Chinese business worlds with Hua Yuan Science and Technology Association, better known as HYSTA.

The networking groups provide opportunities to find teammates, capital, energy, and optimism. They may also offer a window onto the global economy—and an exhilarating raft ride down a new river.

The Possible Dream

In his book *Restless Nation*, James Jasper observes it's no accident that most immigrants, when they can choose their new home, select America.

"They picked this country because of its promise," he writes. "They dreamed the dream."

That vision of America as a land of possibility may be the most inspiring quality of the new immigrants, and the most powerful lesson they impart. Immigrant entrepreneurs are people unsatisfied with the status quo; people dreaming of doing something new, different, and better than before. Their ideas range from modest to bold to world-changing. Typically, they are rolled into a larger dream.

> *The clothes you wear are a form of communication. Clothing starts your conversation when you walk into a room.*
> —Designer Jeffrey Kimathi

Know immigrants, and you will know what it's like to dream again.

In a small shop in Harlem, amidst sewing machines, clothing designs, hangers, and boxes, 33-year-old Jeffrey Kimathi describes himself as an "Afropolitan," an African of the world. He's a proud representative of the African diaspora spreading across America, bringing with it African culture and influences.

To Kimathi, an immigrant from Kenya, the best way to introduce that culture is through clothing.

"The clothes you wear are a form of communication," he said. "Clothing starts your conversation when you walk into a room."

His quest is well on its way. Seven years after arriving in America, Kimathi founded Jamhuri Wear, a clothing line named for the Swahili word for "republic" or "free state." His t-shirts, hoodies, pants, and caps, reflecting a blend of African and American cultures, appeal to the hip-hop generation.

Hip hop-mogul Jay-Z has been seen in the Jamhuri label, as has reggae master Damian Marley. More thrilling to Kimathi, thousands of young people in an increasingly multicultural nation are wearing his designs.

He arrived from Nairobi in 1998, eager for a fresh start in a land he knew only from the movies. He had no training in fashion, but he loved clothes and he knew he could draw. Kimathi pushed his way into an unpaid internship at Ecko Unlimited, an urban-wear clothing company co-founded by immigrant Marc Ecko, and worked his way into the design department.

In 2005, he took the leap and launched his own business. Sales soared when R&B singer Akon wore a Jamhuri sweatshirt in a music video.

The faces of prominent Africans, like Nelson Mandela and Americans with strong African ties like Barack Obama, often grace Kimathi's clothing. He has not yet seen the U.S. president in Jamhuri Wear, but Kimathi has a grander dream.

He sees himself as the African Ralph Lauren, a designer blending Africa into America, and enriching both worlds.

*   *   *

Three hours north of Harlem, in the renovated offices of an old twine mill near the MIT campus in Cambridge, Massachusetts, another immigrant pursues a dream with the power to bring change. Sorin Grama, an immigrant from Romania, founded Promethean Power Systems with his classmate and American-born business partner, Sam White.

Their creation sits in the middle of a room like some unfinished science-fair entry. Wires noodle out of a stack of black, stereo-like boxes that encase a Styrofoam cooler. A slab of solar panel stands nearby, ready to go on top.

The strange tower is a prototype of a solar-powered milk cooler—a practical refrigerator for the Third World. Maybe. The technology is early, the money is tight, and the company did not yet have a nameplate on the door in early 2009.

"That's $200," Grama explained. "I'd rather put that into the research."

But there's momentum. The idea was a runner-up winner at the 2007 MIT $100K Entrepreneurship Competition, which draws hundreds of enterprising teams from the Boston area. A blown-up copy of the $10,000 prize check is pinned to a wall, next to a map of India. On a whiteboard, beside a confusion of algorithms and computer code, is a diagram of the "milk trail" in rural India—dotted lines tracing the routes from farm to dairy to market.

That's a trek that often ends with spoiled milk. Fixing it has become Grama's passion.

His father defected from communist Romania in the early 1980s and gained political asylum in America. It took five years, but a teenaged Sorin, his mother, and his sister were allowed to join him in 1987. A degree in electrical engineering from Ohio State University led to a job in the computer industry in California. In his mid-thirties, feeling the urge to try something new, Grama enrolled at MIT. In 2007, he wrote the business plan for a five-member team that *almost* won the entrepreneurship competition and its $100,000 grand prize.

Afterward, most of the team members pursued other interests. But Grama and White stuck with the idea, which was inspired by a Peace Corps worker. They used their share of the prize money to fly to India and to explore the milk trail. They learned how fresh milk was collected, moved, and packaged. They talked with farmers. They met with a dairy manager.

They changed their plans.

The contest idea called for a mini-power plant for rural villages off the grid. But the pair realized that electricity was not enough. The villages were too poor and too remote.

"The need is for a complete system that can accomplish the task," explained Grama the engineer. "Cold storage."

By blending Grama's knowledge of thermo-electronics with advances in photovoltaics, the pair hopes to manufacture solar-powered refrigerators run by simple microprocessors. They are focusing on chilled milk because that is what everyone drinks. But Grama sees other, life-changing applications. The solar cooler could preserve yogurt, mother's milk, and medicines in villages lacking electricity. It could change life for millions.

His eyes light up at the thought.

"I look at it as one of the last frontiers to conquer," bringing refrigeration anywhere in the world, said Grama the dreamer. "It's not something a lot of people want to bother with. We're crazy enough to try it."

An angel investor, perhaps equally crazy, gave them $50,000 to keep going. Grama hoped to have a prototype solar-powered cold storage system ready by 2010. He'd like to test it in India, then commence production.

He talks like a person in a hurry, like an immigrant entrepreneur. The world is shrinking. Milk is spoiling. He has an idea. But it's more of a dream, really.

Appendix

A growing body of research documents the sucess of immigrant entrepreneurs and their power to innovate and to create jobs. Most of the salient studies were cited in this book. Recent key findings are further illuminated in the charts and tables on the following pages.

You'll find, for example, a graphic representation of the "Kauffman Index of Entrepreneurial Activity," which shows the substantially different rates at which immigrants and native-born start new businesses, from low-income to high-income potential enterprises.

In subsequent illustrations, the study "America's New Immigrant Entrepreneurs" pinpoints the states in which immigrants are busiest, where those immigrants came from, their educational attainment and the businesses they tend to pursue.

The Appendix also includes a listing from the National Venture Capital Association of immigrant-founded companies and the hundreds of thousands of jobs they have created. Many of these corporations are quite well known, though maybe not for their immigrant roots. Did you know that the 2007 market capitalization of immigrant-founded companies was $500 million? That over the past 15 years, immigrant-founded companies accounted for 25 percent of U.S public companies that were venture-backed (40 percent in the high-tech manufacturing sector)?

The Appendix also offers details of the economic impact of international students, their educational attainment, and where they tend to study. Did you know that amount of money that over 600,000 international students collectively brought to the U.S. to pay for their education and support themselves was over $15.5 billion for the 2007–2008 academic year?

The Appendix concludes with a map of immigrant populations for individual states. It's not hard to see the correlation between immigrants and economic growth.

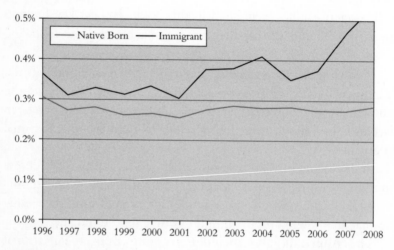

Exhibit A.1   Kauffman Index of Entrepreneurial Activity by Nativity (1996–2008)

Courtesy of Robert W. Fairlie, University of California, Santa Cruz, "The Kauffman Index of Entrepreneurial Activity," 1996–2008.

Appendix

The Kauffman Index of Entrepreneurial Activity, 1996–2008, studied the rate at which people in America start new businesses. The report, issued in April 2009, found that the entrepreneurial activity rate increased sharply for immigrants in 2008, further widening the gap between immigrant and native-born rates. The resulting gap in the entrepreneurial activity rate between immigrants and natives is large. For immigrants, 530 out of 100,000 people start a business each month compared to 280 out of 100,000 native-born people.

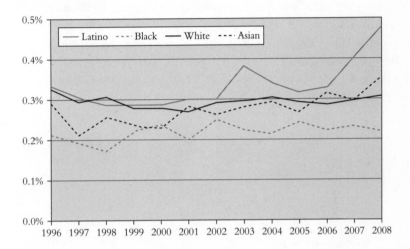

Exhibit A.2   Kauffman Index of Entrepreneurial Activity by Race (1996–2008)

Courtesy of Robert W. Fairlie, University of California, Santa Cruz, "The Kauffman Index of Entrepreneurial Activity, 1996–2008."

Latino and Asian Americans experienced the largest increase in entrepreneurial activity rates between 2007 and 2008. The Latino rate increased from .40 percent in 2007 to .48 percent in 2008. Among Asian Americans, the rate increased from .29 percent in 2007 to .35 percent in 2008.

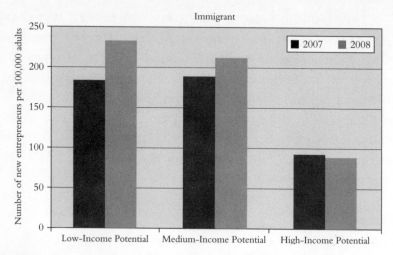

Exhibit A.3a Kauffman Index of Entrepreneurial Activity by Business Income Potential (2007–2008)

Courtesy of Robert W. Fairlie, University of California, Santa Cruz, "The Kauffman Index of Entrepreneurial Activity, 1996–2008"

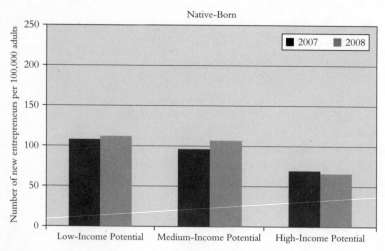

Exhibit A.3b Kauffman Index of Entrepreneurial Activity by Business Income Potential (2007–2008)

Courtesy of Robert W. Fairlie, University of California, Santa Cruz, "The Kauffman Index of Entrepreneurial Activity, 1996–2008."

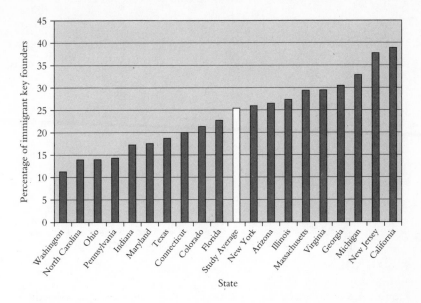

Exhibit A.4   U.S. States Where Immigrants Are Founding Engineering and Technology Companies

Courtesy of Vivek Wadhwa, "America's New Immigrant Entrepreneurs."

The 2007 study, "America's New Immigrant Entrepreneurs,"[1] found that in 25% of engineering and technology companies started in America from 1995 to 2005, at least one key founder was an immigrant. Nationwide, these immigrant-founded tech companies produced $52 billion in sales and employed 450,000 workers in 2005. Over 50% of the Silicon Valley start-ups had one or more immigrants as key founder, compared with the California average of 38.8% or the Ohio average of 14%.

---

[1] By Vivek Wadhwa, Duke University; AnnaLee Saxenian, University of California, Berkeley; Ben Rissing, Duke University; and Gary Gereffi, Duke University.

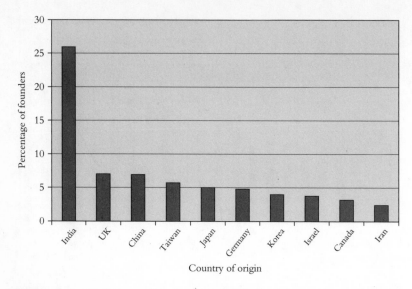

Exhibit A.5 Birthplace of Engineering and Technology Immigrant Founders

Courtesy of Vivek Wadhwa, "America's New Immigrant Entrepreneurs."

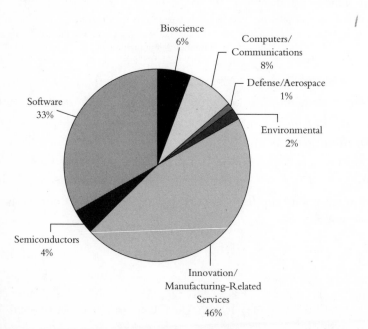

Exhibit A.6 Breakdown of Engineering and Technology Companies Founded by Immigrants from 1995 to 2005 by Industry

Courtesy of Vivek Wadhwa, "America's New Immigrant Entrepreneurs."

Appendix

Industry	Number	Immigrant business owners		All business owners	
		Percent of immigrant total	Percent of U.S. industry total	Number	Percent of U.S. total
All industries	1,436,410	100.0	12.5	11,521,910	100.0
Agriculture and mining	26,740	1.9	3.7	730,800	6.3
Construction	187,030	13.0	9.6	1,945,910	16.9
Manufacturing	73,070	5.1	13.6	535,550	4.6
Wholesale trade	60,900	4.2	15.9	383,370	3.3
Retail trade	182,850	12.7	15.5	1,176,230	10.2
Transportation	71,470	5.0	16.9	423,320	3.7
Information	16,330	1.1	9.2	177,290	1.5
Finance, insurance and real estate	76,900	5.4	8.6	889,800	7.7
Professional services	219,830	15.3	10.4	2,115,610	18.4
Education, health and social services	157,740	11.0	13.0	1,213,690	10.5
Arts, entertainment and recreation	144,240	10.0	21.1	683,390	5.9
Other services	219,320	15.3	17.6	1,247,020	10.8

Notes: 1) The sample includes all business owners with 15 or more hours worked per usual week.
2) All reported estimates use sample weights provided by the 2000 Census.
Source: Author's calculations from 2000 Census microdata.

Exhibit A.7   Number of Immigrant Business Owners by Industry Census 2000

From "Estimating the Contributions of Immigrant Business Owners to the U.S. Economy," 2008, by Robert Fairlie, for the Small Business Administration.
Courtesy of Robert Fairlie.

	Net business income		
Group	Total (thousands of dollars)	Percent of U.S. total	Average per owner (dollars)
U.S. total	577,714,338	100.0	50,141
U.S.-born total	510,757,703	88.4	50,643
Immigrant total	66,956,635	11.6	46,614
Mexico	6,890,546	1.2	26,990
Korea	4,289,510	0.7	47,514
India	4,999,076	0.9	83,023
China	2,612,293	0.5	45,360
Vietnam	1,786,430	0.3	34,540
Canada	3,272,177	0.6	64,924
Cuba	2,421,547	0.4	49,334
Germany	2,322,318	0.4	56,054
Philippines	2,179,736	0.4	59,142
Italy	1,760,395	0.3	51,004
Iran	2,559,450	0.4	76,251
El Salvador	823,997	0.1	26,431
Poland	1,341,773	0.2	43,549
England	1,580,912	0.3	57,427
Colombia	883,144	0.2	34,284
Taiwan	1,367,917	0.2	58,266
Greece	1,253,056	0.2	60,441
Dominican Republic	536,080	0.1	26,860
Jamaica	672,985	0.1	35,448
Guatemala	422,663	0.1	22,588

Notes: 1) The sample consists of all workers with 15 or more hours worked per usual week. The total sample size is 596,550.
2) All reported estimates use sample weights provided by the 2000 Census.
3) Income estimates are reported in 2000 dollars.
4) The reported immigrant groups represent the largest 20 groups based on the number of business owners.
Source: Author's calculations from 2000 Census microdata.

Exhibit A.8   Total Business Income by Immigrant Group, Census 2000

From Estimating the Contributions of Immigrant Business Owners to the U.S. Economy, 2008, by Robert Fairlie, for the Small Business Administration.
Courtesy of Robert Fairlie.

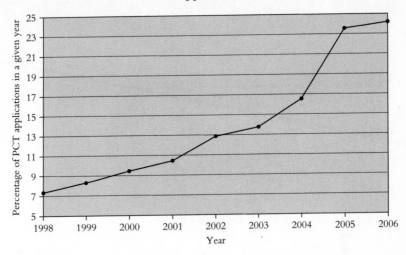

Exhibit A.9 Intellectual Property Contributions of Immigrant Non-Citizens—Estimated Percentage of International Patent Applications (PCT) from 1998 to 2006

Courtesy of Vivek Wadhwa, "America's New Immigrant Entrepreneurs."

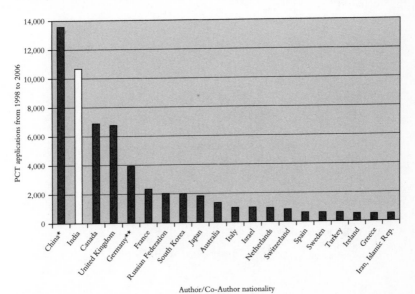

Author/Co-Author nationality

* PCT appplications within the field "China" also include applications from Taiwan. **PCT applications awarded to within the field "Germany" have been calculated using a unique search string; please refer to the Methodology - WIPO Patent Records section for more details.

Exhibit A.10 Intellectual Property Contributions of U.S. Immigrant Non-Citizens—International Patent Applications (PCT) by Nationality—1998 to 2006

Courtesy of Vivek Wadhwa, "America's New Immigrant Entrepreneurs."

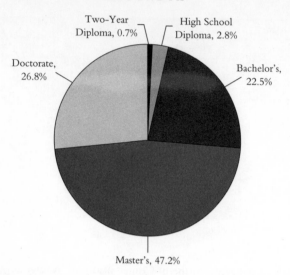

Two-Year Diploma, 0.7%

High School Diploma, 2.8%

Doctorate, 26.8%

Bachelor's, 22.5%

Master's, 47.2%

Exhibit A.11 Highest Completed Degree by Immigrant Founders of Engineering and Technology Companies

Source: Master of Engineering Management Program, Duke University; School of Information, UC-Berkeley; Kauffman Foundation, 2007.

Courtesy of Vivek Wadhwa, "America's New Immigrant Entrepreneurs."

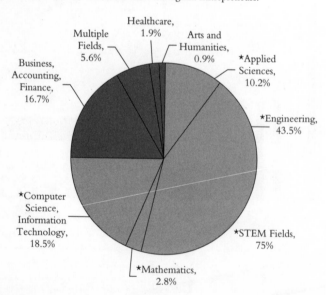

Healthcare, 1.9%

Multiple Fields, 5.6%

Arts and Humanities, 0.9%

Business, Accounting, Finance, 16.7%

★Applied Sciences, 10.2%

★Engineering, 43.5%

★Computer Science, Information Technology, 18.5%

★STEM Fields, 75%

★Mathematics, 2.8%

Exhibit A.12 Fields of Highest Degree by Immigrant Founders of Engineering and Technology Companies

Source: Master of Engineering Management Program, Duke University; School of Information, UC-Berkeley; Kauffman Foundation, 2007.

Courtesy of Vivek Wadhwa, "America's New Immigrant Entrepreneurs."

Appendix

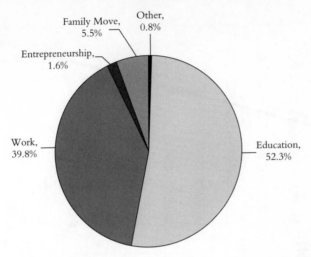

Exhibit A.13 Primary Reason for Which Immigrant Founders of Engineering and Technology Companies Came to the United States

Source: Master of Engineering Management Program, Duke University; School of Information, UC-Berkeley; Kauffman Foundation, 2007.

Courtesy of Vivek Wadhwa, "America's New Immigrant Entrepreneurs."

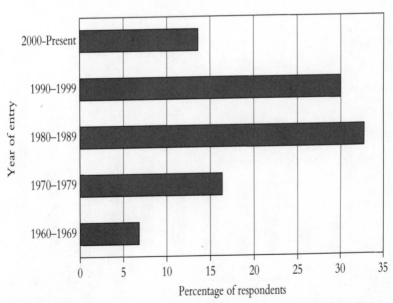

Exhibit A.14 U.S. Immigrant Founders of Engineering and Technology Companies Year of Entry

Source: Master of Engineering Management Program, Duke University; School of Information, UC-Berkeley; Kauffman Foundation, 2007.

Courtesy of Vivek Wadhwa, "America's New Immigrant Entrepreneurs."

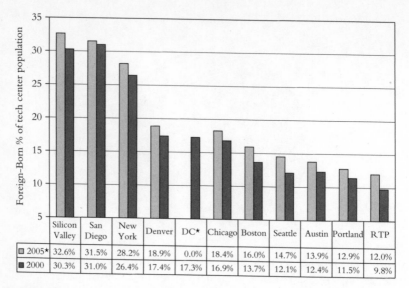

Exhibit A.15 Foreign-Born as Percentage of Tech-Center Populations

*2005 data is currently unavailable for many Washington, D.C., and metro counties.

Source: U.S. Census (2000 and 2005).

Courtesy of Vivek Wadhwa, "America's New Immigrant Entrepreneurs."

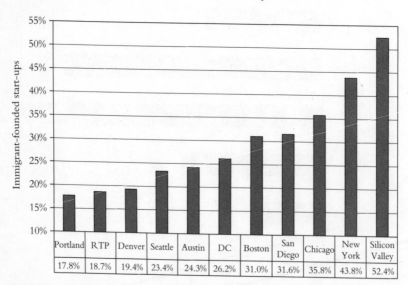

Exhibit A.16 Immigrant-Founded Engineering and Technology Companies as Percent of Total Start-ups in Tech Centers

Source: Master of Engineering Management Program, Duke University; School of Information, UC-Berkeley; Kauffman Foundation, 2007.

Courtesy of Vivek Wadhwa, "America's New Immigrant Entrepreneurs."

Year founded	Immigrant-founded	Native-founded	Total	Immigrant-founded % of all U.S. venture-backed public companies
Prior to 1980	8	115	123	7%
1980–1989	48	198	246	20%
1990–2005	88	268	356	25%

Exhibit A.17   Percentage of Immigrant-Founded Venture-Backed Public Companies by Year Established

Source: Analysis of publicly traded companies from Thomson Financial database.

From "American Made: The Impact of Immigrant Entrepreneurs and Professionals on U.S. Competitiveness," November 2006, by Stuart Anderson and Michaela Platzer for the National Venture Capital Association.
Courtesy of Stuart Anderson and the National Venture Capital Association.

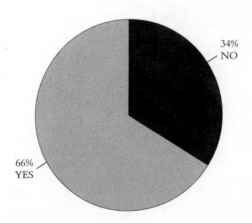

34%
NO

66%
YES

Exhibit A.18   Do the Current U.S. Immigrant Laws on Skilled Professionals Harm American Competitiveness?

From "American Made: The Impact of Immigrant Entrepreneurs and Professionals on U.S. Competitiveness," November 2006, by Stuart Anderson and Michaela Platzer for the National Venture Capital Association.
Courtesy of Stuart Anderson and the National Venture Capital Association.

Company	Immigrant-born founder or co-founder	Country of birth	Employees (FY 2005)	Industry
Intel Corporation	Andy Grove	Hungary	99,900	Semiconductor and Related Device Manufacturing
Solectron Corporation	Winston Chen	Taiwan	53,000	Bare Printed Circuit Board Manufacturing
Sanmina-SCI Corporation	Jure Sola Milan Mandaric	Bosnia Croatia	48,621	Bare Printed Circuit Board Manufacturing
Sun Microsystems, Inc.	Andreas Bechtolsheim Vinod Khosla	Germany India	31,000	Electronic Computer Manufacturing
eBay Inc.	Pierre Omidyar	France	12,600	Electronic Auctions
Yahoo! Inc.	Jerry Yang	Taiwan	9,800	Web Search Portals
Life Time Fitness, Inc.	Bahram Akradi	Iran	9,500	Fitness and Recreational Sports Centers
Tetra Tech, Inc.	Henri Hodara	France	7,200	Engineering Services
UTStarcom, Inc.	Ying Wu	China	6,300	Telephone Apparatus Manufacturing
Google, Inc.	Sergey Brin	Russia	5,680	Web Search Portals
Kanbay International, Inc.	Raymond J. Spencer Dileep Nath John Patterson	Australia India Canada	5,242	Computer Systems Design Services
Cadence Design Systems, Inc.	Alberto Sangiovanni-Vincentelli	Italy	5,000	Software Publishers
Juniper Networks, Inc.	Pradeep Sindhu	India	4,145	Telephone Apparatus Manufacturing
Watson Pharmaceuticals, Inc.	Allen Chao	Taiwan	3,844	Pharmaceutical Preparation Manufacturing
Parametric Technology Corporation	Samuel Geisberg	Russia	3,751	Software Publishers
Pediatrix Medical Group, Inc.	Roger Medel	Cuba	3,013	Offices of Physicians (except Mental Health Specialists)
NVIDIA Corporation	Jen-Hsun Huang	Taiwan	2,737	Semiconductor and Related Device Manufacturing
Salton, Inc.	Lewis Salton	Poland	2,466	Electric Housewares and Household Fan Manufacturing
Lam Research Corporation	David Lam	China	2,200	Semiconductor Machinery Manufacturing
WebEx Communications, Inc.	Subrah S. Iyar	India	2,091	Software Publishers

Exhibit A.19 Leading Immigrant-Founded Venture-Backed Public Companies Ranked by Employment

Note: Employment reflects 2005 worldwide total.

Source: Company 10-k filings and Hoover's.

From "American Made: The Impact of Immigrant Entrepreneurs and Professionals on U.S. Competitiveness," November 2006, by Stuart Anderson and Michaela Platzer for the National Venture Capital Association.

Courtesy of Stuart Anderson and the National Venture Capital Association.

Appendix

Industry	Number of Companies	Employment	% of Immigrant-Foundation Firms by Industry
High-Tech Manafacturing	60	282,442	42%
Information Technology	34	48,794	24%
Life Sciences	30	18,660	21%
Professional, Scientific, and Technical Services	6	17,317	4%
Other Services	5	14,919	3%
Other Manufacturing	5	13,177	3%
Finance and Insurance	2	8,872	1%
E-Commerce	2	234	1%
Total	144	404,415	100%

Exhibit A.20   Immigrant-Founded Venture-Backed U.S. Public Companies by Industry

From "American Made: The Impact of Immigrant Entrepreneurs and Professionals on U.S. Competitiveness," November 2006, by Stuart Anderson and Michaela Platzer for the National Venture Capital Association.
Courtesy of Stuart Anderson and the National Venture Capital Association.

Country of Birth	Number of Companies
India	32
Israel	17
Taiwan	16
Canada	7
France	7
United Kingdom	7
Germany	6
Australia	5
China	5
Iran	5
Italy	4
Korea	3
Switzerland	3
Belgium	2
Hungary	2
All Other Countries	23

Exhibit A.21   Leading Countries of Birth for Immigrant-Founded Venture-Backed U.S. Public Companies

Source: Company 10-k filings and Hoover's.

From "American Made: The Impact of Immigrant Entrepreneurs and Professionals on U.S. Competitiveness," November 2006, by Stuart Anderson and Michaela Platzer for the National Venture Capital Association.
Courtesy of Stuart Anderson and the National Venture Capital Association.

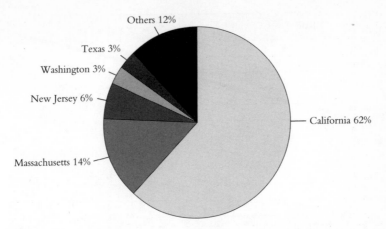

Exhibit A.22 Immigrant-Founded Venture-Backed Firms by State

Source: Analysis of publicly traded companies from Thomson Financial database.

From "American Made: The Impact of Immigrant Entrepreneurs and Professionals on U.S. Competitiveness," November 2006, by Stuart Anderson and Michaela Platzer for the National Venture Capital Association.
Courtesy of Stuart Anderson and the National Venture Capital Association.

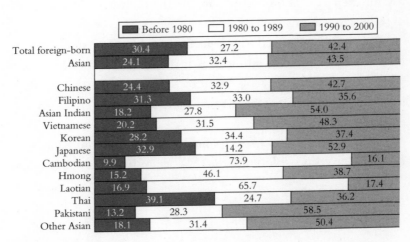

Exhibit A.23 Foreign-Born Asians by Year of Entry to the U.S. in 2000

Source: U.S. Census Bureau, Census 2000 special tabulation.

Courtesy of Vivek Wadhwa, "America's New Immigrant Entrepreneurs."

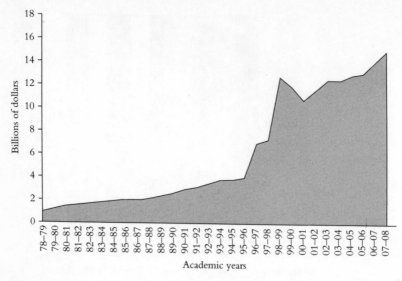

Exhibit A.24 Economic Impact from International Students
Courtesy of Jason Baumgartner, Indiana University—Bloomington.

The economic impact is defined as the amount of money that international students collectively bring into the United States to pay for their education and to support themselves while they (and in some cases, their families) are here.

Research conducted on behalf of NAFSA—Association of International Educators estimates that the annual economic impact which international students bring to the United States to support their education and stay was $15.54 billion for the 2007–2008 academic year.

From research by Jason Baumgartner and Lynn Schoch at Indiana University—Bloomington's Office of International Services.

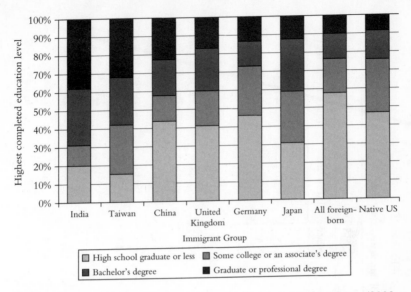

Exhibit A.25 Educational Attainment of Select Immigrant Groups (2000 U.S. Census)

Source: U.S. Census Bureau (2000).

Courtesy of Vivek Wadhwa, "America's New Immigrant Entrepreneurs."

Exhibit A.26 Open Doors 2008 Report on International Educational Exchange

Top 25 Institutions Hosting International Students, 2007/08

Rank	Institution	City	State	Total Int'l Students	Total Enrollment
1	University of Southern California	Los Angeles	CA	7,189	33,408
2	New York University	New York	NY	6,404	44,211
3	Columbia University	New York	NY	6,297	24,842
4	University of Illinois—Urbana-Champaign	Champaign	IL	5,933	41,135
5	Purdue University—Main Campus	West Lafayette	IN	5,772	39,102
6	University of Michigan—Ann Arbor	Ann Arbor	MI	5,748	41,042
7	University of California—Los Angeles	Los Angeles	CA	5,557	38,896
8	University of Texas—Austin	Austin	TX	5,550	50,201
9	Harvard University	Cambridge	MA	4,948	19,987
10	Boston University	Boston	MA	4,789	32,053
11	University of Pennsylvania	Philadelphia	PA	4,610	23,980
12	SUNY University at Buffalo	Buffalo	NY	4,363	27,405
13	Indiana University—Bloomington	Bloomington	IN	4,287	38,247
14	Ohio State University—Main Campus	Columbus	OH	4,259	52,568
15	Michigan State University	East Lansing	MI	4,244	46,045

(Continued)

Exhibit A.26 *(Continued)*

Top 25 Institutions Hosting International Students, 2007/08

Rank	Institution	City	State	Total Int'l Students	Total Enrollment
16	University of Florida	Gainesville	FL	4,228	50,692
17	Texas A&M University	College Station	TX	4,094	46,542
18	Arizona State University—Tempe	Tempe	AZ	3,979	51,481
19	Cornell University	Ithaca	NY	3,928	19,800
20	University of Wisconsin—Madison	Madison	WI	3,910	42,043
21	Stanford University	Palo Alto	CA	3,898	15,856
22	Pennsylvania State University—University Park	University Park	PA	3,860	43,252
23	University of Minnesota—Twin Cities	Minneapolis	MN	3,756	50,883
24	Georgia Institute of Technology	Atlanta	GA	3,616	18,742
25	University of Houston	Houston	TX	3,420	34,663

Courtesy of Institute of International Education, "Open Doors: Report on International Educational Exchange, 2008."

Exhibit A.27 Open Doors 2008 Report on International Educational Exchange

Leading Institutions Hosting International Scholars, 2007/08

		2007/08		
Rank	Institution	City	State	Total
1	Harvard University	Cambridge	MA	3,721
2	Stanford University	Stanford	CA	2,824
3	University of California—Berkeley	Berkeley	CA	2,565
4	University of California—Davis	Davis	CA	2,543
5	Columbia University	New York	NY	2,455
6	University of California—Los Angeles	Los Angeles	CA	2,297
7	University of California—San Diego	La Jolla	CA	2,126
8	Yale University	New Haven	CT	1,920
9	University of Michigan—Ann Arbor	Ann Arbor	MI	1,856
10	University of Washington	Seattle	WA	1,774
11	University of Florida	Gainesville	FL	1,773
12	Massachusetts Institute of Technology	Cambridge	MA	1,748
13	University of Southern California	Los Angeles	CA	1,690
14	Ohio State University—Main Campus	Columbus	OH	1,628
15	University of Illinois—Urbana-Champaign	Champaign	IL	1,541
16	University of Maryland—College Park	College Park	MD	1,491
17	University of Minnesota—Twin Cities	Minneapolis	MN	1,386
18	Washington University in St. Louis	St. Louis	MO	1,362
19	Emory University	Atlanta	GA	1,281
20	University of Wisconsin—Madison	Madison	WI	1,281
21	Cornell University	Ithaca	NY	1,274
22	University of California—Irvine	Irvine	CA	1,211

(Continued)

Appendix

Exhibit A.27 *(Continued)*

Leading Institutions Hosting International Scholars, 2007/08

Rank	Institution	City	State	Total
23	University of North Carolina—Chapel Hill	Chapel Hill	NC	1,161
24	University of Illinois—Chicago	Chicago	IL	1,128
25	Duke University & Medical Center	Durham	NC	1,128
26	Northwestern University	Evanston	IL	1,072
27	Michigan State University	East Lansing	MI	1,019
28	Boston University	Boston	MA	1,018
29	University of Missouri—Columbia	Columbia	MO	982
30	University of California—Santa Barbara	Santa Barbara	CA	881
31	University of Texas—Austin	Austin	TX	865
32	Iowa State University	Ames	IA	854
33	California Institute of Technology	Pasadena	CA	850
34	University of Alabama—Birmingham	Birmingham	AL	755
35	Vanderbilt University	Nashville	TN	749
36	University of Texas Medical Branch—Galveston	Galveston	TX	737
37	North Carolina State University	Raleigh	NC	722
38	Indiana University	Bloomington	IN	709
39	Carnegie Mellon University	Pittsburgh	PA	696
40	Princeton University	Princeton	NJ	694

Courtesy of Institute of International Education, "Open Doors: Report on International Educational Exchange, 2008."

Exhibit A.28   Open Doors 2008 Report on International Educational Exchange

Top 20 Places of Origin of International Scholars, 2006/07 & 2007/08

Rank	Place of Origin	2006/07	2007/08	2007/08 % of Total	2007/08 % Change
	WORLD TOTAL	98,239	106,123	–	8.0
1	China	20,149	23,779	22.4	18.0
2	India	9,138	9,959	9.4	9.0
3	South Korea	9,291	9,888	9.3	6.4
4	Japan	5,557	5,692	5.4	2.4
5	Germany	5,039	5,269	5.0	4.6
6	Canada	4,398	4,758	4.5	8.2
7	France	3,588	3,802	3.6	6.0
8	Italy	3,148	3,273	3.1	4.0
9	United Kingdom	2,877	2,823	2.7	−1.9
10	Spain	2,193	2,320	2.2	5.8
11	Taiwan	1,813	2,185	2.1	20.5
12	Brazil	1,862	2,071	2.0	11.2
13	Russia	2,102	1,945	1.8	−7.5
14	Israel	1,591	1,698	1.6	6.7
15	Turkey	1,362	1,539	1.5	13.0
16	Mexico	1,218	1,396	1.3	14.6
17	Australia	1,175	1,163	1.1	−1.1
18	Netherlands	959	1,018	1.0	6.2
19	Poland	877	840	0.8	−4.2
20	Argentina	834	781	0.7	−6.3

Courtesy of Institute of International Education, "Open Doors: Report on International Educational Exchange, 2008."

Exhibit A.29   International Student and Total U.S. Enrollment

Open Doors 2008 Report on International Educational Exchange International Student and U.S. Higher Education Enrollment Trends, Selected Years 1954/55−2007/08

Year	Int'l Students	Annual % Change	Total Enrollment	% ¹Int'l
1954/55	34,232	–	2,499,800	1.4
1959/60	48,486	2.6	3,640,000	1.3
1964/65	82,045	9.7	5,280,000	1.6
1965/66	82,709	0.8	5,921,000	1.4
1966/67	100,262	21.2	6,390,000	1.6
1967/68	110,315	10.0	6,912,000	1.6
1968/69	121,362	10.0	7,513,000	1.6
1969/70	134,959	11.2	8,005,000	1.7
1970/71	144,708	7.2	8,581,000	1.7
1971/72	140,126	−3.2	8,949,000	1.6
1972/73	146,097	4.3	9,215,000	1.6
1973/74	151,066	3.4	9,602,000	1.6
1974/75²	154,580	2.3	10,224,000	1.5
1975/76	179,344	16.0	11,185,000	1.6
1976/77	203,068	13.2	11,012,000	1.8
1977/78	235,509	16.0	11,286,000	2.1
1978/79	263,940	12.1	11,260,000	2.3
1979/80	286,343	8.5	11,570,000	2.5
1980/81	311,882	8.9	12,097,000	2.6
1981/82	326,299	4.6	12,372,000	2.6
1982/83	336,985	3.3	12,426,000	2.7
1983/84	338,894	0.6	12,465,000	2.7
1984/85	342,113	0.9	12,242,000	2.8
1985/86	343,777	0.5	12,247,000	2.8
1986/87	349,609	1.7	12,504,000	2.8
1987/88	356,187	1.9	12,767,000	2.8
1988/89	366,354	2.9	13,055,000	2.8
1989/90	386,851	5.6	13,539,000	2.9
1990/91	407,529	5.3	13,819,000	2.9

1991/92	419,585	3.0	14,359,000	2.9
1992/93	438,618	4.5	14,487,000	3.0
1993/94	449,749	2.5	14,305,000	3.1
1994/95	452,635	0.6	14,279,000	3.2
1995/96	453,787	0.3	14,262,000	3.2
1996/97	457,984	0.9	14,368,000	3.2
1997/98	481,280	5.1	14,502,000	3.3
1998/99	490,933	2.0	14,507,000	3.4
1999/00	514,723	4.8	14,791,000	3.5
2000/01	547,867	6.4	15,312,000	3.6
2001/02	582,996	6.4	15,928,000	3.7
2002/03	586,323	0.6	16,612,000	3.5
2003/04	572,509	−2.4	16,911,000	3.4
2004/05	565,039	−1.3	17,272,000	3.3
2005/06	564,766	−0.05	17,487,000	3.2
2006/07	582,984	3.2	17,672,000	3.3
2007/08	623,805	7.0	17,958,000	3.5

[1]Data from the National Center for Education Statistics. % Int'l data is not entirely comparable to previous *Open Doors*.

[2]The data collection process was changed in 1974/75. Refugees were counted from 1975/76 to 1990/91.

Courtesy of "Institute of International Education, Open Doors: Report on International Educational Exchange, 2008."

Appendix

(Civilian noninstitutional population plus Armed Forces
living off post or with their families on post)

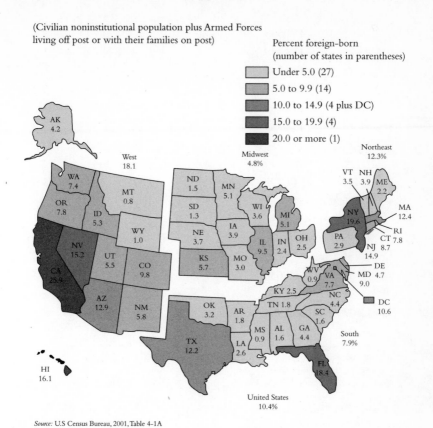

Percent foreign-born
(number of states in parentheses)

Under 5.0 (27)
5.0 to 9.9 (14)
10.0 to 14.9 (4 plus DC)
15.0 to 19.9 (4)
20.0 or more (1)

Source: U.S Census Bureau, 2001, Table 4-1A

Exhibit A.30 Foreign-Born Population for Individual States: 2000

About the Authors

Robert L. Smith is a veteran journalist who covers international cultures and immigration issues for the Cleveland *Plain Dealer*. He grew up in Cleveland, where he lives with his wife, Cleveland Orchestra violinist Chul-In Park, and their two children, Jae, 5, and Sun-Hee, 3.

Richard T. Herman, an immigration and business attorney, is the founder of Richard T. Herman & Associates, LLC, a multilingual law firm in Cleveland, Ohio, which serves immigrant entrepreneurs and companies that hire foreign-born talent. He is a co-founder of TiE Ohio, the 50th chapter of TiE, a global network of entrepreneurs. Richard is one of the architects of a movement to revitalize the Rust Belt through federal and local policies to attract job-creating high-skill, entrepreneurial, and investor immigrants, American-born, formerly residing in Moscow, Richard is married to Kimberly Chen, a physician born in Taiwan. They have two children, Nathan, 7, and Isabella, 5.

The Conversation Continues

The authors invite you to continue this conversation about immigrants, entrepreneurship, and America. They welcome your observations and ideas.

Write them at:

Feedback@ImmigrantInc.com

Visit their web site at **www.ImmigrantInc.com** where you can further research the topic, post comments, see the faces of America's immigrant enterpreneurs, and sign-up for the e-newsletter for more updates.

Richard Herman will continue exploring the culture of Immigrant, Inc. at his blog, curiously titled *Immigrant, Inc.* which can be found at **http://blog.immigrantinc.com.**

Finally, to help you to "think like an immigrant," we encourage you to visit the authors' web site and find links to immigrant entrepreneur and innovation networks such as:

The Indus Entrepreneurs Association(TiE), Hua Yuan Science & Technology Association (HYSTA), Society of Hispanic Engineers, SiliconFrench, TechWadi, The African Network, and many others.

Index

A123Systems, Inc.
  American battery industry and, 93–95
  background of fathers of, 83–88
  characteristics of founders of, 81–82
  culture of immigrant entrepreneurs and, 4–5
  dreams of founders of, 3–4
  founding of, 1–3
  immigrant personality of, 93
  naming of, 3
  partnership with Chrysler, 95–97
  physical location of, 79–80
  request for federal stimulus money, 80–81
  at start of its eighth year, 82–83
  startup of, 88
  venture capitalism and, 21, 88–89, 92–93
Abboud, Soo Kim, 174–175
*Accelerating Decline in America's High-Skilled
    Workforce: Implications for Immigration Policy,
    The* (Kirkegaard), 144
Adefuye, Adedeji, 66–67
Advanced technology, immigrant culture in, 4–5
Advanced Technology Vehicles Manufacturing
    Incentive Program, 96
Adventure, immigrant trait of, 169–171
African Americans, 131, 186
African immigrants, 65, 66–67, 178–179
Aggarwal, Raj, 170
Ahuja, Monte, 25
  accomplishments of, 38–39
  arrival in Cleveland, 27–28

in business administration graduate school,
    37–38
  on business environment in America, 41, 42
  early years in America, 35–36
  in engineering graduate school, 35–36
  goal to come to America, 33–34
  home of, 41
  on immigrant experience, 39–41
  launching Transtar Industries, 38
  at Lemco Industries, 36–38
  sense of adventure in, 169
  success of, 28–29
  trip to America, 34–35
Ahuja, Usha, 36
Akroyd, Dan, 159
Alberta, Canada, 147
Albright, Madeleine, 101
Alex de Tocqueville Institute, 126
Alfalfa Nail Supply, 105
America. *See* United States
American Association of Physicians of Indian
    Origin, 31
American Community Survey, 2007
    (U.S. Census Bureau), 64
American Dream, the, xxiv, xxv
  immigrant belief in, 5
  immigrant traits and, 164–165
American-made products
  A123 batteries, 94–96
  by Farouk Systems, 59

213

*American Made: The Impact of Immigrant
  Entrepreneurs and Professionals on U.S.
  Competitiveness* (National Venture Capital
  Association), 22, 196, 197, 198, 199, 200
Americans. *See* Native-born Americans
"America's New Immigrant Entrepreneurs," 12,
  188–189, 192–195, 202
Amin, Jignesh, 173
Ammonia-free hair coloring system, 57
Anderson, Stuart, 147, 196, 197, 198,
  199, 200
Andretti, Mario, xv
Anti-immigrant sentiments, 50–51
Anti-Semitism, 99–100
Arab American business community, 120
Arepa, 84
Argentina, international scholars from, 207
Arizona State University, 204
Arsenel on the Charles (Watertown,
  Massachusetts), 79
Artists, immigrant, 157–158
Arvizu, Dan, 144–145
Asian American Convenience Stores
  Association, 30
Asian American Hotel Owners Association, 30
Asian Americans. *See also* individual country
  names in Asia
  Kauffman Index of Entrepreneurial Activity
    by, 186
  number of, by year of entry to the U.S., 200
Asian students, 174
Atlant, Georgia, 119
Austin (TX), foreign-born population in, 195
Austin, John, 120
Australia
  business ownership by immigrants in, 16
  international scholars from, 207
  number of companies founded by immigrants
    from, 199
Auto batteries. *See* A123Systems, Inc.
Auto parts company (Transtar Industries), 2, 25,
  29, 38–39

Babson College, 84
Bahena, Geno, 25, 51–55, 64
Ballmer, Steve, 163
Baltimore, Maryland, 119
Barrett, Craig, 142–143, 144
Baton Rouge, Louisiana, 105
Battery company. *See* A123Systems, Inc.
Baumgartner, Jason, 201
Bayless, Rick, 54
Bechtolsheim, Andy, 176
Belda, Alain, xxiii
Belgium, number of immigrant-founded compa-
  nies from, 199
Bell Labs, 31

Bernanke, Ben, 149
Bioscience industry, 189
BioSilk shampoo, xiv, 56
Biotech companies, xxi
Black & Decker tools, 3, 82
The Blade (newspaper), 72
Blue jeans, 20
Boat people, Vietnamese, 102–103
Boston, Massachusetts, 119, 195
Boston Red Sox, 126
Boston University, 121, 203, 206
Brazil, xxiv, 207
Brin, Eugenia, 99–100, 107–111
Brin, Michael, 100, 107–111
Brin, Samuel, 111
Brin, Sergey, xxi, 20, 22. *See also* Google, Inc.
  family of, 106–111
  goal of, 101–102
  personality of, 107
  speaking to Israeli high school students,
    111–112
Broadband2Wireless, 84
"Broken Borders" series, 138
Brookings Institution, 117
Brooklyn Polytechnic, 86
Brown University, 159
Buckley, Patricia, xx
Buffalo, New York, 47, 119
Burger King, 141
Business income potential, Kauffman Index
  of Entrepreneurial Activity by, 187

Cadence Design Systems, 68, 197
Cadence Research Laboratory@ Berkeley, 68
California. *See also* Silicon Valley
  high-tech companies launched by
    immigrants in, 11
  immigrant-founded firms in, 200
  percentage of immigrant-owned
    businesses in, 16
California Institute of Technology, 206
Cambodian immigrants, 200
Cambodians, 19
Canada
  business ownership by immigrants in, 16
  recruiting immigrants from U.S. into, 147
Canadian immigrants, 112, 113
  net business income of, 191
  number of companies founded by, 199
  percentage of engineering and technology
    businesses founded by, 189
Caracas, Venezuela, 83
Carey, Drew, 1
Carnegie, Andrew, 158, 159
Carnegie Corporation of New York, 158
Carnegie Endowment for International
  Peace, 16

Index

Carnegie Mellon University, 206
Carnegie Steel Company, xxii, 158
Carnival Cruises, xxii
Cascade Communications, 90
Castillo, Carmen, xiv, 64
 on anti-immigrant sentiments, 50–51
 immigrant experience of, 45–47
 Richard Stenclik and, 47–48
 Superior Design International and, 48–50
Celebrity doctors, Indian immigrant, 41
Census. See U.S. Census
Chandigarh, India, 33
Chaudary, Khalid, 135
Chaudary, Rukhsana, 135
Chavez, Pablo, 113
Chefs, immigrant, 25, 51–55
Chen, Kimberly, xiii
Cheriton, David, 23, 112
Chiang, Yet-Ming
 on American battery industry, 95
 biography, 1, 86–87
 founding of A123Systems, xiv, 2–4, 3, 4, 88
 on opportunities with auto batteries, 97
 Ric Fulop and, 1–2, 80, 85–86
Chicago, Illinois
 Adedeji Adefuye in, 66–67
 Chef Geno Bahena's restaurants in, 51–55
 foreign-born population in, 195
 immigrant growth in, 118
Chicago State University, 66, 67
CHI iron, 58
China, xxiv
 current immigration from, 76–77
 immigrants returning to, 145, 146, 147
 international scholars from, 207
 science/engineering undergraduates in, 142
 sending students abroad for graduate school, 73
 Tianenmen Square incident in, 74
CHI nail polish, 56
Chinese immigrants
 college education of, 65
 educational attainment of, 202
 nationality quota system for visas and, 150
 net business income of, 191
 networking group for, 177
 number of, by year of entry to U.S., 200
 number of companies founded by, 199
 patents filed by, 20
 percentage of engineering and technology
  businesses founded by, 189
 Xunming Deng and Liwei Xu, 61–63, 72–77
Chinook Communications, 84
Choi, Benjamin, 173–174
Choi, Judy, 173–174
Chrysler, 95–96
Chrysler Machining plant (Perrysburg,
  Ohio), 71

Chu, Steven, 172
Cirrus Logic, 5, 31
Cities, immigrant-driven renewal of, 18–19
 Cleveland's lack of efforts for, 129–130
 efforts to attract immigrants and,
  119–121
 High-Skill Immigration Zone and, 154–155
 home values and, 124–125
 home values impacted by, 126
 by Jason Lin, 127–129
 job growth impacted by, 126–127
 job loss and, 131
 in the 1990s, 118–119
 in Philadelphia, Pennsylvania, 118, 130,
  133–136
 research on economic growth and, 126
 in Schenectady, New York, 123–125
 wages impacted by, 125
Citizenship, swearing-in ceremony for, 115
Claiborne, Liz, 159
Clean technology, xxii, 141, 144–145. See also
  A123Systems, Inc.
Cleveland, Ohio, 18
 High-Skill Immigration Zone and, 154–155
 immigrant-driven renewal bypassing, 119
 immigrant labor force in, 131
 Jason Lin in, 127–129
 Jewish population in, 107
 Kumon Learning Center in, 172–174
 lack of immigrant-attraction efforts in,
  129–130
 Monte Ahuja's experience in, 27–28, 35–38
 nail salon company in, 105
Cleveland Plain Dealer (newspaper), xiii, 130
Cleveland State University, 29, 37, 39
Clinton, Bill, 142
CNN, 137, 138, 141
Codex Corporation, 90
College education. See also International college
  students
 of African immigrants, 65
 of Chinese immigrants, 65
 immigrants in science and technology, 143
 of Indian immigrants, 65
 as indicator of success, 65
 of Israeli immigrants, 65
 research on correlation between high-tech
  companies and, 67–68
 of Russian immigrants, 65
 successful immigrants without, 64
 of Taiwanese immigrants, 65
 value of international students, 143
 of Xunming Deng and Liwei Xu, 73–74
Colombia, net business income of immigrants
  from, 191
Columbia University, 203, 205
Columbus, Ohio, 19, 119, 155

Companies. *See* Immigrant businesses

Computers/communications industry, 189

Convenience stores, Indian immigrants
operating, 30

Coral Networks, 90, 92

Cornell University, 204, 205

"The Cost of Illegal Immigration" (Lou Dobbs
Tonight), 138

Credit Suissee First Boston, 8

Crespi, Gregory, 155

Cuban immigrants, net business income of, 191

Darwin, Charles, 137

Defense/aerospace industry, 189

Democracy in America (Tocqueville), 87

Deng Xiaoping, 73

Deng, Xunming. *See* Xunming Deng

Denmark, immigrant from, 42

Denver, Colorado, foreign-born population in, 195

Deportation of illegal immigrants, 139

Deshpande Center for Technological
Information, 91

Deshpande Foundation, 91

Deshpande, Gururaj "Desh," xiv
A123Systems and, 2–3, 4, 80, 89
biography, 2, 89–91
business ventures of, 90–91
on entrepreneurs, 91–92
on going outside of America, 170, 171

Deshpande, Jaishree, 90

Detroit, Michigan
High-Skill Immigration Zone and, 155
immigrant-led revival of, 120

Discrimination, 14, 18, 40, 108

Distinguished Teaching Award, University
of California, 69

Dobbs, Lou, 137–138

Doctors
Adedeji Adefuye, 66–67
number of immigrant, 31, 63

Doerr, John, 163

Dominican Republic, net business
income of, 191

Dot.com era, 5

Dow Chemical, xxii, 170

Dream Act (Development, Relief, and Education
for Alien Minors Act), 140

*Dreams from My Father: A Story of Race and
Inheritance* (Obama), 156

Drucker, Peter, 170

Duke University, 8, 9, 206

Dun & Bradstreet, 10

DuPont, xxii

EB-5 Foreign Investor green card program, 164

EBay, 22

EBay Inc., 197

EB visas, 150

Ecko, Marc, 178–179

Ecko Unlimited, 178–179

Economic Club of Washington D.C., xx

Economy, immigrant contribution to, 15–16. *See
also* New Economy, the; Recession

Education. *See also* College education
arriving with limited education, 64
high and low ends of immigrant, 64–65
highest degree completed by immigrant entrepreneurs, 193
of immigrants in high-skill jobs, 63
immigrant trait of valuing, 171–175
of Indian immigrants, 30–31, 33, 34
science and education, 142–143
of select immigrant groups, 202
United States inheriting benefits of
overseas, 147

Einstein, Albert, 101

Electric cars, 2

Eli Lilly and Company, xxiii

El Salvador, net business income of immigrants
from, 191

Emory University, 205

Employment-based green cards, 150

Employment visas, restrictions on, 150–151

Energy Conversion Devices, 74

Engineers/engineering companies, xxi, xxii, 31,
63. *See also* Science and engineering
birthplace of immigrant founders of, 189
breakdown by industry, 189
U.S. states where immigrants are
founding, 188

England, 66, 67, 70, 191

Entrepreneurism. *See also* Immigrant
entrepreneurs
coming out of MIT, 87
Deshpande on, 91–92

Entrepreneur Next Door, The (Wagner), 82

Environmental industry, 189

Evans, Harold, 165

Expired visas, 138

Fairlie, Robert, 15–16, 186, 187, 190, 191

Family, respect and love for, 175–176

Family reunification, 32, 150, 152

Farouk Systems, 56–59

Fashion designer company, 178–179

Federal Immigration and Nationality Act
(1952), 149

Federal Immigration and Nationality Act (1965),
149, 150–151

FedEx, 141

Fiat, 96

Filipino immigrants

Index

net business income of, 191
number of, by year of entry into U.S., 200
Filmmakers, Indian immigrant, 31
First Solar, 71–72
Flake, Robert, 153
Florida, 16, 19, 47, 48
Folk wisdom on immigrant entrepreneur, 14
Foreclosure crisis, 155
Foreign companies, U.S. based, xxiii
Foreign direct investment, xxiii
Fortune (magazine), 9
France
  immigrants from, 22
  international scholars from, 207
  number of companies founded by, 199
  rigid social class in, 70
  science/engineering undergraduates in, 142
Friedman, Thomas, 141–142
Frontera Grill, 54
Fulop, Ric, xiv
  on American dream, 5
  biography, 1–2, 83–84
  Gururaj Deshpande and, 2–3
  in immigrant experience, 84–85
  on importance of American-made batteries, 94, 95
  MBA earned at MIT, 85
  pairing up with Chiang, 2, 80, 85–86
  request for federal stimulus money, 80–81
  startup of A123Systems, Inc., 3, 88
Future of Small Business Series, 171
"The Future of the Center: The Core City in the New Economy" (Kotkin), 119

Gaia Power Technologies, 42
Gallagher, Ellen, 165–166
Gamesa, xxiii
Garage Technology Ventures, 23
Gartner, John, xxv, 13, 16–17, 167
Gas Light, Ohio, 35
Gates, Bill, 64
Gauthier-Loiselle, Marjolaine, 21
General Electric, 89
Geno's Steaks (Philadelphia, PA), 116
Georgia Institute of Technology, 204
Gereffi, Gary, 188n1
German immigrants
  educational attainment of, 202
  Klaus Kleinfeld, xxiii
  Levi Strauss, 20
  net business income of, 191
  number of companies founded by, 199
  percentage of engineering and technology businesses founded by, 189
  Vilcek Prize awarded to, 158
  von Bechtolsheim, Andreas, 22, 23, 112

Germany, international scholars from, 207
Gladwell, Malcolm, 172
Global Detroit, 120
Goddard Flight Center, 111
Google, Inc., xx, 5, 197
  founder of, 100–101
  goal of Sergey Brin for, 101–102
  immigrant innovation and, 20
  immigrant leadership in, 112–113
  venture capitalism and, 21, 22
Google Story, The (Vise/Malseed), 111–112
Gore, Al, 84
Gosplan, 109
Grama, Sorin, 179–181
Greater Cleveland Partnership, 154
Great Lakes Chambers of Commerce, 154
Greek immigrants, net business income of, 191
Green cards
  employment or skill-based, 150
  family-based, 150
  immigration reform and, 153, 154
  Indian immigrants given employment related, 33
  loosening restrictions on, 148
  nationality quota system for, 151
Green technology, xxii, 180–181. *See also* A123Systems, Inc.; Clean technology
Gregorian, Vartan, 158–159
Grove, Andrew, xxi, 22, 102, 168
Guatemala, net business income of immigrants from, 191
Gupta, Sanjay, 31
Guyanese families, 120, 123–125

H-1B visas, 147, 148, 151–152, 153
Hair-care industry, 56–59
Harvard Business School, 19
Harvard University, 203, 205
Hayek, Salma, 159
Hebrew Immigration Aid Society, 100
Herman, Richard
  immigrant experience of, xi–xv
  on immigration reform, 154–155
  TiE and, 161–164
  visiting Brin family, 106
Hewlett-Packard, 141
High, Howard, 144
High-Skill Immigration Zone, 154–155
High-technology. *See also* Technology companies
  backed by venture capital, 22
  correlation between higher education and, 67–68
  guest worker visas and, 151
  immigrant contribution in, xx, 5, 11
  Indian immigrants in, 31

High-technology (*continued*)
link between education and immigrant
founders of, 12–13
patent filings and, 20–21
percentage of immigrants launching, 11
High-tech trade group (TiE), 162–164
Hispanic-Net, 177
HIV/AIDS Research and Policy
Institute, 66
Hmong immigrants, 119, 200
Ho, David, 159
Holzle, Urs, 113
Home Depot, 41
Home values, 124–125, 126
Hospitality industry, 18, 30
Hotel owners, 30
Hotmail, 5
Houston Chronicle, 59
"How Much Does Immigration Boost Inno-
vation?" (Hunt/Gauthier-Loiselle), 21
Hua Yuan Science and Technology Association
(HYSTA), 177
Hudson, Ohio, 37
Huffington, Arianna, 159
Hungarian immigrants
Andrew Grove, 22, 102, 168
number of companies founded
by, 199
Tom Szaky, 41–42
Hunting Valley, Ohio, 28
Hunt, Jennifer, 21
Hypomania, 17
*Hypomanic Edge: The Link Between (A Little)
Craziness And (A Lot of) Success In America*
(Gartner), 16, 167
HYSTA (Hua Yuan Science and Technology
Association), 177

Ibargüen, Alberto, 156
Illegal immigrants, 13
comprehensive immigration reform and,
139–140
Dream Act and, 140
issues with legalizing, 139
media portrayal of, 137–138
public opinion on, 138–139
*Illusions of Entrepreneurship: the Costly Myths that
Entrepreneurs, Investors and Policy Makers Live
By, The* (Shane), 15
Immigrant businesses. *See also* Engineers/engi-
neering companies; Technology companies
A123Systems .*See* A123Systems, Inc.
backed by venture capital, 21–23, 197
companies started by native-born
Americans *vs.,* 15
compliance with rules, 122–123
creative shopkeepers, 121–122

Farouk Systems, 56–59
First Solar, 71–72
founded by Indian immigrants, 32
Gaia Power Technologies, 42
Google .*See* Google, Inc.
impact of shopkeepers, 121–122
Intel .*See* Intel Corporation
Jamhuri Wear, 178–179
Lam Research Corporation, 175
leading countries of birth for
venture-backed, 199
leading, ranked by employment, 197
misperceptions on government help for, 122
nail salon, 103–105
number of, by industry, 198
percentage of, by state, 200
percentage of venture-backed public, 196
Poly-Carb, 170
Promethean Power Systems, 179
Relativity Technologies, Inc., 8–9
reviving neighborhoods and cities, 18–19
Seer Technologies, 8
solar-energy, 71–72
Sun Microsystems, 5, 22, 31, 112, 176
Superior Design International, 46, 48–51
TerraCycle, Inc., 41
Transtar Industries, Inc., 25, 29, 38–39, 169
Xunlight Corporation, 61–62, 72, 74–76
Immigrant entrepreneurs. *See also* Immigrant
businesses; individual names of immigrant
entrepreneurs
"accidental," 13
on American business environment, 41–43
in American folk wisdom, 14
America's impact on, 23–24
coming out of MIT, 87
education of, 12–13
fields of highest degree, 193
highest degree completed, 193
high rate of, 5
high-tech trade group for, 162–164
hurdles overcome by, 14
images of, 81
impact of Indian, xx
impact on the New Economy, 9–10
job creation through, xx–xxii
Kauffman Index, 186–187
number of, by industry, 190
optimism of, 164–165
in other developed countries, 16
primary reason for immigrating to the
U.S., 194
promoting, 143–145
refugee, 101–102
research on contributions of, 15–16
research on economic impact of, 10–12
Russian, xii

Index

self-reliance, 122
year of entry, 194
Immigrant experience
  of Alberto Sangiovanni-Vincentelli, 69
  ancestry of Americans and, xxv
  Brin family, 107–111
  of Carmen Castillo, 45–47
  of Geno Bahena, 54–55
  harshness of, 40
  of Monte Ahuja, 27–28, 33–41
  Ric Fulop on, 84–85
  in Russia, xi–xii
  three stages of, 39
  of Ton Quy, 102–103
  of Xunming Deng and Liwei Xu, 75–77
Immigrant, Inc., xiv, xv, 168
  explained, xix–xx
  ideals of, xxiv–xxv
Immigrant Learning Center, xxi, 121
Immigrants. See also Countries of origin
  acknowledging contributions of,
    157–159
  Asian, by year of entry to U.S., 200
  culture of entrepreneurship among,
    xiv–xv, 5–6
  education of .See Education
  exodus of, 145–148
  at Google, 112–113
  in higher education, 143
  illegal .See Illegal immigrants
  illegal immigrants dominating spotlight
    over, 138, 140
  impact of high-skilled, 63–64
  native-born Americans related or
    married to, 167
  number of, 13, 119, 167
  percentage of, in tech-center
    populations, 195
  in Philadelphia, PA, 115–118
  population for individual states, 210
  primary reason for immigrating, 194
  refugee .See Refugee immigrants
  scientists and engineers with doctorate
    degrees, xxii
  start-ups by, vs. native-born start-ups, 15
  success in U.S., xii–xiii
  urban renewal through .See Cities, immigrant-
    driven renewal of
  U.S. Nobel Laureate, 19
  venture capital, 23
Immigrants, traits of, xv, xxiv, 24
  epitomizing American Dream, 165–166
  Gururaj Deshpande on, 93
  hard work and persistence, 70
  hypomania, 17
  of Monte Ahuja, 29, 39–40
  native-born Americans learning from, 166–167

optimism, 164–165
  respect and love for the family, 175–176
  risk-taking, 17
  sense of adventure, 169–171
  social cohesiveness, 18
  spirit of striving, xiii–xiv
  for success, 169
  tendency to dream, 177–181
  value on education, 171–175
Immigrant visas. See Green cards
Immigration and Nationality Act (1965), 33
Immigration laws, 144, 149, 150–151
  as harming competitiveness, 196
Immigration reform
  changes in attitudes and, 155–159
  changes in quota system, 149–152
  clean technology and, 144–145
  Dream Act, 140
  exodus of highly-skilled immigrants
    and, 145–148
  high-skill, 153–155
  illegal immigration dominating debate
    on, 140
  job creation and entrepreneurial
    innovation with, 140–144
  under Obama, 156–157
  pubic opinion on, 138–139
  targeting complexities of illegal
    immigration, 140
Immigration system/policy. See also
    Immigration reform
  as antiquated, 148–149
  employment through H-1B visas, 151–152
  with equal emphasis on family ties and job
    creation, 152
  favoring family reunification, 32, 150
  nationality quota system and, 150–151
  promotion of immigration during economic
    downturn, 140–145
  visa backlog in, 146
  waiting for visas, 148
Income
  of average Indian-owned business, 19
  by immigrant group, 2000 Census, 191
  impact of immigrant-driven renewal of
    cities on, 125
  of Indian immigrants, 31
India, xxiv
  immigrants returning to, 145, 146
  international scholars from, 207
  "milk trail" in, 180
Indiana University, 203, 206
Indian immigrants
  Ahuja, Monte .See Ahuja, Monte
  celebrity doctor, 41
  college education of, 65
  education of, 30–31, 33, 34, 65, 202

Indian immigrants *(continued)*
  at Google, 112, 113
  green cards for, 33
  Gururaj Deshpande, 2–3, 4, 89–91
  in hospitality industry, 18
  income, 19, 31
  job creation in Silicon Valley by, xx
  as the model minority, 30–33
  nationality quota system for visas and, 150
  net business income of, 191
  number of, by year of entry to U.S., 200
  number of companies founded by, 199
  patents filed by, 20
  percentage of engineering and technology
    businesses founded by, 189
  Ratanjit Sondhe, 170–171
  Vinod Khosla, 22
  Vivek Wadhwa . *See* Wadhwa, Vivek
Indian Institute of Technology (IIT), 31, 65, 90
Indian University-Bloomington, 201
Institute of International Education, 203–209
Intel Corporation, 5, 102, 144, 197
  economic recession, 141
  founder, 102, 168
  job creation by, xxi
  patents filed by, 21
  venture capital and, 22
Intellectual diversity, 69, 70
International college students, 143–144
  economic impact from, 201
  enrollment, 1954-2008, 208–209
  leading institutions hosting, 205–206
  top 20 places of origin, 207
  top 25 institutions hosting, 23–24
International Migration Policy Program, 16
International patent applications, 11–12
Internet, as inspiration for Relativity
    Technologies, Inc., 8–9
Into Networks, 84
Intuit Inc., 170
Inventors. *See also* Patents
  immigrant innovation and, 20–21
  percentage of immigrant, 63
Iowa State University, 206
Iranian immigrants
  net business income of, 191
  number of companies founded by, 199
  Omid Kordestani, 113
  percentage of engineering and technology
    businesses founded by, 189
Israel, xxiv
  international scholars from, 207
  Sergey Brin speaking to high school students
    in, 111–112
Israeli immigrants
  college education of, 65

founders of engineering and technology
    businesses, 189
  number of companies founded by, 199
Issues in Science and Technology (journal), 145–146
Italian immigrants
  net business income of, 191
  number of companies founded by, 199
Italy
  international scholars from, 207
  rigid social class in, 70

Jackson, Frank, 130
Jamaica, net business income of immigrants
    from, 191
Jamhuri Wear, 178
Japan
  international scholars from, 207
  percentage of engineering and technology
    businesses founded by, 189
Japanese immigrants, 200, 202
Jasper, James, 165, 167–168, 177
Jefferson, Thomas, 125
Jewish Family Service Association of
    Cleveland, 107
Jews, 99–100, 106–111
Jindal, Bobby, 31
Job creation, xx–xxi. *See also* Immigrant
    businesses
  by Farouk Systems, 59
  by high-skill immigrants, 141
  promoting immigration and, 140–145
  through U.S.-based affiliate foreign
    companies, xxiii
  urban-renewal power of immigrants
    and, 126–127
John S. and James L. Knight Foundation, 156
Juniper Networks, Inc., 197
Junming Le, 157
Jurczynski, Albert, 123–124

Kanbay International, Inc., 197
Kane, Tim, 153
Kauffman Foundation, 12, 87, 141, 153
Kauffman Index, 15
  Entrepreneurial Activity by Business Income
    Potential, 187
  Entrepreneurial Activity by Nativity
    (1996-2008), 185–186
  Entrepreneurial Activity by Race, 186
Kawaski, Guy, 23
Kedar, Ruth, 113
Kennedy, John F., 7, 166
Kent, Muhtar, xxiii
Kent State University, 37
Kenyan immigrant, 178–179
Kerr, William, 20

Index

Khosla, Vinod, xx, 22, 31, 163
Kimathi, Jeffrey, 178
Kim, Jane, 174–175
Kingery, W. David, 87
Kirkegaard, Jacob Funk, 144
Kleinfeld, Klaus, xxiii
"Knowledge Economy Immigration: A Priority
    for U.S. Growth Policy" (Kane/Litan), 153
Koppel, Ted, 159
Kordestani, Omid, xxv–xxvi, 113
Korea
    battery companies in, 94
    international scholars from, 207
    science/engineering undergraduates
        in, 142
Korean immigrants
    emphasis on education by, 173–175
    net business income of, 191
    number of, by year of entry to U.S., 200
    number of companies founded by, 199
    percentage of engineering and technology
        businesses founded by, 189
Kotkin, Joel, 119
Kumon Learning Centers, 172–174

Labor laws, 42
Lafayette, Louisiana, 57
Lagos, Nigeria, 66
Lam, David, 175–176
Lam Research Corporation, 175, 197
Lantos, Thomas, 101
Laotian immigrants, 200
Latino immigrants. See also Mexican immigrants
    education of, 64
    entrepreneurial activity of, 186
    networking group for, 177
Leahy, Anne. See O'Callaghan, Anne
Lebanese immigrant, Vilcek Prize awarded to, 158
Lemco Industries, 36–37
Le Su, 105
Lewiston, Maine, 155
Liberian community, 133
Life Time Fitness, Inc., 197
Liljenquist, Katie, xxiii
Lin, Jason, 127–129
LinkedIn, 21
Lithium-ion batteries, 88. See also
    A123Systems, Inc.
Liwei Xu, 25
    in China, 72–73
    at University of Chicago, 73–74
    Xunlight Corporation and, 61–63, 74–76
L. & J.G. Stickley, 104
"Lou Dobbs Tonight," 138
Louisiana State University, 103
Lowell, Massachusetts, 19

Malawi, 151
Malden, Massachusetts, 121
Malik, Mansoor, 162, 163–164
Mallorca (island), 45
Malseed, Mark, 111–112
Manufacturing-related businesses, 189
Martinez, Mel, 159
Massachusetts
    battery plant in, 96
    high-tech companies launched by
        immigrants in, 11
    immigrant-founded firms in, 200
Massachusetts Institute of Technology
    (MIT), xxi
    A123Systems, Inc. and, 83
    entrepreneurism and innovation at, 87
    international scholars at, 205
    Ric Fulop and, 84, 85
    Sorin Grama at, 180
Massagué, Joan, 158
"Mau ve" nail art, 104
McMaster, Harold, 71
McNealy, Scott, 176
Melville, Herman, 45
Mexican American communities, 120
Mexican immigrants
    in Chicago, Illinois, 118
    education of, 64
    Geno Bahena, 25, 51–55
    illegal, 118, 137, 139
    net business income of, 191
Mexico, international scholars from, 207
Miami, Florida, 19
Miami Herald (newspaper), 156
Michigan battery plants, 96–97
Michigan State University, 203, 206
Microchip design companies, 69–70
Microsoft, 141, 147–148
Migration Policy Institute, 63–64
Million Dollar Database (Dun & Bradstreet), 10
Minneapolis, Minnesota, 119
MIT. See Massachusetts Institute of
    Technology (MIT)
MIT $100K Entrepreneurship Competition,
    179–180
Mom and pop shops, 121–122
Monte Ahuja Hall, Cleveland State University, 39
Monte Jade Science and Technology
    Association, 177
Moritz, Michael, 21, 23, 93, 112
Moscow State University, 108
Mother Teresa, 115
Motorola, 89, 90
Motwani, Rajeev, 112
MTV, 141
Muhammad, Fatimah, 133–134

Murdoch, Rupert, 159
Musk, Elon, 22, 113

NAFSA, 201
Nail salons, 103–105
Nairobi, 178
NASA (National Aeronautic Space
    Administration), 99, 111
Nash, Betty Joyce, 12
National Academy of Sciences, 63, 142
National Center for Education Statistics, 209n1
National Foundation for American
    Policy, 147, 151
National Inventors Hall of Fame, 63
Nationality quotas, 33, 149, 150–151, 152
National Renewable Energy Laboratory, 144
National University of Science and
    Technology, 163
National Venture Capital Association, 22, 32, 196,
    197, 198, 199, 200
Nation of Immigrants, A (Kennedy), 166
Native-born Americans
    average income of, 19
    education of, 64, 202
    entrepreneurship in 1990s by, 16
    going outside of America, 171
    learning from immigrant traits, 166–167
    net business income of, 191
    start-ups by, vs. immigrant start-ups, 15
    thinking and acting like immigrants, 167–168
Naturalization ceremony, 115, 116
Negroponte, Nicholas, 163
Neitzel, Robert, 37
Netherlands, international scholars from, 207
Netravali, Arun, 31
Networking groups, 177
New Economy, the, xiv, xix
    businesses becoming icon of, 22
    defined, 12
    foreign-born executives leading American
        companies in, xxiii
    Indian immigrants in, 31–32
    job creation in, xx, xxi
    opportunities abroad, 145
    refugee immigrant of, 101–102
    research on skilled immigrants as drivers
        of, 10–12
    thinking like an immigrant and, xxv–xxvi
    types of entrepreneurs driving, 82
    venture capital and icons of, 22
New Jersey
    high-tech companies launched by
        immigrants in, 11
    immigrant-founded firms in, 200
    percentage of immigrant-owned
        businesses in, 16
New Orleans, Louisiana, 103

New York (city), foreign-born population
    in, 195
New York Library System, 159
New York (state), percentage of immigrant-
    owned businesses in, 16
New York Times (newspaper), 141–142
New York University, 203
Nguyen, Thuong, 105
Nichols, Mike, 158
Nigeria, xxiv
Nigerian immigrants (Adedeji Adefuye), 66–67
Nixon, Rob, 99
Nobel Prize, the, 19, 63
Nooyi, Indra, xxiii, 159
North American International Auto Show
    (2009), 3
North Carolina State University, 8, 206
Northwestern University, 206
Nutter, Michael, 116, 118, 135–136
Nvidia, 21
NVIDIA Corporation, 197
NYU's School of Medicine, 157

Obama, Barack (Cabinet of), 156–157
O'Callaghan, Anne, 130, 131–133
Ohio. See Cleveland, Ohio; Toledo, Ohio
Ohio State University, 27, 34, 180, 203, 205
Olsen, Ib, 42
Only the Paranoid Survive (Grove), 168
"Open Doors: Report on International
    Exchange" (Institute of International
    Education), 203–209
Otellini, Paul, xxi
Ottaviano, Gianmarco, 125
Outliers: The Story of Success (Gladwell), 172

Page, Jimmy, 161n1
Page, Larry, 101, 111–112, 113
Pakistani immigrants, 176–177, 200
Pakistanis, 135
Palestinian immigrants (Farouk Shami), 56–59
Palm Beach, Florida, 47
Paral, Rob, 131
Parametric Technology Corporation, 197
Park, Chul-In, xiii
Patel Hotel, 30
Patel, Jyodi, 18
Patel, Vinu, 17, 18
Patent research, 20
Patents
    examination of ethnic names and, 20
    growth in immigrant innovation and, 20–21
    immigrants vs. native-borns filing, xx
    increase in immigrants applying for, 11–12
    percentage of international
        applications, 192
Patil, Suhas, 31

Index

PayPal, 21, 22, 113
Pediatric Medical Group, Inc., 197
Pennsylvania, xxiii. *See also* Philadelphia,
    Pennsylvania; Pittsburgh, Pennsylvania
Pennsylvania State University-University
    Park, 204
PepsiCo, xxiii
Peri, Viovanni, 125
Perrysburg, Ohio, 71
Pew Hispanic Center, 13
Pew Research Center, 139
Pfizer, xxii
Philadelphia, Pennsylvania
    agency helping immigrants in, 131–133
    growth of immigrants in, 117–118
    immigrant-driven renewal of, 118, 130,
        133–136
    naturalization ceremony in, 115–116
    suspicion of immigrants in, 116–117
Philipines. *See* Filipino immigrants
Photovoltaics, 62
Phuong Le, 105
Pittsburgh, Pennsylvania, 119, 155
Plant, Robert, 161n1
Platzer, Michaela, 196, 197, 198, 199, 200
Poland, international scholars from, 207
Polish immigrants, net business income
    of, 191
Politecnico di Milano University, 69
Politicians, Indian immigrant, 31
Poly-Carb, 170
Porter, Michael, 19, 126
Portland, Oregon, 119, 195
Pratt School of Engineering, 9
Prejudices, 158
Press, James, 95–96
Princeton University, 206
Proctor & Gamble, xxii, 89
Promethean Power System, 179
Punjab Engineering College (Chandigarh,
    India), 33
Pupin, Michael, 79
Purdue University, 203

Qualcomm, 89
Quotas, visa
    denial of visas for high-skilled immigrants and,
        150–151
    nationality, 33, 149, 150, 152
    refugee, 101, 155
    two types of, 149
Qureshi, Safi, 176–177

Race, Kauffman Index of Entrepreneurial
    Activity by, 186
Racism, 40
Real Tenochtitlan (restaurant), 52

Recession
    optimism during, 164–165
    promoting smart immigration during,
        140–145
Red Herring (magazine), 2, 84
Refugee immigrants, 101–102. *See also*
    Brin, Sergey
    defined, 101
    number of, 119
    Ton Quy, 103–106
Refugee quotas, 101, 155
Regal Nails salon, 103
Relativity Technologies, Inc., 8–9
Remicade, 157
Research
    on education of immigrants,
        67–68, 147
    on immigrant-driven revival of cities, 121–122
    on impact of immigrant entrepreneurs, 10–12,
        15–16, 141
    on impact of immigrant entrepreneurship,
        10–12
    patent, 20
    by Ric Fulop, 84
    on urban-renewal power of immigrants, 126
    on venture capital funding, 32
Research Triangle, North Carolina, 7, 8
Restaurants, of Geno Bahena, 51–55
Restless Nation: Starting over in America (Jasper),
    165, 167, 177
"Reverse brain drain," 145
Richard T. Herman & Associates, xii
Richwine, Jason, 32–33
Riley, Bart, 3, 88
Risk-taking, immigrant trait of, 17
Rissing, Ben, 188n1
Roberts, Edward, xix
Romanian immigrant, 179–181
Romans, Christine, 137
Russia
    immigrant experience in, xi–xii
    international scholars from, 207
Russian immigrants
    college education of, 65
    Michael and Eugenia Brin, 107–111
    Sergey Brin .*See* Brin, Sergey
Rust Belt cities, 154

Salton, Inc., 197
San Diego, foreign-born population in, 195
Sangiovanni-Vinventelli, Alberto
    businesses of, 69–70
    immigrant experience of, 69
    on opportunities in America, 70–71
    at UC berkeley, 68, 70
Sanmina-SCI Corporation, 197
Santana, Carlos, 159

Santo, Mark, 154–155
Satram, Mohabir, 124, 125
Saxenian, AnnaLee, xxi, 10, 141, 188n1
Schenectady, New York, 19, 120, 123–125
Schoch, Lynn, 201
Schramm, Carl, 143
Schwarzenegger, Arnold, 27, 113, 163
Science and engineering. *See also* High-
    technology; Technology companies
    America losing competitive edge in, 142–143
    exodus of immigrants in, 145–146
    immigrant contribution in, xxii, 12, 20, 63
    immigration law discriminating against immi-
        grants in, 149
    Indian immigrants in, 65
    offering visas to graduates in, 153–154
Seattle, Washington, 119, 195
Seer Technologies, 8
Semiconductor industry, 189
Seng, Wong Kan, 148
September 11th terrorist attacks, 152
Sequoia Capital, 21, 89, 112
Serbian immigrant (Nikola Tesla), 20
Shah, Baiju, 163
Shalikashvili, John, 101
Shami, Farouk, xiv, 56–59
Shami, Rami, 58
Shane, Scott, 14–15
Shaw, Richard, 59
Shriram, Ram, 23, 113
Shyamalan, M. Night, 31
Sierra Leone, 166
Silicon Valley
    foreign-born population in, 195
    immigrant contribution in, 5, 11, 31, 63
    immigrant entrepreneurs in, xiii, 10
    Indian immigrants in, xx
    percentage of immigrant startups in, 188
    TiE founded in, 162
"Silicon Valley's New Immigrant Entrepreneurs"
    (Saxenian), 10
Singapore
    appreciation of foreign talent, 148
    science/engineering undergraduates in, 142
Sixth Sense, The (film), 31
Skill-based green cards, 149, 150
Smith, Robert, xiii–xiv
Social class, movement from, 70
Social cohesiveness, immigrant trait of, 18
Software industry, 189
Solar-energy companies
    First Solar, 71–72
    Xunlight Corporation, 25, 61–62, 74–76
Solar-powered cold storage system, 180–181
Solectron Corporation, 197
Somali refugees, 19, 119
Sondhe, Ratanjit, 170–171

Sonis, Olga, 106–107, 108
Soros, George, 101
South African immigrant (Elon Musk), 22
South Asia. *See* India
South Korea. *See* Korea
Soviet Union, immigrants from, 99–100. *See also*
    Russian immigrants
Spain
    international scholars from, 207
    Vilcek Prize awarded to immigrant from, 158
Speiser, Mike, 23
Spelling bees, Indian immigrant success in, 30
Spencer, Raymond, xxii
Stabenow, Debbie, 96
Stack, Charles, 154–155
Stahl, Leslie, xx
Stanford University, 159, 204, 205
"Staple Act," 153–154
St. Augustine College, 54
STEM fields (science, technology, engineer-
    ing and mathematics), 13. *See also* High-
    technology; Science and engineering
Stenclik, Richard, 47–48
"Stopping Trained in America Ph.D.s from
    Leaving the Economy Act," 153–154
St. Paul, Minnesota, 119, 155
Strauss, Levi, 20
Street, John, 130
Striver class, the, 64–65
SunGlitz hair dye, 56, 57–58
Sun Microsystems, Inc., xx, 5, 22, 31, 112,
    176, 197
SUNY University at Buffalo, 203
Superior Design International, 46, 48–51
Superior Group of Companies, 47, 49
Sutter Hill Ventures, 23
Switzerland, immigrants from, 113, 199
Sycamore Networks, 3, 91
Szaky, Tom, 41–42

Taiwan, xxiv, 207
Taiwanese immigrants
    college education of, 65
    educational attainment of, 202
    Jerry Yang, 22
    net business income of, 191
    networking group for, 177
    number of companies founded by, 199
    percentage of engineering and technology
        businesses founded by, 189
    Yet-Ming Chiang .*See* Chiang, Yet-Ming
Taurel, Sidney, xxiii
Technology companies
    birthplace of immigrant founders of, 189
    Cadence, 69–70
    job creation in, xx, xxi
    Relativity Technologies, Inc., 8–9

Seer Technologies, 8
Synopsys, 69
U.S. states where immigrants are founding, 188
Technology patents, xx
Technology Policy Institute, 148
Temporary visas. *See* H-1B visas
TerraCycle, Inc., 41
Tesla Motors, 113
Tesla, Nikola, 20, 113
Tesla Roadstar, 113
Tetra Tech, Inc., 197
Texas A&M University, 204
Texas, immigrant-founded firms in, 200
Thai immigrants, 200
The Indus Entrepreneurs (TiE), 161–164, 177
They Made America (Evans), 165
Tiananmen Square incident (1989), 74
TiE (The Indus Entrepreneurs). *See* The Indus
    Entrepreneurs (TiE)
TiE convention, 163
Tobocman, Steve, 120
Tocqueville, Alexis de, 87
Tolani, Hitesh, 166
Toledo, Ohio, 61–62, 72, 76
Ton, Quy "Charlie," 102–106
*Top of the Class: How Asian Parents Raise High
    Achievers-And How You Can Too* (Abboud/
    Kim), 174
Toronto, Canada, 119
Tran, Ham, 158
Transmission repair part, 38
Transtar Industries, Inc., 2, 25, 29, 38–39, 169
Trident Capital, 72
Truong, Vi, 135–136
Turkey, international scholars from, 207
Twin Cities, Minnesota, 119

Undocumented immigrants. *See* Illegal
    immigrants
Unemployment, 131
Ung, Loung, 101
United Kingdom
    business ownership by immigrants
        from, 16, 189
    educational attainment of immigrants
        from, 202
    international scholars from, 207
    number of companies founded by immigrants
        from, 199
United States. *See also* Native-born Americans
    exodus of skilled immigrants from, 145–148
    freedom in, 99–100
    immigrant patriotism toward, 94
    immigrants on business environment in, 41–43
    losing competitive edge in science and tech-
        nology, 142–143
    number of refugees accepted into, 101

opportunities for immigrants in, 70–71
    promoting immigrant entrepreneurs in,
        140–145
United States Citizenship & Immigration
    Services, 165
University Hospitals of Cleveland, 39
University of Alabama-Birmingham, 206
University of Arkansas, 57
University of California-Berkeley, 68, 69, 205
University of California-Davis, 205
University of California-Irvine, 205
University of California-Los Angeles, 203, 205
University of California-San Diego, 205
University of California-Santa Barbara, 206
University of California-Santa Cruz, 15–16
University of Chicago, 73–74
University of Florida, 204, 205
University of Houston, 204
University of Illinois-Chicago, 66–67, 206
University of Illinois-Urbana-Champaign,
    203, 205
University of Maryland, 111, 205
University of Michigan-Ann Arbor, 74,
    203, 205
University of Minnesota-Twin Cities,
    204, 205
University of Missouri, 206
University of North Carolina at Chapel
    Hill, 8, 206
University of Pennsylvania, 203
University of Pennsylvania's School of
    Dentistry, 166
University of Southern California, 203, 205
University of Texas-Austin, 203, 206
University of Texas Medical Branch-
    Galveston, 206
University of Toledo (UT), 62, 74
University of Washington, 205
University of Wisconsin-Madison, 204, 205
Urban legend, on success of immigrant entrepre-
    neurs, 14–18
Urban renewal. *See* Cities, immigrant-driven
    renewal of
U.S. Agency for International Development
    (USAID), 66
U.S. Census
    American Community Survey (2007), 64
    on business income by immigrant
        group, 191
    on education of Taiwanese immigrants, 65
    on foreign born population for individual
        states, 210
    immigrant self-employment reflected in, 16
    on Indian immigrant income, 31
    2007, 13
U.S. Citizenship and Immigration Service
    (USCIS), 150

U.S. Department of Energy, 89, 96
U.S. Patent and Trademark Office, 20
U.S. Small Business Administration, xxi, 15
U.S. Steel, xxii, 158
UTStarcom, Inc., 197

Vancouver, Canada, 147
Vanderbilt University, 206
Vator TV, 176
VCs (venture capitalists). See Venture
    capitalists (VCs)
Venezuela, immigrants from. See Fulop, Ric
Venture capitalists (VCs), 21–23
    for A123Systems, Inc., 88–89, 92–93
    Indian immigrants and, 32
    leading companies backed by, 197
    percentage of immigrant businesses backed
        up by, 196
    for Sunlight Corporation, 62
Vieau, David, 83, 96
Vietnamese immigrants
    Jason Lin, 127–129
    net business income of, 191
    number of, by year of entry to U.S., 200
    shopkeepers, 122
    Ton Quy, 102–106
    Vilcek Prize awarded to, 158
Vilcek Foundation, 157–158
Vilcek, Jan, 157
Vilcek, Marica, 157
Vilcek Prizes, 158
Visas
    available to high-skill immigrants, 150
    based on kinship ties, 152
    categories of employment, 150
    expediting wait for, 148
    expired, 139
    H-1B, 147, 148, 151–152, 153
    nationality quota system for, 150–151
    offered to immigrants with science, math,
        engineering, or technology degrees,
        153–154
    waiting for, 145, 146
Vise, David A., 111–112
Volvo, 96
Von Bechtolsheim, Andreas, 22, 23, 112

Wadhwa, Tarun, 8
Wadhwa, Tavinder, 7–8

Wadhwa, Vineet, 8
Wadhwa, Vivek, xxi
    "America's New Immigrant Entrepreneurs"
        study, 188–189, 192–195, 202
    biography, 8
    on exodus of young scientists and engineers,
        145–146
    on hurdles of immigrant entrepreneurs, 14
    near-death experience of, 7–8
    patent research by, 20
    research on economic impact of immigrants,
        9–12, 141
    research on education of immigrants,
        67–68, 147
Wages. See Income
Wagner, Bill, 82
Wales, immigrant from, 112
Wal-Mart, 105
Washington (state), immigrant-founded
    firms in, 200
Washington University in St. Louis, 205
Watertown, Massachusetts, 79
Watson Pharmaceuticals, Inc., 197
WebEx Communications, Inc., 197
Welcoming Center for New Pennsylvanians,
    130, 132–134
White, Sam, 179
Will, George, 154
Windows Vista operating system, 84
World Intellectual Property Organization
    (WIPO), 11
World is Flat: A Brief History of the 21st Century,
    The (Friedman), 141

Xu, Liwei. See Liwei Xu
Xunlight Corporation, 25, 61–62, 74–76
Xunming Deng, 25
    in China, 72–73
    at University of Chicago, 73–74
    Xunlight Corporation and, 61–63, 74–76

Yahoo, 5, 21, 22, 197
Yale University, 205
Yang, Jerry, 22, 159
YMCA of Cleveland, 28, 35
York, James, 81
YouTube, 21

Zoghbi, Huda, 158